The
Rinehart Guide
to Grammar and Style

About the Title of This Book

Stanley M. Rinehart, Jr. (1897-1969), was a distinguished book publisher. In 1929, he, his brother Frederick, and editor John Farrar founded the publishing house of Farrar & Rinehart, which later became (in 1946) Rinehart & Company, and then (in 1960) Holt, Rinehart and Winston. As president of Rinehart & Company, Stanley Rinehart published such works as Norman Mailer's *The Naked and the Dead,* the "Nero Wolfe" detective novels of Rex Stout, and Rinehart Editions, a series of quality paperback editions of classic literature. The firm began its college department in 1934 and soon became a major publisher in the field, specializing in the humanities and social sciences. Today, Harcourt Brace College Publishers carries on this same tradition of publishing excellence through such noteworthy volumes as *The Rinehart Handbook for Writers, The Rinehart Guide to Grammar and Style,* and *The Rinehart Reader.*

The
Rinehart Guide
to Grammar and Style

Fourth Edition

Bonnie Carter

Craig Skates
formerly of
The University of Southern Mississippi

Harcourt Brace College Publishers

Fort Worth   Philadelphia   San Diego

New York   Orlando   Austin   San Antonio

Toronto   Montreal   London   Sydney   Tokyo

Publisher	Christopher P. Klein
Executive Editor	Michael Rosenberg
Developmental Editor	Michell Phifer
Senior Project Editor	Cliff Crouch
Project Editor	Deanna Johnson
Senior Production Manager	Tad Gaither
Production Manager	Jane Tyndall Ponceti
Senior Art Director	Don Fujimoto

Book design adapted from original text design by Caliber Design Planning
and cover design by Albert D'Agostino

International Standard Book Number: 0-15-503561-4

Address for editorial correspondence: Harcourt Brace College Publishers, 301 Commerce Street, Suite 3700, Fort Worth, Texas 76102

Address for orders: Harcourt Brace, Inc., 6277 Sea Harbor Drive, Orlando, Florida, 32887

Phone: 800/782-4479, or (in Florida only) 800/433-0001

Printed in the United States of America

5 6 7 8 9 0 1 2 3 4 5   016   9 8 7 6 5 4 3 2 1

To the Instructor

The Rinehart Guide to Grammar and Style, Fourth Edition, is designed for students at different levels of proficiency as well as for instructors with different priorities and teaching techniques. For example, the *Guide* can function solely as a reference manual for use outside of class. When grading papers, instructors can use tab numbers and symbols to send students to appropriate sections of the text. Students can then refer to those sections when editing and correcting papers or when writing new papers.

If instructors prefer another approach, the *Guide* can serve as a source for in-class explanation and discussion. For example, Part I (Review of the Basics) describes English grammar in traditional terms: parts of speech and the components of phrases, clauses, and sentences. An in-class review of this material can help students with minimal skills to use the *Guide* effectively on their own. For ESL students, Part I and Appendix B (English as a Second Language) can provide a concise overview of English grammar.

Part II (Structural and Grammatical Problems) addresses errors common to inexperienced writers such as fragments, faulty pronoun reference, and tense shifts. ESL students will profit from the explanations of grammatical principles such as agreement, case, and placement of modifiers. Instructors can review all of Part II or only those sections most needed by an individual class.

Part III (Punctuation and Mechanics) covers the current conventions for punctuation marks as well as for quotations, italics, hyphens, abbreviations, numbers, and capitalization. The chapters are divided into brief sections, allowing instructors to focus on the material that students find most troublesome.

Part IV (Style) has only two chapters, yet it contains a great deal of information about stylistic choices—a concept that intrigues most students. Typically, inexperienced writers feel at the mercy of the language. They are accustomed to ask, "Is this correct?" Part IV encourages them to ask, "Do I like the way this sounds?" As a result, students can learn to judge not only their own style but also the style of other writers.

Appendix A (Spelling) helps students make sense of the peculiarities of the English spelling system. ESL students as well as native speakers will profit from the practical advice about spelling patterns and anomalies. Appendix B (English as a Second Language) acquaints ESL students with the underlying principles of English grammar. This appendix uses efficient ESL methods to explain such common English puzzles as the use of articles and other determiners, order of modifiers in the noun phrase, order of components in the verb phrase, and recognition of complete sentences.

The Glossary of Usage supplements material on usage that appears throughout the text. For example, this glossary addresses questions such as when to use *affect* and *effect, amount* and *number, bad* and *badly, all ready* and *already.* The Glossary of Terms not only defines key terms in the text but also includes a complete verb conjugation and a complete list of irregular verbs with their principal parts.

A book of exercises is available for instructors who wish to use it as reinforcement. As this exercise book also accompanies *The Rinehart Handbook for Writers,* a longer text, instructors will use only those exercises that cover material in *The Rinehart Guide to Grammar and Style* (Parts I–IV and the two appendices, on spelling and English as a second language, respectively). Instructors may assign the appropriate exercises to students for practice or use them for tests.

A book of answers to exercises is also available. It features an instructor's manual with suggestions for using Parts I through IV. Instructors may request that both the exercises and answer books be packaged with *The Rinehart Guide to Grammar and Style,* Fourth Edition.

Although *The Rinehart Guide to Grammar and Style* is concise, it contains a wealth of information. Moreover, it accommodates a diversity of student abilities, course objectives, and teaching techniques.

Acknowledgments

We thank the following colleagues for the comments and advice on previous editions: Steve Adams, Northeast Louisiana University; Joy Allameh, Eastern Kentucky University; Kristine Anderson, Southern Technical Institute; Bruce Appleby, Southern Illinois University; Tracey Baker, University of Alabama—Birmingham; Conrad Bayley, Glendale Community College; Jane Bouterse, Texarkana College; Henry Brown, Midwestern State University; Alma Bryant, Fort Valley State College; Rebecca Butler, Dalton College; James Bynum, Georgia Tech; Joe Christopher, Tarleton State University; Peggy Cole, Arapahoe Community College; Deborah Core, Eastern Kentucky University; James Creel, Alvin Community College; Joseph Davis, Memphis State University; Ralph Dille, University of Southern Colorado; Charles Dodson, University of North Carolina; Linda Doran, Volunteer State Community College; Joseph Dunne, St. Louis Community College at Meramec; Elizabeth Fifer, Lehigh College; Eleanor Garner, George Washington University; Jan Goodrich, Embry-Riddle Aeronautical University; George Haich, University of North Carolina—Wilmington; Charles Hall, Memphis State University; June Hankins, Southwest Texas State University; Stephen Hathway, Wichita State University; David Higgins, Cameron University; Gertrude Hopkins, Harford Community College; Peggy Jolly, University of Alabama—Birmingham; Edwina Jordan, Illinois Central College; Edward Kline, University of Notre Dame; Cheryl Koski, Louisiana State University; Ruth Laux, Arkansas Technical University; Jane E. Lewis, University of Southern Mississippi; Russell Long, Tarleton State University; Andrea Lunsford, University of British Columbia; Robert Lynch, New Jersey Institute of Technology; Lisa McClure, Southern Illinois University—Carbondale; Beverly McKay, Lenoir Community College; Louis Molina, Miami-Dade Community College South; Sam Phillips, Gaston College; Kenneth Rainey, Memphis State University; Sally Reagan, University of Missouri—St. Louis; Edward Reilly, St. Joseph's College; John Reuter, Florida Southern College; Michael Rossi, Merrimack College; Cheryl Ruggiero, Virginia Polytechnic Institute and State University; Gary Simmers, Dalton College; Mike Slaughter, Illinois Central College; Joyce Smoot, Virginia Polytechnic Institute and State University; Charles Sphar, Delmar College; Jo Tarvers, University of North Carolina—Chapel Hill; John Taylor, South Dakota State University; Elizabeth Thomas, University of New Orleans—Lake Front; George Trail, University of Houston; Daryl Troyer, El Paso Community College; Gloria Tubb, Jones County Junior College; Richard Vandeweghe, University of Colorado at Denver; Harold Veeser, Wichita State University; Art Wagner, Macomb Community College; Laura Weaver, University of Evansville; Betty Wells, Central Virginia Community College; Jack White, Mississippi State University; Marie Wolf, Bergen Community College; Peter Zoller, Wichita State University; Carolyn Drakeford, Benedict College; Chick White, West Texas State University; Noel Mawer, Edward Waters College; Patricia Phillips, Detroit College of Business; Donald Anderson, Marist College; David Rosenwasser, Muhlenberg College; Virginia Polanski, Stonehill College; Richard Kleinman, Cumberland College; Charlotte Perlin, University of Miami; Chris Baker, Lamar University; and Albert Wilhelm, Tennessee Technical University.

We are especially indebted to Penny Stewart for her work on Appendix B (English as a Second Language). Her expertise eased our burdens and improved the book. In addition, we thank the following colleagues for their comments and advice on the fourth edition: George Crandell, Auburn University; Edward Palm, Glenville State College; Donna Smith, Odessa College; Mary Sauer, Indiana University—Purdue University at Indianapolis; Margaret Arnold, Baker College—Flint; Lennet Daigle, North Georgia College; Judith Bentley, South Seattle Community College; Michael Kleeberg, Ball State University; Harry Papagan, Lord Fairfax Community College; and David Miller, Fayetteville Technical Community College.

Many thanks to the staff at Harcourt Brace who made the fourth edition possible. Thanks to Michell Phifer, our developmental editor, for keeping us on track. Thanks to Michael Rosenberg, our executive editor, for his innovative ideas and unfailing good nature. Finally, we owe a very special debt to Clifford Crouch, our senior project editor, who tackled all problems with patience and solved them with skill.

B.C.
C.S.

To the Student

A guide should be handy. In other words, you should have no difficulty finding in it the material you need. If you are using *The Rinehart Guide to Grammar and Style,* Fourth Edition, in class, your instructor can help you learn how to locate information. Remember, however, that you will not always have an instructor to guide you. Therefore, you should become familiar with the organization so that you can find information quickly and easily.

Look carefully at the table of contents to determine what material is available and where it appears. Learn to use the index and glossaries. Make sure you understand the correction symbols and the numbering system of the book. Pay close attention to cross-references; they direct you to related sections of the text.

The Rinehart Guide to Grammar and Style contains all the grammar and usage information you need for writing in the classroom and most of what you need for writing in a professional setting. If you use the book effectively, you may be surprised at how much your writing skills improve—and with them your confidence in yourself and your future.

Contents

Part II

Structural and Grammatical Problems   53

Part III

Punctuation and Mechanics   127

Helpful Lists and Charts

The
Rinehart Guide
to Grammar and Style

I

A REVIEW OF
THE BASICS

The grammar of a language is a system of predictable patterns: words fit together to form phrases; phrases join to form clauses; clauses create sentences. If you can recognize the system's components, you can understand descriptions of acceptable or effective constructions, and you can look up information in an index or glossary. In short, recognition underlies improvement of your writing skills.

1 Nouns
2 Pronouns
3 Adjectives and Adverbs
4 Verbs and Verb Phrases

5 Verbals and Verbal Phrases
6 Function Words
7 Clauses and Sentences

1

NOUNS

Nouns are commonly defined as "words that name persons, places, or things." Although this definition is rather limited, it does contain a key word—*name.* Anything in the physical and mental worlds can be named with a noun.

PEOPLE:	Susan, doctor, singer, family
PLACES:	ocean, Canada, home, campus
THINGS:	popsicle, shoe, fingernail, crater
QUANTITIES:	pound, quart, inch, dollar
SENSES:	sound, smell, taste, feel
FEELINGS:	hope, disappointment, anxiety, peace
OCCURRENCES:	earthquake, wedding, party, contest
ACTIONS:	handshake, smile, leap, wink

You can usually recognize a noun by its function, that is, the position it fills in a phrase or a sentence.

• Nouns follow the articles *a, an,* and *the.*

a field	the light
an apple	the car

- Nouns appear in phrases after descriptive words known as modifiers.

    a muddy <u>field</u>   the bright <u>light</u>

    a red <u>apple</u>   the new <u>car</u>

- Nouns join with prepositions to form prepositional phrases.

    through a <u>field</u>   behind the <u>light</u>

    in an <u>apple</u>   under the <u>car</u>

- Nouns join with other nouns to form compounds and phrases.

    <u>field</u> house   <u>light</u> bulb

    <u>apple</u> pie   <u>car</u> wreck

- Nouns join with verbs to form sentences.

    A <u>field</u> lay between the house and the lake.

    Pat gave the <u>teacher</u> an apple.

    The <u>light</u> was brilliant.

    My most pressing problem was my <u>car</u>.

1a PROPER AND COMMON NOUNS

Proper nouns are official names, such as names of people, organizations, geographical locations, holidays, languages, and historical events. You can easily recognize proper nouns in prose because they begin with capital letters. **Common nouns,** all other nouns, are usually not capitalized unless they appear as the first word in a sentence. (See Chapter 31.)

PROPER NOUNS	COMMON NOUNS
Muhammad Ali	athlete
United Kingdom	country
Saks	store

Okefenokee	swamp
English	language

1b   SINGULAR AND PLURAL NOUNS

Nouns have **number**—that is, they are either **singular** or **plural.** Singular nouns refer to one person, place, or thing; plural nouns to more than one. Disregarding number can lead to errors in agreement of subject and verb. (See Chapter 10.)

(1)   Simple nouns

Most nouns form plurals with the addition of *-s* or *-es,* sometimes with a slight adjustment in spelling, such as changing *y* to *i* or doubling a consonant.

SINGULAR	PLURAL
week	weeks
box	boxes
quiz	quizzes
destiny	destinies
hero	heroes

Some nouns form plurals in unpredictable ways.

SINGULAR	PLURAL
leaf	leaves
foot	feet
mouse	mice
child	children
salmon	salmon
criterion	criteria

(2) Compound nouns

A compound noun is made up of two or more words functioning as a single noun. The forms of compounds are somewhat unpredictable. In some, the words are separated (*half dollar*); in others, hyphenated (*man-of-war*); and in others, written together (*holdup*).

In addition, the plurals of compounds are formed in different ways. Regularly, the last word in the compound is plural (*gentlemen, backlogs, pocket knives*). But sometimes, the first word is plural (*sisters-in-law, leaves of absence*). And occasionally, either way is acceptable (*attorney generals* or *attorneys general*). Consult a dictionary for the correct forms of compound nouns. If no plural appears, then consider the noun regular and pluralize the last word.

1c POSSESSIVE NOUNS

Nouns have **possessive forms,** which indicate a variety of meanings.

OWNERSHIP:	my sister's house (house belonging to my sister)
AUTHORSHIP:	Ibsen's plays (plays by Ibsen)
SOURCE:	the mayor's permission (permission from the mayor)
MEASUREMENT:	a year's leave (leave of a year)
DESCRIPTION:	men's dormitory (dormitory for men)

You can recognize possessive nouns in prose because they contain apostrophes. Some possessive nouns are formed by the addition of an apostrophe and an *s;* others, by just an apostrophe after a final *s: institution's, James's, doctors', Raiders'.*

For a more detailed discussion of the forms and uses of possessive nouns, see 26a.

2

PRONOUNS

The word **pronoun** means literally "for a noun," and pronouns do, in fact, occur in most of the same positions as nouns and noun phrases.

NOUN: Students can have identification cards made at the sports arena.

PRONOUN: You can have identification cards made at the sports arena.

NOUN PHRASE: I left your coat with the attendant at the door.

PRONOUN: I left your coat with someone at the door.

NOUN PHRASE: The collie ate the whole turkey.

PRONOUN: The collie ate what?

Often, pronouns substitute for previously stated nouns or noun phrases, called **antecedents.**

Voters did not turn out today. They were deterred by the weather.

The curry was so hot that few people could eat it.

A taxpayer whose returns are audited should hire an accountant.

Although they make up a relatively small class of words, pronouns are in constant use. Notice that of the two passages that follow, the one without pronouns sounds unnatural.

WITHOUT PRONOUNS

Emily Dickinson is regarded as a great American poet. Even though Emily Dickinson lived in seclusion, Dickinson's poems have universal significance: Dickinson's poems concern the relationship between the inner self and the outer world. Dickinson regarded the relationship between the inner self and the outer world as tragic. Dickinson examined the relationship between the inner self and the outer world with irony and wit.

WITH PRONOUNS

Emily Dickinson is regarded as a great American poet. Even though she lived in seclusion, her poems have universal significance: they concern the relationship between the inner self and the outer world. She examined this relationship, which she regarded as tragic, with irony and wit.

2a PERSONAL PRONOUNS

The seven **personal pronouns** have different forms for different functions.

I, me, my, mine

you, your, yours

he, him, his

she, her, hers

it, its

we, us, our, ours

they, them, their, theirs

These personal pronouns can be described by four characteristics: number, person, gender, and case.

- **Number** is either singular (*I, you, he, she, it*) or plural (*we, you, they*).

- **Person** identifies whether the pronoun is speaking, spoken to, or spoken about.

FIRST PERSON SINGULAR: *I* [speaker] hear the phone.

FIRST PERSON PLURAL: *We* [speaker and others] demand a recount.

SECOND PERSON: *You* [person spoken to] must apply before June 1.

THIRD PERSON: *She* [person spoken about] is a new client.

- **Gender** is the sex represented by third-person singular pronouns:

    masculine (*he*), feminine (*she*), neuter (*it*)

- **Case** involves the various forms a pronoun takes according to its use in a sentence. (Case forms and their uses are discussed in Chapter 14.)

    They [subject form] are my friends.

    Don't call *them* [object form].

    Their [possessive form] house is on Main Street.

The *-self/-selves* personal pronouns

In addition to case forms, personal pronouns also have compound forms, made by adding the suffixes (endings) *-self* or *-selves: myself, yourself, himself* (not *hisself*), *herself, itself, ourselves, yourselves, themselves* (not *theirselves*). These forms are used in two ways.

- As **reflexives,** the *-self/-selves* pronouns function as objects that rename the subjects of sentences (*we enjoyed ourselves*).

- As **emphatics,** the *-self/-selves* pronouns repeat, for emphasis, the words and phrases they refer to (*she races the boat herself*).

2b   DEMONSTRATIVE PRONOUNS

The only **demonstrative pronouns** are *this* and *that,* along with their corresponding plurals, *these* and *those.* A demonstrative can be used alone to point out that something is relatively near to or far from the speaker.

This certainly has been a better year than that. [*This* year is the present year; *that* is past.]

I prefer these to those. [*These* are closer to the speaker than *those*.]

A demonstrative pronoun usually precedes a noun and functions like the determiner *the* to indicate that something has been previously mentioned.

Dieters should avoid beef, pork, and lamb when dining out, since these meats are high in both calories and fat. [*These meats* refers to beef, pork, and lamb.]

In the last game of the season, the coach threw a chair at the referee; that tantrum cost him his job. [*That tantrum* refers to the coach's behavior.]

2c RELATIVE PRONOUNS

The **relative pronouns** are as follows.

who,* whom* (referring to people)

which, what (referring to things)

that, whose* (referring to either people or things)

Since their function is to introduce adjective clauses (7c.2) and noun clauses (7c.3), you can use relative pronouns to combine sentences and eliminate choppy prose.

CHOPPY: I voted for the candidate. He promised the least.

IMPROVED: I voted for the candidate who promised the least.

CHOPPY: Julia arrived in a limousine. She had rented it at great expense.

IMPROVED: Julia arrived in a limousine, which she had rented at great expense.

---

*These forms represent different cases: subjective (*who*), objective (*whom*), and possessive (*whose*). See Chapter 14.

CHOPPY: Only one creature recognized Ulysses. It was his dog.

IMPROVED: The only creature <u>that</u> recognized Ulysses was his dog.

The relatives *who, which,* and *what* sometimes appear with the suffix *-ever* in noun clauses.

<u>Whoever</u> raises the most money wins the trip.

Discuss first <u>whichever</u> question seems easiest to you.

He said <u>whatever</u> came to his mind.

2d INTERROGATIVE PRONOUNS

The **interrogative pronouns** (*who, whom, whose, which,* and *what*) introduce questions that ask for information, rather than a yes or no answer. (For the distinction between *who* and *whom,* see 14c.)

<u>Who</u> painted the ceiling of the Sistine Chapel?

<u>Whose</u> idea was it to tell stories on the way to Canterbury?

<u>Which</u> house was Liberace's?

<u>What</u> did Arthur call his sword?

2e INDEFINITE PRONOUNS

Most **indefinite pronouns** need not refer to specific people or things and can be completely general, such as those in the following two sentences.

<u>Anyone</u> can raise tropical fish.

To an adolescent, <u>everything</u> seems a crisis.

However, indefinites can also refer to something definite—a noun or noun phrase already named or about to be named.

Numerous needleleaf trees grow in the Southeast, but <u>few</u> are as graceful as the loblolly pine.

<u>Many</u> of the North American totems depict birds and fish.

Many indefinite pronouns can serve as determiners, modifying nouns. (See 6c.)

> <u>Neither</u> apartment had enough closet space.

> We expected <u>some</u> support from the local media.

Indefinite Pronouns		
all	everyone	no one
another	everything	nothing
any	few	one
anybody	many	other
anyone	more	others
anything	most	several
both	much	some
each	neither	somebody
either	nobody	someone
everybody	none	something

Two indefinites, called **reciprocal pronouns,** require antecedents. *Each other* refers to two persons or things; *one another,* to more than two.

> The two participants debated <u>each other</u> for an hour.

> The four directors communicate with <u>one another</u> by telephone.

3

ADJECTIVES AND ADVERBS

Adjectives and **adverbs** are modifiers—that is, they describe, limit, or qualify some other word or words. Most modifiers flesh out basic sentence structure but do not change it. For example, if the underlined modifiers were deleted, the structure of the following sentence would be unaltered.

> Suddenly I came over a steep rise and saw a panoramic sweep of brilliantly blue water and alabaster sand.

On the other hand, some modifiers are not merely descriptive additions but part of the basic sentence structure. For example, if the underlined words in the following sentences were deleted, the structures would be unfinished.

> The water is cold.

> Grady seemed angry.

> The court declared the law unconstitutional.

> The auditor is here.

3a ADJECTIVES

Adjectives modify nouns and a few pronouns to express attributes such as quality, quantity, or type. You can usually identify adjectives by their characteristic positions, or functions.

- Before nouns (and occasionally pronouns)

    <u>rusty</u> scissors

    <u>flexible</u> plastic

    <u>new</u> one

- After *very*

    very <u>rusty</u>

    very <u>flexible</u>

    very <u>new</u>

- After forms of the verb *be*

    The scissors are <u>rusty</u>.

    This plastic is <u>flexible</u>.

    That one is <u>new</u>.

3b ADVERBS

Adverbs modify adjectives, other adverbs, verbs, and whole clauses. Consequently, you will find adverbs in a variety of forms and positions.

- Most adverbs are made by the addition of -*ly* to adjectives: *boldly, smoothly, actively, gracefully, suddenly.* These adverbs can usually be moved about in sentences.

    <u>Suddenly</u>, all the lights went out.

    All the lights <u>suddenly</u> went out.

    All the lights went out <u>suddenly</u>.

- A small but widely used group of adverbs includes *now, then, soon, still, last, here, there, always, never, once*—expressions of time, place, distance, and frequency. These adverbs, too, can often be moved about in sentences.

    <u>Now</u> we hope to buy a condominium.

    We <u>now</u> hope to buy a condominium.

    We hope to buy a condominium <u>now</u>.

- Also movable are the conjunctive adverbs: *furthermore, however, therefore, also, thus, instead, consequently,* and so forth. Sometimes called transitional expressions, the conjunctive adverbs modify whole clauses and provide transition between sentences and paragraphs. (See *Transitional Expression* in the Glossary of Terms.)

  The commercial is extremely annoying; also, it is insulting to women.

  The commercial is extremely annoying; it is also insulting to women.

- Another type of movable adverb is produced by the combination of *some, any, every,* and *no* with words like *how, place, where,* and *way: somehow, someplace, anywhere, anyway, everywhere, nowhere.*

  Somehow we managed to get the canoe righted.

  We somehow managed to get the canoe righted.

  We managed somehow to get the canoe righted.

  We managed to get the canoe righted somehow.

- The suffixes *-ward* and *-wise* produce adverbs like *backward, southward, lengthwise,* and *clockwise.* These adverbs usually occur after a verb or its object.

  The man was walking backward.

  Cut the board lengthwise.

- Some adverbs, the qualifiers, restrict or intensify adjectives and other adverbs: *very, quite, really, rather, hardly, somewhat,* and so forth. The qualifiers appear immediately before the words they modify.

  The boat was hardly visible from shore.

  He turned down my request very cheerfully.

- When not coupled with nouns, some prepositions can also function as adverbs: *in, out, up, down, over, under, inside, outside,* and so forth. These adverbs usually express place or direction and appear with verbs.

We were locked <u>inside</u>.

Don't look <u>down</u>.

- Adverbs that function as interrogatives—*when, where, why,* and *how*—normally appear at the beginning of a clause or before an infinitive.

    <u>Where</u> is the next meeting?

    We don't know <u>when</u> the funds will be available.

    The first chapter explains <u>how</u> to string a guitar.

3c ADJECTIVE AND ADVERB FORMS

Most adjectives and adverbs have three forms, sometimes called **degrees.** The **positive** form is the simple form of a modifier (*a <u>new</u> building*). The **comparative** form makes a comparison between two people or things (*the <u>newer</u> of the two buildings*) and between a person or thing and other individual members of a group (*a building <u>newer</u> than any other in town*). The **superlative** form compares three or more people or things (*the <u>newest</u> of the three buildings*) and describes the position of a person or thing within its group (*the <u>newest</u> building in town*).

Most one-syllable and some two-syllable adjectives and adverbs show degree with *-er/-est* forms (*short, shorter, shortest; funny, funnier, funniest; near, nearer, nearest*).

Adjective

Positive:	The lake is <u>large</u>.
Comparative:	Sardis is the <u>larger</u> of the two lakes.
Superlative:	Superior is the <u>largest</u> of the Great Lakes.

Adverb

Positive:	I arrived <u>early</u> for the dinner party.
Comparative:	I arrived <u>earlier</u> than anyone else.
Superlative:	Of all the guests, I arrived <u>earliest</u>.

Some adjectives and adverbs have irregular comparative and superlative forms, for example, *good, better, best; many, more, most; badly, worse, worst.*

POSITIVE:	In light years, Mercury is not <u>far</u> from the sun.
COMPARATIVE:	Saturn is <u>farther</u> from the sun than Jupiter.
SUPERLATIVE:	Pluto is <u>farthest</u> from the sun.

Adjectives and adverbs without *-er/-est* forms show degree with *more* and *most* or *less* and *least.* These adjectives and adverbs have at least two but usually three or more syllables (*careful, more careful, most careful; important, less important, least important; fully, more fully, most fully; suddenly, less suddenly, least suddenly*).

Adjective

POSITIVE:	The kitchen was <u>spacious</u>.
COMPARATIVE:	The kitchen was <u>more spacious</u> than the den.
SUPERLATIVE:	The kitchen was the <u>most spacious</u> room in the house.

Adverb

POSITIVE:	The campaign was <u>carefully</u> planned.
COMPARATIVE:	This year's campaign was <u>less carefully</u> planned than last year's.
SUPERLATIVE:	This year's campaign was the <u>least carefully</u> planned of the three.

You can be sure that any word with degree is either an adjective or an adverb. For a discussion of the appropriate use of comparatives and superlatives, see 15b.

4

VERBS AND VERB PHRASES

Verbs and **verb phrases** make up the most versatile word class in the language. They state action, occurrence, and existence. In addition, their various forms and functions can express an enormous range of meaning and subtle distinctions. Without doubt, the effective use of English requires mastering the verb system.

4a BASIC FORMS

All verbs and verb phrases include one of the basic forms. Three of these forms—base, past, and past participle—are often called the three **principal parts.** As the charts illustrate, regular verbs make their past forms and past participles by adding -*d* or -*ed* to the base; irregular verbs do not follow this predictable pattern.

In addition to the three principal parts, two other forms exist for all verbs, both regular and irregular: the -*s* form, made by adding -*s* or -*es* to the base, and the present participle, made by adding -*ing* to the base. Thus, all verbs (except *be,* which is treated separately) can be said to have a total of five possible forms.

Examples of Regular Verbs				
Base	*-s Form*	*Past*	*Past Participle*	*Present Participle*
assume	assumes	assumed	assumed	assuming
drag	drags	dragged	dragged	dragging
dry	dries	dried	dried	drying
enjoy	enjoys	enjoyed	enjoyed	enjoying
fix	fixes	fixed	fixed	fixing

Examples of Irregular Verbs				
Base	*-s Form*	*Past*	*Past Participle*	*Present Participle*
begin	begins	began	begun	beginning
cut	cuts	cut	cut	cutting
draw	draws	drew	drawn	drawing
eat	eats	ate	eaten	eating
leave	leaves	left	left	leaving
think	thinks	thought	thought	thinking

You will find a complete list of irregular verbs and their principal parts under *Irregular Verb* in the Glossary of Terms. Also, for information about correct use of verb forms, see Chapter 11.

The verb *be* does not follow the patterns of other verbs; it has eight forms, including three for the *-s* form and two for the past form.

Forms of *Be*				
Base	*-s Form*	*Past*	*Past Participle*	*Present Participle*
be	am	was	been	being
	is	were		
	are			

4b AUXILIARIES AND VERB PHRASES

Frequently, the verb in a sentence is not a single word but a phrase. In the phrase, the last verb is the **main verb,** and all preceding verbs are **auxiliaries.**

Intense heat does not affect the paint.

The orchestra has been rehearsing.

The wallet might have been stolen.

There are four categories of auxiliaries that combine with one another and with main verbs to create a variety of structures and subtle shades of meaning: auxiliaries that use *be, have,* or *do* and modal auxiliaries.

(1) *Be* auxiliary

The *be* auxiliary appears in one of eight forms (*am, is, are, was, were, be, being, been*) and is always followed by the present or past participle.

AUXILIARY + PRESENT PARTICIPLE OF *LEAVE:*	He is leaving.
AUXILIARY + PAST PARTICIPLE OF *FIRE:*	I was fired today.

(2) *Have* auxiliary

The *have* auxiliary appears in one of four forms (*have, has, had, having*) and is always followed by a past participle.

AUXILIARY + PAST PARTICIPLE OF *FORGET:*	I have forgotten the combination.
AUXILIARY + PAST PARTICIPLE OF *BREAK:*	The quarterback had broken his ankle.

(3) Modal auxiliaries

The modal auxiliaries influence the "mood" of verbs by expressing ideas such as ability, obligation, necessity, and possibility. For example, the verb *complete* takes on slightly different meanings when accompanied by different modal auxiliaries.

ABILITY: The crew can complete the job in one week.

OBLIGATION: You should complete the investigation before you begin the report.

NECESSITY: We must complete the remodeling by June.

POSSIBILITY: I may complete the course in time for graduation.

The common modal auxiliaries are *will, would, can, could, shall, should, may, might,* and *must.* These auxiliaries are followed by the base form of either the main verb, the *be* auxiliary, or the *have* auxiliary.

AUXILIARY + BASE FORM OF *ARRANGE:* The director will arrange a meeting.

AUXILIARY + BASE FORM OF *BE* AUXILIARY: She might be living in Paris.

AUXILIARY + BASE FORM OF *HAVE* AUXILIARY: I could have taken three courses this summer.

(4) *Do* auxiliary

The *do* auxiliary appears in one of three forms (*do, does, did*) and is always followed by the base form of the main verb. This auxiliary is unique in that it cannot combine with other auxiliaries.

AUXILIARY + BASE FORM OF *REVEAL:* The studies do reveal current trends.

AUXILIARY + BASE FORM OF *BLOOM:* The tree did not bloom this year.

4c TENSE

Tense places the verb in a time frame. For example, past tense can express an action already completed, and present perfect tense can express an action begun in the past but not yet completed. Nevertheless, tense is not always equivalent to time, and the uses of tenses can overlap. Present and future tense, for instance, often convey the same idea.

PRESENT TENSE: Intense heat causes the surface to crack.

FUTURE TENSE: Intense heat will cause the surface to crack.

The following charts show the range of meanings that can be expressed by the three simple tenses (present, past, and future) and the three perfect tenses (present perfect, past perfect, and future perfect).

Simple Tenses		
Formation	*Uses*	*Examples*
Present -*s* form in third-person singular; base form everywhere else	present time with certain verbs, especially referring to senses	I hear a car in the driveway.
	statements of fact	The Amazon empties into the Atlantic.
	repetitive action	She walks to school.
	references to works of art and literature	In the *Mona Lisa,* the woman smiles enigmatically.
	future time	The races start tomorrow.
Past past form	past occurrences	The Rams won the game.
Future *will* + base form and sometimes *shall* + base form*	future time	The store will open in May.
	results of conditions	If suddenly heated, air will expand violently.

*In current usage, *shall* and *will* often suggest different meanings. *Shall we go?* is an invitation meaning "Would you like to go?" *Will we go?* asks "Are we going?" *Shall* also occurs in set expressions (*we shall overcome*), in laws and resolutions (*the court shall set the fine*), and in heightened prose (*we shall never surrender*).

Perfect Tenses		
Formation	*Uses*	*Examples*
Present Perfect *have/has* + past participle	occurrences completed at an unspecified time in the past	He has sung at the Met.
	action begun in the past and continuing to the present	We have always gone to Vermont in June.
Past Perfect *had* + past participle	past action occurring before some other past action	The troops had reached the river when the mes- sage arrived.
Future Perfect *will* + *have* + past participle	action that will occur before or by the time of another future action	We will have left by the time he arrives.

4d PROGRESSIVE FORMS

The six tenses have **progressive forms** that indicate actions in progress. A progressive verb is made with a form of the verb *be* followed by a present participle (an *-ing* form of the verb). The following charts explain the progressive forms and their uses.

Simple Progressive Forms		
Formation	*Uses*	*Examples*
Present Progressive *am/is/are* + present participle	action currently in progress	Crowds are lining the streets.
	future time	He is sailing Monday.
Past Progressive *was/were* + present participle	past action in progress	I was sleeping when he called.
Future Progressive *will be* + present participle	future action in progress	Kathy will be traveling next month.
	future action that is not continuous	She will be arriving at noon.

Perfect Progressive Forms		
Formation	*Uses*	*Examples*
Present Perfect Progressive		
have/has + *been* + present participle	continuous past actions still occurring or occurring until recently	The committee has been considering the issue all week.
Past Perfect Progressive		
had + *been* + present participle	past action in progress until another past action occurred	He had been lifting weights daily before his doctor advised restraint.
Future Perfect Progressive		
will + *have* + *been* + present participle	continuous future action that will be complete at some other future time	He will have been pitching for fifteen years by the time the season ends.

4e VOICE

Some verbs can be expressed in both active and passive voice. In **active voice,** the subject acts or in some way controls the action of the verb, and the object receives the action. Active-voice sentences have this pattern:

ACTOR	VERB	RECEIVER
An auditor	has checked	the figures.
Snow	covers	the mountains.
My dog	ate	my lunch.
Disney	is filming	the movie.

In **passive voice,** the subject receives the action. The actor or agent, if named, appears in a prepositional phrase beginning with *by* or *with.* It is easy to recognize passive-voice verbs: they always contain a form of *be* plus the past participle. Sentences with passive-voice verbs have this pattern:

RECEIVER	FORM OF *BE*	PAST PARTICIPLE	*BY* OR *WITH*	ACTOR
The figures	have been	checked	by	an auditor.
The mountains	are	covered	with	snow.
My lunch	was	eaten	by	my dog.
The movie	is being	filmed	by	Disney.

Often in passive voice, the agent is not named: the *by* or *with* phrase is omitted.

ACTIVE: The horse threw the rider over the fence.

PASSIVE: The rider was thrown over the fence by the horse.

PASSIVE: The rider was thrown over the fence.

ACTIVE: Trash littered the streets.

PASSIVE: The streets were littered with trash.

PASSIVE: The streets were littered.

For a discussion of when to avoid and when to use the passive voice, see 33c.2.

4f MOOD

The **mood** of a verb indicates whether the idea expressed is a fact (indicative mood), a command (imperative mood), or a matter of desire or possibility (subjunctive). The three moods are expressed through special verb forms.

(1) Indicative mood

The **indicative mood** is used to make statements and ask questions.

She paints murals.

Squirrels ate the birdseed.

Who is your senator?

Has the mail arrived?

This mood has six tenses, explained by the charts in 4c and 4d.

(2)   Imperative mood

The **imperative mood** is used to give commands. The omitted but understood subject of all imperative verbs is the singular or plural *you.* In addition, for all verbs except *be,* the imperative is the form used with *you* in the present tense.

POSITIVE	NEGATIVE
Answer the memo.	Do not/Don't answer the memo.
Order the sirloin.	Do not/Don't order the sirloin.

The imperative of the verb *be* is always *be* for positive commands and *do not/don't be* for negative commands.

POSITIVE	NEGATIVE
Be serious.	Do not/Don't be serious.
Be an observer.	Do not/Don't be an observer.

(3)   Subjunctive mood

The forms of **subjunctive** verbs (other than *be*) are the same as the forms of the indicative except in one respect: the *-s* is not added in the third-person singular present tense.

SUBJUNCTIVE: Heaven forbid.

INDICATIVE: Heaven forbids.

With *be,* the present-tense subjunctive is always *be;* the past-tense subjunctive is always *were.*

SUBJUNCTIVE: We demand that the accused be tried in a court of law.

INDICATIVE: The accused is tried in a court of law.

SUBJUNCTIVE: Even if the movie were free, I would not see it.

INDICATIVE: The movie was free, but I did not see it.

In current English, the subjunctive mood has limited use, appearing only in three special contexts.

- The subjunctive is present in a few traditional expressions, such as farewells and blessings.

  SUBJUNCTIVE: Peace be with you.

  INDICATIVE: Peace is with you.

  SUBJUNCTIVE: Long live the queen.

  INDICATIVE: The queen lives long.

- The subjunctive is used in clauses introduced by conjunctions such as *if, as if,* and *as though* to express hypothetical situations or conditions contrary to fact.

  SUBJUNCTIVE: If a left turn signal were installed, traffic flow would improve.

  INDICATIVE: When a left turn signal was installed, traffic flow improved.

  SUBJUNCTIVE: If I were you, I would not smoke.

  INDICATIVE: I am not you, but I don't think you should smoke.

- The subjunctive occurs in *that* clauses naming demands, recommendations, wishes, and needs.

  SUBJUNCTIVE: We demand that the terms of the contract be met.

  INDICATIVE: The demands of the contract are met.

SUBJUNCTIVE: The committee recommended that he submit a proposal.

INDICATIVE: He submits a proposal.

SUBJUNCTIVE: I wish I were good at math. [*That* is understood after
wish.]

INDICATIVE: I am good at math.

SUBJUNCTIVE: It is urgent that the police department enforce zoning
regulations.

INDICATIVE: The police department enforces zoning regulations.

5

VERBALS AND VERBAL PHRASES

A **verbal** is a present participle (*winning*), a past participle (*won*), or an infinitive (*to win*) functioning in a sentence as something other than a verb. A verbal may function as a noun, an adjective, or an adverb.

<u>Winning</u> was all that mattered to him.

Teams are rated by the number of games <u>won</u>.

We were surprised <u>to win</u>.

A **verbal phrase** is a verbal plus any words that complete its meaning.

<u>Winning the game</u> was all that mattered to him.

Teams are rated by the number of games <u>won within the conference</u>.

We were surprised <u>to win so easily</u>.

5a INFINITIVES AND INFINITIVE PHRASES

Infinitives begin with *to,* followed by a verb (*to go, to think, to seem*). These verbals appear alone or in phrases and can function as adverbs, adjectives, and nouns.

- As adverbs

  The audience rose to cheer the performance. [modifying *rose*]

  This exercise machine is difficult to use. [modifying *difficult*]

  The river flows too slowly to do much damage. [modifying *slowly*]

  To return to my question, is the government interfering in another country's affairs? [modifying the rest of the sentence]

- As adjectives

  Many writers have a tendency to use too many commas. [modifying *tendency*]

  A poison to kill fire ants is now available. [modifying *poison*]

- As nouns

  To invest successfully in oil requires the instincts of a good gambler. [subject of *requires*]

  Darwin believed natural selection to be important in the origin of plants and animals. [object of *believed*]

  The delegates argued about how to cast the votes. [object of *about*]

The "sign" of the infinitive, *to,* is omitted after certain verbs like *let, help, make, hear, see,* and *feel.*

  Let the record show that only four people were present.

  We saw her steal the necklace.

5b PARTICIPLES AND PARTICIPIAL PHRASES

Participles exist in two forms: the present participle and the past participle. You can always identify a present participle by its *-ing* ending—for example, *walking, thinking, singing.* The past participle is the form that can follow *have* in a verb phrase—for example, *walked, thought, sung.* Participles, alone or in phrases, can act as adjectives to modify nouns or pronouns.

  The missing passengers apparently drowned after the ferry capsized. [present participle modifying *passengers*]

The passengers, <u>missing after the ferry capsized</u>, apparently drowned. [present participial phrase modifying *passengers*]

The <u>frightened</u> people panicked and fled the hostile "Martians." [past participle modifying *people*]

<u>Frightened by the broadcast</u>, people panicked and fled the hostile "Martians." [past participial phrase modifying *people*]

5c   GERUNDS AND GERUND PHRASES

Gerunds are present participles (*walking, believing, feeling*) functioning as nouns. Like other verbals, gerunds can appear alone or in phrases.

<u>Selling beer without a license</u> is illegal. [subject of *is*]

The patient had lost <u>his hearing</u> because of a childhood illness. [object of *had lost*]

Mendel devoted his time to <u>studying genetics</u>. [object of *to*]

5d   ABSOLUTE VERBAL PHRASES

An **absolute phrase** does not modify any one element in a sentence but instead modifies the rest of the sentence. Thus, the absolute phrase seems rather loosely connected. There are two types of absolute verbal phrases.

- The first is a familiar expression containing a participle or an infinitive.

  <u>Speaking of friends</u>, Susan let me use her credit card when I was broke.

  <u>To tell the truth</u>, my vacation was more work than my job.

- The second is the nominative absolute—a phrase beginning with a noun or pronoun that acts as the subject of the verbal. The nominative absolute is somewhat formal and usually explains causes or adds details to sentences.

  <u>His fortune squandered on cards and horses</u>, he went to work as a valet.

The seas being rough, we put into harbor.

The estate will be liquidated, everything to be sold at auction.

The gunfighter of Hollywood westerns was casually sinister—guns slung low on his hips, hat cocked rakishly over one eye, steps measured and slow.

6

FUNCTION WORDS

Nouns, verbs, adjectives, and adverbs make up the greater part of our vocabulary and convey most of the semantic meaning of sentences. However, meaning also depends on **functions words:** prepositions, conjunctions, determiners, and expletives. These words create structure. If the function words are removed from a sentence, all that remains is a list of unrelated vocabulary items.

WITH FUNCTION WORDS: Under the canopy sat a man and a woman waiting for the bus.

WITHOUT FUNCTION WORDS: canopy sat man woman waiting bus

You might think of the vocabulary items as bricks and of the function words as the mortar that holds them together: both are necessary to build meaning.

6a PREPOSITIONS AND PREPOSITIONAL PHRASES

A **prepositional phrase** contains a preposition and its object, usually a noun, noun phrase, or pronoun. The following list includes some of the most common prepositions. Those made up of two and three words are called **phrasal prepositions.**

above	during	onto
across	except	out
after	except for	outside of
against	for	over
around	from	past
as	in	since
at	in front of	through
away from	in spite of	toward
because of	into	under
before	like	until
beneath	near	up
between	of	with
by	off	within
by means of	on	without
down		

As the following examples demonstrate, prepositional phrases can modify a variety of elements.

boats <u>in the harbor</u> [modifying a noun]

a rusty bicycle <u>without wheels</u> [modifying a noun phrase]

everything <u>on the back porch</u> [modifying a pronoun]

ran <u>through the alley</u> [modifying a verb]

performing <u>at Christmas</u> [modifying a verbal]

optimistic <u>about the future</u> [modifying an adjective]

In addition to their use as modifiers, prepositional phrases can also function like nouns, usually as objects but occasionally as subjects.

The creature emerged from <u>behind the snow bank</u>. [object of *from*]

<u>After Thursday</u> will be too late. [subject of sentence]

6b CONJUNCTIONS

Conjunctions are grammatical connectors that link sentence elements and express relationships between ideas. For instance, conjunctions attribute causes and effects; signal time sequences; indicate alternatives, parallels, or contrasts. As you can see from reading the following passage, prose without conjunctions can be disjointed.

WITHOUT CONJUNCTIONS

We rarely think in terms of meters/liters. We are accustomed to inches/pounds. There has been an effort to change to the metric system. The changeover has met strong opposition. We are familiar with a foot. We can estimate length fairly accurately in feet. We can easily stride off a distance to measure it in yards.

The addition of conjunctions makes clear the relationships of the ideas.

WITH CONJUNCTIONS

We rarely think in terms of meters and liters because we are accustomed to inches and pounds. Although there has been an effort to change to the metric system, the changeover has met strong opposition. We are so familiar with a foot that we can estimate length in feet fairly accurately, and we can easily stride off a distance to measure it in yards.

(1) Coordinating conjunctions

Coordinating conjunctions connect words, phrases, and clauses to grammatically coordinate, or equal, structures. Five coordinators—*and, but, or, nor,* and *yet*—can join any structures that are grammatically equal.

NOUNS:	I always order fish or chicken.
VERBS:	We did not eat nor sleep for five days.
ADJECTIVES:	The singer was loud but off-key.
PREPOSITIONAL PHRASES:	The road runs through the valley and up the mountains.
CLAUSES:	He was a stern man, yet he was patient.

Two coordinators—*for* and *so*—connect only independent clauses.

INDEPENDENT CLAUSES:	The conductor stopped, for the cellist had begun to snore.

INDEPENDENT CLAUSES: English has only a few inflections, <u>so</u> it does not have a very flexible word order.

(2) Correlative conjunctions

A special type of coordinating conjunction, the **correlative,** has two parts that connect elements of equal grammatical structure— two nouns, two verbs, two adjectives, two dependent clauses, two independent clauses, and so forth. The correlatives *both . . . and* and *not . . . but* connect elements within clauses.

ADJECTIVES: The program includes <u>both</u> isometric <u>and</u> aerobic exercise.

NOUNS: The problem is <u>not</u> the hardware <u>but</u> the software.

Three sets of correlatives—*not only . . . but also, either . . . or, neither . . . nor*—can connect two independent clauses as well as elements within independent clauses.

ADJECTIVES: The stove is <u>not only</u> compact <u>but also</u> fuel efficient.

PREPOSITIONAL PHRASES: Paper is made <u>either</u> by a mechanical process <u>or</u> by a chemical process.

NOUNS: <u>Neither</u> Melville <u>nor</u> Hawthorne is as popular with students as Poe is.

CLAUSES: <u>Not only</u> did the Egyptians distinguish between planets and stars, <u>but also</u> they devised a 365-day calendar.

(3) Subordinating conjunctions

Subordinating conjunctions introduce dependent clauses (7c) and express relationships such as cause, contrast, condition, manner, place, and time. Some commonly used subordinators are listed here.

after	except that	than
although	if	that

as	in case	unless
as if	in that	until
as though	now that	when
because	once	whenever
before	since	where
even though	so that	while

The following examples suggest the versatility of subordinate clauses, but for a more complete discussion, see 7c.1.

MODIFYING A VERB: You should act <u>as though you are accustomed to such elegance</u>.

MODIFYING AN ADJECTIVE: I am sure <u>that he has forgotten the appointment</u>.

MODIFYING A CLAUSE: <u>When the movie began</u>, the theater was empty.

(4) Comparative conjunctions

A special type of subordinating conjunction has two parts—for example, *so . . . that* and *as . . . as.* These conjunctions usually introduce clauses of measurement or degree; that is, they introduce ideas that express how much or to what extent. The following are the most common **comparatives.**

- *as . . . as*

  She is not <u>as</u> clever <u>as</u> I thought she was.

- *so . . . that*

  Paul was <u>so</u> scared <u>that</u> he was shaking.

- *such . . . that*

  He is <u>such</u> a nice man <u>that</u> people take advantage of him.

- A comparative form of an adjective or adverb . . . *than*

  The river is clean<u>er</u> <u>than</u> it was last year.

  This pump works <u>more</u> efficiently <u>than</u> the old one did.

- A superlative form of an adjective . . . *that*

  ~~His Thunderbird was the fanciest car that I had ever seen.~~

  The game is the <u>most</u> complicated <u>that</u> the company has designed.

6c DETERMINERS

Determiners signal that a noun will follow, if not immediately, then shortly. Some words are always determiners.

- The articles—*a, an, the*

  <u>A</u> new theory about dinosaurs has been proposed.

  Where did you hide <u>the</u> chocolate chip cookies?

- Some possessive pronouns—*my, her, its, our, your, their, whose*

  <u>Her</u> German accent sounds authentic.

  <u>Whose</u> music did they play?

- An indefinite pronoun—*every*

  <u>Every</u> item was marked down 50 percent.

In addition, some nouns and pronouns frequently function as determiners.

- Possessives: *his, everyone's, Kathy's, today's,* and so on

  DETERMINER: Leading the discussion is <u>his</u> responsibility.

  PRONOUN: The responsibility is <u>his</u>.

- Demonstrative pronouns: *this, that, these, those*

  DETERMINER: You must pack <u>these</u> provisions for the trip.

  PRONOUN: The necessary provisions are <u>these</u>: food, water, and first-aid equipment.

- Indefinite pronouns: *each, either, neither, all, some, many, much, any, few, more, less,* and so on

DETERMINER: Few inventors achieve success.

PRONOUN: Of the thousands of inventors, few achieve success.

- Interrogative pronouns: *which, what*

DETERMINER: We could not determine which virus was present.

PRONOUN: A virus was present, but we could not determine which.

- Cardinal numbers—*one, two, three,* and so on

DETERMINER: The terrorists showed pictures of four hostages.

NOUN: There were six hostages, but the terrorists showed pictures of only four.

6d EXPLETIVES

The two **expletives,** *it* and *there,* are "filler words" that introduce clauses and allow the real subjects to be delayed until after the verbs or verb auxiliaries. *There* usually introduces a clause with a noun or noun phrase as the subject.

SUBJECT FIRST: A phone is ringing.

SUBJECT DELAYED: There is a phone ringing.

SUBJECT FIRST: A notice from the bank is on your desk.

SUBJECT DELAYED: There is a notice from the bank on your desk.

When the real subject of a clause is an infinitive or a *that* clause, beginning with the expletive *it* sounds more natural than beginning with the subject.

SUBJECT FIRST: To call is important.

SUBJECT DELAYED: It is important to call.

SUBJECT FIRST: That the dam will break is unlikely.

SUBJECT DELAYED: It is unlikely that the dam will break.

The expletive *it* has an additional function—to introduce constructions that have no real subject.

It is raining.

It is noisy in here.

CAUTION: The words *it* and *there* are not always expletives. *There* can function as an adverb; *it* is frequently a pronoun. Compare the following pairs of sentences:

EXPLETIVE: There are three horses in the paddock.

ADVERB: Three horses are there in the paddock.

EXPLETIVE: It is dangerous to jog after eating.

PRONOUN: Jogging after meals is dangerous. It should be avoided.

CHAPTER

7

CLAUSES AND SENTENCES

A **clause** is a grammatical construction with both a subject and a predicate. The simple subject consists of at least one noun (or noun equivalent); the complete subject consists of the noun and its modifiers. The predicate consists of at least one verb and its modifiers. In addition, the predicate may include one or more complements, that is, words necessary to complete the meaning of the verb. As the following examples show, the predicate makes an assertion about its subject.

SUBJECT	PREDICATE
Travis	defended the Alamo.
Everyone in the elevator	panicked.
The convention	will be in Des Moines next year.

An independent, or main, clause expresses a complete idea and can occur by itself as a **sentence** (see 7b). A dependent, or subordinate, clause must occur as part of a sentence. Both independent and dependent clauses have the same structural patterns.

7a CLAUSE PATTERNS

In all clause patterns, the subject is a noun (or noun equivalent) and any modifiers. What distinguishes the patterns from one another is the predicate structure, which is determined by the type of verb it contains—intransitive, transitive, or linking.

(1) Intransitive verb pattern

Technically, an **intransitive verb** is complete by itself and is the only element needed in the predicate structure.

SUBJECT +	INTRANSITIVE VERB
The doctor	smiled.
The prisoner	has escaped.
They	were leaving.

Frequently, however, the pattern is fleshed out by an adverbial modifier following the verb.

The doctor smiled sheepishly.

The prisoner has escaped through a tunnel.

They were leaving before the party was over.

(2) Transitive verb patterns

A **transitive verb** in the active voice requires a direct object, a complement that receives the action. Notice that without the direct objects, the verbs in the following sentences do not seem complete. In addition, some transitive verbs allow indirect objects, and some allow object complements. As a result, there are three transitive verb patterns.

- In one pattern, the subject performs the verb's action, and the direct object receives or is affected by the verb's action.

SUBJECT +	TRANSITIVE VERB +	DIRECT OBJECT
The FBI	investigated	him.
A local press	has published	her memoirs.
Energy shortages	would change	our lifestyles.

One way that you can test this pattern is to convert it to the passive voice (see 4e). In this conversion, you move the direct object to the subject position, where it still receives the verb's action.

> He was investigated by the FBI.
>
> Her memoirs have been published by a local press.
>
> Our lifestyles would be changed by energy shortages.

- Another kind of complement, the indirect object, is common with a few transitive verbs—including *give, make, tell, show, bring, send, sell,* and *offer.* This object appears between the verb and the direct object; like the direct object, it completes the verb's meaning.

SUBJECT	TRANSITIVE VERB	INDIRECT OBJECT	DIRECT OBJECT
Our courts	cannot deny	a felon	due process.
My uncle	knitted	me	a wool sweater.
The professor	asked	us	only one question.

You can identify an indirect object by converting it to a prepositional phrase (with *to, for,* or occasionally *of*) and shifting it to follow the direct object.

> Our courts cannot deny due process to a felon.
>
> My uncle knitted a wool sweater for me.
>
> The professor asked only one question of us.

- Still another kind of complement, the object complement, can occur with a few transitive verbs—including *make, consider, call, elect, appoint, declare, name,* and *choose.* In this pattern, the complement is an adjective or a noun that follows the direct object and refers to it. Without the complement, the verb often means something a bit different or makes no sense. For instance, try reading the following examples with and then without the object complement.

SUBJECT	TRANSITIVE VERB	DIRECT OBJECT	OBJECT COMPLEMENT
The fog	will make	travel	dangerous.
The reporter	called	the senator	devious.
I	kept	the letter	a secret.
Most people	consider	the tomato	a vegetable.

You can identify an object complement by making a kind of equation between it and the direct object: *Travel is dangerous. The senator is devious. The letter is a secret. The tomato is a vegetable.*

(3) Linking verb patterns

A **linking verb** requires a subject complement, which completes the meaning of the verb and refers to the subject.

- An adjective can fill the position of subject complement with almost all linking verbs—*be;* verbs with meanings similar to *be* (including *seem, appear, become, grow, remain*); and verbs that refer to the senses (*look, taste, smell, sound,* and *feel*).

SUBJECT +	LINKING VERB +	ADJECTIVE SUBJECT COMPLEMENT
Most of the guests	were	obnoxious.
The surface	feels	rough.
The crowd	grew	restless.
The witness	seemed	hostile.

Notice that you can test the pattern by making a noun phrase with the subject and subject complement: *obnoxious guests, rough surface, restless crowd, hostile witness.*

- Sometimes the subject complement is a *predicate nominative*—a noun or pronoun that names or refers to the subject. The most common verbs in this pattern are *be, become, remain, seem,* and *appear.*

SUBJECT +	LINKING VERB +	NOUN OR PRONOUN SUBJECT COMPLEMENT
The main problem	is	you.
Stacy	became	a jockey.
All the cousins	remained	friends.

You can test the pattern by making an equation of the subject and the subject complement: *problem = you; Stacy = jockey; cousins = friends.*

- With *be* and *become,* the subject complement can be a possessive:

SUBJECT +	LINKING VERB +	POSSESSIVE SUBJECT COMPLEMENT
That Jaguar	is	Karen's.
The responsibility	became	mine.
The loss	would be	everyone's.

Notice that the subject and complement make a noun phrase: *Karen's Jaguar; my responsibility; everyone's loss.*

- Finally, with *be* only, the complement can be an adverb or an adverb phrase that locates the subject in time or space.

SUBJECT +	LINKING VERB +	ADVERB SUBJECT COMPLEMENT
A police officer	is	outside.
The meeting	will be	tomorrow.
The game	was	at 7:30.

In this pattern, the subject and subject complement can combine to form a noun phrase. The complement, however, follows the subject: *police officer outside; meeting tomorrow; game at 7:30.*

7b INDEPENDENT CLAUSES

Independent clauses (sometimes called *main clauses*) may stand by themselves as sentences.

SUBJECT	PREDICATE
The book	examines human cruelty.
The ideas	are not pessimistic.
A hostile crowd	had gathered.
Serbian assassins	waited.

In addition, independent clauses can be joined to produce compound sentences.

The book examines human cruelty, but the ideas are not pessimistic.

A hostile crowd had gathered; the Serbian assassins waited.

7c DEPENDENT CLAUSES

Like independent clauses, **dependent clauses** (also called *subordinate clauses*) have subjects and predicates. Unlike independent clauses, they cannot stand alone as sentences, and they usually begin with an introductory word that signals dependence.

INTRODUCTORY WORD	SUBJECT	PREDICATE
because	it	causes tarnishing
that	we	call Baalbeck
if	their tires	are underinflated

Because they are not complete in themselves, dependent clauses must be attached to independent clauses:

Pewter articles no longer contain lead because it causes tarnishing.

The town that we call Baalbeck was known to the Greeks as Heliopolis.

Drivers waste gasoline if their tires are underinflated.

Dependent clauses function in sentences as modifiers or as nouns and are generally classified as adverb clauses, adjective clauses, and noun clauses.

(1) Adverb clauses

The most versatile of dependent clauses is the **adverb clause,** which can modify verbs, adjectives, adverbs, and whole clauses. In fact, any dependent clause that does not act as a noun or modify a noun can safely be called an adverb clause.

Adverb clauses are introduced by subordinating conjunctions to express relationships such as time, cause, purpose, condition, contrast, comparison, place, and manner. Most of the subordinating conjunctions can be grouped according to these relationships.

- **Time:** *when, whenever, while, after, before, as, just as, as soon as, until, since, ever since, once, as long as*

    The British blockaded Germany when World War II broke out.

    As soon as a dolphin is born, the mother pushes it to the water's surface for its first breath of air.

- **Cause:** *because, since, now that, once, as, in case*

    Because some years produce better wines, experts often judge quality by the vintage year.

    In Nebraska, most farmers must install irrigation systems in case rainfall is under 10 inches a year.

- **Purpose:** *so that, in order that*

    So that his arrival would be noticed, the star hired teenagers to mob the airport.

    Place bluebird houses facing south in order that the birds can avoid the north wind.

- **Condition:** *if, unless, once, provided that, whatever, whoever, whichever, whether or not, no matter how (which, what, when, who, were), assuming that*

    Please check the color-coded map if you do not know the correct subway line.

No matter how much he eats, he never gains weight.

- **Contrast:** *although, even though, even if, though, except (that), whereas*

  Even though the superhighways have made travel faster, they have also made it less scenic.

  The Aztec capital was as large as a European city, although the Indians neither domesticated animals nor used wheels.

- **Comparison:** *as . . . as, so . . . as, so . . . that, more . . . than, most . . . that, than*

  The Royal Canadian Mounted Police are as effective in reality as they are in legend.

  The Imperial Hotel in Tokyo was so well built that it survived the destructive 1923 earthquake.

- **Place:** *where, wherever*

  We saw nothing but litter where the fair had been.

  The migrant workers went wherever jobs were available.

- **Manner:** *as, as if, as though, just as, just as if*

  She walked with her shoulders squared and head erect as though life were her adversary.

  The Celtics played as if the championship were at stake.

(2) Adjective clauses

Adjective clauses modify nouns and pronouns. These clauses are often called *relative clauses* because they are introduced by relative pronouns (*who/whom/whose, which, that*) or relative adverbs (*when, where, why*). Unlike a subordinating conjunction, which merely connects an adverb clause to a main clause, a relative introducer functions within an adjective clause as a noun or an adverb. Also, the relative introducer follows and refers to the word or phrase being modified.

One-fifth of the water that runs off the Earth's surface is carried by the Amazon.

Afghanistan is a landlocked country whose strategic location has affected its history.

Ellen Terry, who played all of Shakespeare's heroines, was a celebrated actress for almost fifty years.

A tax on tea brought about the Boston Tea Party, which triggered the Revolutionary War.

In Connecticut, November is the month when the wild animals and insects retreat to shelter.

Sometimes an adjective clause appears without a relative introducer. In such cases, the introducer is understood to be *that*.

The playwright [that] he emulates is Tennessee Williams.

The robots [that] they manufacture are installed in chemical plants.

The adjective clause is sometimes set off with commas and sometimes not, depending on its relationship to the noun it modifies. For a discussion of how to punctuate adjective clauses, see 21c. For a discussion of when to use *who/whom* and *whoever/whomever,* see 14c.

(3) Noun clauses

Noun clauses function in the same ways that all nouns do—as subjects, objects, and complements. These clauses are introduced with a variety of words, most of which begin with *wh-*.

that, who, whom, whose, which, what

whoever, whomever, whatever, whichever, however

whether, where, when, how, if

* **Noun clauses as subjects**
  A noun clause functioning as a subject can appear at the beginning of a sentence.

  Whatever you decide is acceptable to me.

This pattern, however, is not very common. More often, the expletive *it* begins the sentence, and the subject clause is moved to the end. (See 6d.)

That a need will arise is unlikely.

It is unlikely that a need will arise.

What you study doesn't matter.

It doesn't matter what you study.

- **Noun clauses as direct objects**
  Noun clauses probably appear most frequently as direct objects after verbs like *say, believe, think, decide, propose, hope,* and *prove*—usually verbs that name some sort of mental activity.

  The scientist calculated that a million black holes exist in our galaxy.

  The group proposed that San Francisco ban the building of more skyscrapers downtown.

  Sometimes the subordinator *that* is left out, although it is understood by a reader.

  Ecologists hope [that] the whooping crane can be saved.

  Buddhists believe [that] monks should live a life of poverty.

- **Noun clauses as objects of prepositions**
  When the noun clause appears as the object of a preposition, the clause usually begins with *whether, how, what, whatever, whoever,* or some other interrogative word.

  After improving the telephone, Edison turned his attention to how one might permanently record sound.

  When he received his "visions," Edgar Cayce was totally unconscious of what went on around him.

- **Noun clauses as subject complements**
  Sometimes, after the verb *be,* noun clauses function as subject complements (predicate nominatives) to rename the subject.

  The problem was that Edward the Confessor died without an heir.

  The candidate will be whoever can afford to run.

7d   ELLIPTICAL CLAUSES

In an **elliptical clause,** one or more words that can be readily understood by the reader are dropped from the complete structure. The most common omissions in elliptical clauses are a relative pronoun (*that* or *whom*), the subject and a form of *be,* or a previously stated verb or predicate.

Most economists believe [that] the bond market is improving.

Dylan Thomas died at age thirty-nine while [he was] on an American tour.

The Appalachian National Scenic Trail is longer than any other hiking trail in the country [is long].

As a rule, private colleges charge more tuition than public colleges [charge].

Bats of some species roost in colonies of millions; others [roost], in solitude.

7e   KINDS OF SENTENCES

Independent clauses appear alone or in combinations—with other independent clauses or with dependent clauses. One method of classifying sentences is based on the number and kinds of clauses in a single construction. According to this classification system, there are four categories of sentences: simple, compound, complex, and compound-complex.

(1)   Simple sentence

A **simple sentence** is made up of only one independent clause. The sentence may contain modifiers and compound elements (for example, compound subjects and verbs), but it may not contain more than one subject-predicate structure.

Cigarette smoke contains carbon monoxide.

For most college students, computers and calculators have become essential.

The Rhone flows south through France and then <u>empties</u> into the Mediterranean.

(2)   Compound sentence

A **compound sentence** is made up of two or more independent clauses. The primary ways to coordinate independent clauses are with commas and coordinating conjunctions (*and, but, or, for, nor, so, yet*) and with semicolons.

> For centuries, Brittany was an independent state, but now the area is part of France.

> The restaurant was dark, the air was filled with smoke, and the music was deafening.

> Socrates wrote nothing; his thoughts are known only through the works of Plato and Xenophon.

(3)   Complex sentence

A **complex sentence** is made up of one independent clause and one or more dependent clauses—adverb, adjective, or noun.

> Although most rifle experts have 20/20 vision, pistol experts are often very nearsighted.

> The game involves three contestants who spin a roulette wheel.

> Whoever could solve the riddle of the Sphinx would be spared her wrath.

(4)   Compound-complex sentence

A **compound-complex sentence** is made up of two or more independent clauses and one or more dependent clauses.

> London's Great Exhibition, which opened in 1851, was designed to show human progress; it brought together in the "Crystal Palace" industrial displays remarkable for their day.

Alchemists believed that they could change lesser metals into gold, and although they failed, they helped establish the science of chemistry.

The fathom once was the distance that a Viking could encompass in a hug; a gauge was the distance that lay between the wheels of a Roman chariot; an acre was an area that could be plowed in one day by a team of two oxen.

II

STRUCTURAL AND GRAMMATICAL PROBLEMS

When you write, you must concentrate on matters such as content, organization, purpose, and audience. Naturally, incorrect constructions are likely to appear in early drafts of a composition. Therefore, before you complete a final draft, read your work carefully and revise any sentences that contain structural or grammatical problems. Careful revision will ensure clear and logical prose.

8

SENTENCE FRAGMENTS

A **sentence fragment** is an incomplete structure punctuated as a complete sentence but lacking the necessary independent clause. The following passage shows how confusing sentence fragments can be.

> Humans accept death as their certain destiny. In nature, however, everything does not die. The hydra, a freshwater, tube-shaped creature. The hydra's body cells regenerate every two weeks. Giving it an unlimited life expectancy. Except for predators and diseases, some fish might never die. Because they never stop growing. In a sense, the amoeba doesn't die. It simply divides. And thus not only survives but also multiplies.

The six complete sentences in the passage express complete thoughts, even out of context.

> Humans accept death as their certain destiny.
>
> In nature, however, everything does not die.
>
> The hydra's body cells regenerate every two weeks.
>
> Except for predators and diseases, some fish might never die.
>
> In a sense, the amoeba doesn't die.
>
> It simply divides.

In contrast, the four fragments seem meaningless.

The hydra, a freshwater, tube-shaped creature.

Giving it an unlimited life expectancy.

Because they never stop growing.

And thus not only survives but also multiplies.

In a few special instances, fragments do not handicap communication.

- **Dialogue:** "Now," thought William. "<u>Now.</u>"

- **Deliberate sylistic effects:** The play catches everyone and everything in its swirl. <u>Rather like a tornado.</u>

- **Questions and answers:** <u>When?</u> <u>Only ten years from now.</u>

- **Interjections:** <u>Oh!</u> <u>Well.</u>

- **Advertising:** <u>The best hardware for your best software.</u>

- **Idioms:** <u>The sooner the better.</u> <u>So much for that.</u>

As a general rule, however, you should avoid fragments. If you do find a fragment while revising your prose, you can either attach it to a complete sentence or convert it to a complete sentence.

8a DEPENDENT CLAUSE FRAGMENTS

A dependent clause contains a subject and a predicate and begins with a subordinating word such as *since, if, because, although, who, which, that* (see 7c). When punctuated as a complete sentence, a dependent clause is considered a fragment.

FRAGMENT:	Registration was a nightmare. <u>Although I did get the courses I wanted.</u>
REVISED:	Registration was a nightmare, although I did get the courses I wanted.
REVISED:	Registration was a nightmare. I did, however, get the courses I wanted.
FRAGMENT:	At age twenty-six, Jefferson began Monticello. <u>Which he did not complete until he was sixty-eight.</u>

REVISED: At age twenty-six, Jefferson began Monticello, which he
did not complete until he was sixty-eight.

REVISED: At age twenty-six, Jefferson began Monticello, but he did
not finish it until he was sixty-eight.

8b PHRASE FRAGMENTS

A phrase is a construction without a subject and a predicate. Ordinarily, a phrase should not appear alone, punctuated as though it
were a complete sentence.

FRAGMENT: Manufacturers will hold a trade fair in St. Louis next month.
The fair to promote new sports equipment.

REVISED: Manufacturers will hold a trade fair in St. Louis next month
to promote new sports equipment.

REVISED: Manufacturers will hold a trade fair in St. Louis next month.
The event will promote new sports equipment.

FRAGMENT: The department's bloodhound has trailed 165 missing people. And has found 85 percent of them.

REVISED: The department's bloodhound has trailed 165 missing people and has found 85 percent of them.

REVISED: The department's bloodhound has trailed 165 missing people; she has found 85 percent of them.

FRAGMENT: Spider Man's strength and climbing ability came from a remarkable source. The bite of a radioactive spider.

REVISED: Spider Man's strength and climbing ability came from a remarkable source: the bite of a radioactive spider.

REVISED: Spider Man's strength and climbing ability came from a remarkable source. He was bitten by a radioactive spider.

FRAGMENT: She quit smoking last Christmas. Because of a chronic cough.

REVISED: She quit smoking last Christmas because of a chronic cough.

REVISED: She quit smoking last Christmas. At that time, her cough
had become chronic.

9

COMMA SPLICES AND FUSED SENTENCES

Two independent clauses joined with only a comma create a **comma splice,** so called because the clauses are "spliced" together. Two clauses run together without a conjunction or proper punctuation create a **fused sentence,** also called a *run-on* or *run-together sentence.*

COMMA SPLICE: Pickpockets have become a serious problem, tourists should be especially alert in crowded areas.

FUSED SENTENCE: Pickpockets have become a serious problem tourists should be especially alert in crowded areas.

Neither of these constructions is acceptable in standard written English. If you find a comma splice or a fused sentence in your rough drafts, you can revise it in one of five ways.

- Use a comma and a coordinating conjunction.
- Use a semicolon.
- Use a colon.
- Create two sentences.
- Create a dependent structure.

57

9a REVISION WITH A COMMA AND A COORDINATING CONJUNCTION

Comma splices and fused sentences can often be revised by connecting the clauses with both a comma and a coordinating conjunction (*and, but, or, nor, for, so, yet*). This option works well when the sentence does not contain much internal punctuation and one of the conjunctions expresses the proper relationship between the two clauses.

COMMA SPLICE: Winter lasts six months in Wyoming, life gets hard at 20 to 40 degrees below zero.

FUSED SENTENCE: Winter lasts six months in Wyoming life gets hard at 20 to 40 degrees below zero.

REVISED: Winter lasts six months in Wyoming, and life gets hard at 20 to 40 degrees below zero.

COMMA SPLICE: My dormitory room is supposed to house two people comfortably, actually it has only enough space for a six-year-old child.

FUSED SENTENCE: My dormitory room is supposed to house two people comfortably actually it has only enough space for a six-year-old child.

REVISED: My dormitory room is supposed to house two people comfortably, but actually it has only enough space for a six-year-old child.

9b REVISION WITH A SEMICOLON

A semicolon works well when the clauses in a comma splice or fused sentence do not have a relationship easily expressed by one of the coordinating conjunctions.

COMMA SPLICE: The novel is remarkable, Mr. Wright has written over 50,000 words without once using the letter *e*.

FUSED SENTENCE: The novel is remarkable Mr. Wright has written over 50,000 words without once using the letter *e*.

REVISED: The novel is remarkable; Mr. Wright has written over ~~50,000 words without once using the letter *e*.~~

The semicolon can also be used in addition to a coordinating conjunction when the first clause has internal punctuation.

COMMA SPLICE: Standing on the pier, her blond hair blowing in the breeze, she looked frail, innocent, and vulnerable, she was actually planning a robbery.

REVISED: Standing on the pier, her blond hair blowing in the breeze, she looked frail, innocent, and vulnerable; <u>yet</u> she was actually planning a robbery.

The semicolon is especially appropriate when the second independent clause begins with a transitional expression (or conjunctive adverb) such as *therefore, consequently, finally, for example, nevertheless, however, then.* (For a more complete list of these expressions, see *Transitional Expression* in the Glossary of Terms.)

Be careful not to confuse coordinating conjunctions and transitional expressions. A conjunction actually links clauses grammatically and cannot move from its position between the two.

POSSIBLE: They discovered that the library ceiling contained asbestos, <u>but</u> the school could not afford to have the material removed.

IMPOSSIBLE: They discovered that the library ceiling contained asbestos; the school could not, <u>but</u>, afford to have the material removed.

A transitional expression, on the other hand, is not a conjunction but an adverb and can move about in its clause.

POSSIBLE: They discovered that the library ceiling contained asbestos; <u>however</u>, the school could not afford to have the material removed.

POSSIBLE: They discovered that the library ceiling contained asbestos; the school could not, <u>however</u>, afford to have the material removed.

An easy way to distinguish between the two types of words is to remember that all the coordinating conjunctions have only two or three letters, whereas all the transitional expressions have four or more.

9c REVISION WITH A COLON

Occasionally, one independent clause is followed by another that explains or amplifies it. In this very special case, you can join the two clauses with a colon.

COMMA SPLICE: The economics of the country caused the 1848 revolution, harvests and commerce were at a low.

REVISED: The economics of the country caused the 1848 revolution: harvests and commerce were at a low.

9d REVISION BY CREATING TWO SENTENCES

You can effectively revise many comma splices and fused sentences by creating two separate sentences—particularly when you want a major break between the clauses. This revision is especially useful when the two clauses are long or when you want to emphasize each clause.

COMMA SPLICE: Unlike most of my friends, I cannot abide watching those silly, mindless situation comedies, for one thing, I resent having the laugh track tell me when to be entertained.

REVISED: Unlike most of my friends, I cannot abide watching those silly, mindless situation comedies. For one thing, I resent having the laugh track tell me when to be entertained.

9e REVISION WITH A DEPENDENT CLAUSE OR PHRASE

Often you can correct a comma splice or fused sentence by changing one of the independent clauses to a dependent clause or phrase.

This correction is a good solution when you want to indicate a special relationship—a relationship such as time, place, condition/result, cause/effect, contrast, and so forth.

FUSED SENTENCE:	Sometimes I craved fried foods floating in grease then I ate in the school cafeteria.
REVISED WITH A DEPENDENT CLAUSE:	When I craved fried foods floating in grease, I ate in the school cafeteria.
REVISED WITH A PHRASE:	Craving fried foods floating in grease, I ate in the school cafeteria.

This correction also works well when the two independent clauses have a noun or noun phrase in common.

COMMA SPLICE:	We desperately need zoning laws, the construction of unsightly commercial buildings could be prevented by zoning laws.
REVISED WITH A DEPENDENT CLAUSE:	We desperately need zoning laws, which could prevent the construction of unsightly commercial buildings.
REVISED WITH A PHRASE:	We desperately need zoning laws to prevent the construction of unsightly commercial buildings.

10

SUBJECT-VERB AGREEMENT

Standard English requires **subject-verb agreement**—that is, a verb form appropriate for the subject. In general, agreement depends on three factors: person, number, and tense.

- **Person** refers to whether the subject is speaking, spoken to, or spoken about.

  FIRST PERSON: The subject is *I* or *we*.

  SECOND PERSON: The subject is *you*.

  THIRD PERSON: The subject is any noun or pronoun except *I*, *we*, or *you*.

- **Number** refers to singular (one) and plural (more than one).

- **Tense** is the verb feature that indicates time (see 4c). All verbs require agreement in the third person of the present tense and the present perfect tense. Notice the *-s* form of the verb (4a) appears in the singular of these tenses but not in the plural.

Present Tense

PERSON	SINGULAR	PLURAL
FIRST:	I upset him.	We upset him.
SECOND:	You upset him.	You upset him.
THIRD:	Anything upsets him.	All things upset him.

Present Perfect Tense

PERSON	SINGULAR	PLURAL	
FIRST:	I have upset him.	We have upset him.	**s/v agr 10**
SECOND:	You have upset him.	You have upset him.	
THIRD:	Something <u>has upset</u> him.	Several things <u>have upset</u> him.	

The verb *be* requires agreement in more instances than other verbs. Notice in the following examples that the singular and plural forms differ in the first and third persons of the present tense, in the first and third persons of the past tense, and in the third person of the present perfect tense.

Present Tense

PERSON	SINGULAR	PLURAL
FIRST:	I <u>am</u> a student.	We <u>are</u> students.
SECOND:	You are a student.	You are students.
THIRD:	She <u>is</u> a student.	They <u>are</u> students.

Past Tense

PERSON	SINGULAR	PLURAL
FIRST:	I <u>was</u> a student.	We <u>were</u> students.
SECOND:	You were a student.	You were students.
THIRD:	Amy <u>was</u> a student.	Amy and Jake <u>were</u> students.

Present Perfect Tense

PERSON	SINGULAR	PLURAL
FIRST:	I have been a student.	We have been students.
SECOND:	You have been a student.	You have been students.
THIRD:	The professor <u>has been</u> a student.	Professors <u>have been</u> students.

When the subject of a sentence is simple and appears next to its verb, subject-verb agreement usually presents no problems. But some subjects are tricky. As you edit your writing, watch for constructions such as the following that can cause agreement problems.

10a   INTERVENING WORDS BETWEEN SUBJECT AND VERB

Often the subject of a sentence is followed by a phrase or clause that contains a noun. Be sure that the verb agrees with the true subject and not with a noun that follows the subject.

Emission that pours from the smokestacks has polluted the area.

The instructions outlined in the manual were not clear.

A collection of glass animals was arranged on the table.

The development of new techniques leads to increasingly accurate test results.

10b   SUBJECTS JOINED BY *AND*

In general, when a sentence has two or more subjects joined by *and,* use a plural verb.

The governor and the attorney general drive limousines.

Sun and wind cause skin burn.

McDonald's, Wendy's, and Burger King have been waging commercial warfare.

CAUTION: This convention does not apply to subjects joined by phrases such as *as well as, together with, in addition to.*

The governor, as well as the attorney general, drives a limousine.

Hot sun, together with strong wind, causes severe skin burn.

McDonald's, in addition to Wendy's and Burger King, has been waging commercial warfare.

EXCEPTIONS: Use a singular verb in two instances.

* When *each* or *every* precedes subjects joined by *and*

    Each governor and each attorney general was assigned a limousine.

    Every hamburger chain and every fried chicken franchise has been engaged in commercial warfare.

* When the subjects joined by *and* refer to a single person, thing, or idea

Red beans and rice <u>is</u> a popular Cajun dish.

My best friend and confidant <u>has betrayed</u> me.

10c   SUBJECTS JOINED BY *OR/NOR*

When the subjects of a sentence are joined by *or* or *nor* (or *either . . . or, neither . . . nor*), make the verb agree with the subject closer to it. If the closer subject is singular, the verb is singular; if the closer subject is plural, the verb is plural.

Neither the boxwood nor the <u>roses</u> <u>have survived</u> the ice storm.

Neither the roses nor the <u>boxwood</u> <u>has survived</u> the ice storm.

CAUTION: This practice can cause awkward constructions, particularly with the verb *be* when the subjects are in different persons: *Either Steve or I am in charge.* Although this sentence is technically correct, you may want to avoid awkwardness by using two clauses instead of one: *Either Steve is in charge, or I am.*

10d   INDEFINITE PRONOUNS AS SUBJECTS

Some indefinite pronouns are always singular, some are always plural, and some can be either.

• Singular verbs are required with the following indefinite pronouns used as subjects.

another	everybody	nothing
anybody	everyone	one
anyone	everything	other
anything	neither	somebody
each	nobody	someone
either	no one	something

<u>Neither</u> <u>is</u> acceptable.

<u>Each</u> <u>was</u> published in 1989.

<u>Everyone</u> <u>comments</u> on the vivid colors.

When phrases and clauses follow these indefinite pronouns, be careful not to mistake an intervening noun for the subject of the verb.

Neither of these essays is acceptable.

Each of the studies was published in 1989.

Everyone who sees the paintings comments on the vivid colors.

- Plural verbs are required with the following indefinite pronouns used as subjects.

    both   few   several

    many   others

    Both have graduated with honors.

    Many claim to have seen UFOs.

- When the following indefinite pronouns are used as subjects, meaning determines whether the verb is singular or plural.

    all   more   none

    any   most   some

If the indefinite pronoun refers to a noncountable noun (*confusion, laughter, art*), use a singular verb. If the indefinite pronoun refers to a plural, countable noun (*residents, pages, machines*), use a plural verb.

NONCOUNT/SINGULAR:	Most of the confusion was over.
COUNT/PLURAL:	Most of the residents were elderly.
NONCOUNT/SINGULAR:	Some of the laughter was dying.
COUNT/PLURAL:	Some of the pages were missing.

Some writers always use a singular verb with *none,* even when it refers to a plural, countable noun.

None of the players was fined.

Nevertheless, most contemporary writers prefer a plural verb when the reference is plural.

> <u>None</u> of the players <u>were fined</u>.

10e   RELATIVE PRONOUNS AS SUBJECTS

When a relative pronoun (*that, which, who*) is the subject of a clause, make the verb agree with the pronoun's antecedent—the word or phrase that the pronoun stands for.

> The Phantom is powered by <u>engines</u> <u>that</u> <u>deliver</u> 17,900 pounds of thrust. [<u>engines</u> <u>deliver</u>]

> Her celebrated <u>collection</u> of photographs, <u>which</u> <u>documents</u> Christmas in rural America, is on display during December. [<u>collection</u> <u>documents</u>]

When the relative pronoun is preceded by *one of those* . . . or *one of the* . . . make the verb plural.

> He is <u>one of those students</u> <u>who</u> always <u>study</u> early. [<u>students</u> <u>study</u>]

When the relative pronoun is preceded by *the only one of* . . ., make the verb singular.

> He is <u>the only one of the students</u> <u>who</u> always <u>studies</u> early. [<u>one</u> <u>studies</u>]

10f   SUBJECTS OF LINKING VERBS

A linking verb may connect a singular subject with a plural complement or a plural subject with a singular complement. (See 7a.3.) Regardless of the number of the complement, the verb agrees with its subject.

> My chief <u>entertainment</u> <u>was</u> the old movies on television.

> The old <u>movies</u> on television <u>were</u> my chief entertainment.

10g   SUBJECTS THAT FOLLOW VERBS

Verbs agree with their subjects even when normal sentence order is inverted and the subjects are delayed.

There <u>are</u> three <u>reasons</u> for the mistake.

**s/v
agr
10f**

There <u>is</u> a good <u>reason</u> for the mistake.

Covering the wall <u>were</u> <u>dozens</u> of ancestral portraits.

Covering the wall <u>was</u> a medieval <u>tapestry</u>.

10h   COLLECTIVE NOUNS AND AMOUNTS AS SUBJECTS

A collective noun refers to a group that forms some sort of unit, for example, *team, class, audience, enemy, orchestra, panel, crew, family, club.* When these nouns refer to the group as a whole, use a singular verb; when they refer to the individual members of the group, use a plural verb.

<u>Parliament</u> <u>sits</u> in majestic houses along the Thames. [*Parliament* refers to the governing body as a unit.]

<u>Parliament</u> <u>disagree</u> on the tax issue. [*Parliament* refers to the individuals within the group since a unit cannot disagree with itself.]

The <u>team</u> <u>is</u> on the court. [*Team* refers to the group as a unit.]

The <u>team</u> <u>are</u> taking their practice shots. [*Team* refers to the individuals within the group since each team member must take practice shots by himself or herself.]

A plural verb with a collective noun (*team are*) sounds peculiar to most people and is therefore uncommon. Instead, writers usually prefer to pair a plural verb with a subject that is obviously plural.

The <u>members</u> of Parliament <u>disagree</u> on the tax issue.

The <u>players</u> <u>are taking</u> their practice shots.

When the subject refers to a unit amount, a kind of lump sum, use a singular verb. When the subject refers to several units, use a plural verb.

<u>Four days</u> <u>seems</u> a reasonable time.

<u>Four days</u> <u>were</u> marked off on the calendar.

With some amounts, either a singular or a plural verb is appropriate.

Three truckloads of gravel <u>was</u> (or <u>were</u>) needed to fill the hole.

~~When the word *number* is the subject and is preceded by *the*,~~ use a singular verb. When *number* is preceded by *a*, use a plural verb.

The number of students taking workshops <u>has increased</u>.

A number of students <u>have signed up</u> for the workshop.

10i TITLES AS SUBJECTS

Titles are considered singular, regardless of whether the words in them are singular or plural.

African Kingdoms <u>is</u> assigned reading.

Gulliver's Travels <u>satirizes</u> human nature.

10j FOREIGN NOUNS AS SUBJECTS

Some nouns borrowed from foreign languages have retained their foreign plurals and do not "look" plural to an English speaker. If you are not sure about the number of a foreign noun, consult an up-to-date, standard dictionary. There you will find, for example, that *genera* is the plural form of *genus; stimuli,* the plural of *stimulus,* and *media,* the plural of *medium.*

Data is probably the most commonly used of these foreign nouns because it occurs frequently in technical literature. Traditionally, *datum* is the singular form and *data* is the plural.

The data <u>were gathered</u> over a six-month period.

Increasingly, however, *data* is treated as a noncountable noun (such as *information*) and is used with a singular verb.

The data <u>was gathered</u> over a period of six months.

10k SUBJECTS ENDING IN *-ICS*

A number of words in English end in *-ics: linguistics, physics, mathematics, economics, ceramics, statistics, ballistics, athletics, aerobics, gymnastics, calisthenics, acoustics, politics, ethics,* and so on.

When referring to a body of knowledge or a field of study, a noun ending in *-ics* requires a singular verb. When referring to activities, the same noun requires a plural verb.

Politics is one of the major industries in this country.

His politics make me nervous.

Calisthenics is required in the qualification trials.

Calisthenics are simple gymnastic exercises.

101   "WORDS" AS SUBJECTS

A word cited as the word itself is marked in one of three ways: enclosed in quotation marks, underlined, or italicized. Whether singular or plural, the word cited requires a singular verb.

"Fiddlesticks" was my grandmother's favorite expression.

In law, *person* means either a human being or an organization with legal rights.

People is a plural noun.

11

NONSTANDARD VERB FORMS

Nonstandard verb forms occur most commonly for three reasons.

1. A writer does not know the correct principal parts of irregular verbs and thus writes a verb such as *had went* for *had gone.*
2. A writer transfers the sounds of speech to writing and drops a letter, producing a verb such as *use to* for *used to.*
3. A writer confuses a verb with a word that closely resembles it, using *loose,* for example, instead of *lose.*

The wrong verb form may not always obscure meaning. If you make the errors just described, a reader will possibly understand what you mean but will judge you uneducated—or at the very least, careless. Therefore, when revising your prose, make sure you have used verbs and their forms correctly.

11a NONSTANDARD PRINCIPAL PARTS

The principal parts of verbs include three forms—the base, or infinitive form; the past-tense form; and the past participle. (See 4a.) Ordinarily, problems do not arise with regular verbs because the past form and the past participle are identical (*cure, cured, cured; look, looked, looked*). Irregular verbs, however, have unpredictable forms for the past tense and the past participle (*do, did, done; break, broke, broken*). Furthermore, the forms have different uses. The past form expresses a past occurrence and is used

71

alone—without auxiliaries. The past participle is used after forms of *have* to express the perfect tenses and after forms of *be* to express the passive voice.

vb form 11b

PAST:	The axle broke for the third time.
PRESENT PERFECT:	The axle has broken for the third time.
PASSIVE VOICE:	The axle was broken by the impact.

The wrong form of an irregular verb is considered nonstandard English. If you are ever unsure of the principal parts of a verb, check the forms in a dictionary or in the Glossary of Terms under the heading *Irregular Verbs.*

NONSTANDARD:	The letter come Monday.
STANDARD:	The letter came Monday.
STANDARD:	The letter had come Monday.

NONSTANDARD:	Someone had stole my tennis racquet.
STANDARD:	Someone had stolen my tennis racquet.
STANDARD:	Someone stole my tennis racquet.

11b   DROPPED -*S*/-*ES* AND -*D*/-*ED* VERB ENDINGS

Two important verb endings are -*s*/-*es* and -*d*/-*ed*. The -*s*/-*es* occurs with all verbs in the present-tense singular, except those whose subjects are *I, we,* and *you*. The -*d*/-*ed* occurs with regular verbs to form the past tense and past participle. In conversation, speakers sometimes drop these endings, producing verb forms such as the ones in the following sentences.

-*s* DROPPED:	He exist on potato chips and sodas.
-*d* DROPPED:	We use to go to New Orleans every year.
-*ed* DROPPED:	They box the equipment yesterday.

In writing, however, you must retain the -*s*/-*es* and -*d*/-*ed*, regardless of whether you would pronounce them. Dropping these important endings will result in nonstandard verb forms:

NONSTANDARD:	That reporter always <u>ask</u> personal questions.
STANDARD:	That reporter always <u>asks</u> personal questions.
NONSTANDARD:	The players are <u>suppose</u> to practice every day.
STANDARD:	The players are <u>supposed</u> to practice every day.
NONSTANDARD:	You cannot successfully reheat <u>bake</u> potatoes.
STANDARD:	You cannot successfully reheat <u>baked</u> potatoes.

11c VERBS CONFUSED WITH SIMILAR WORDS

Writers sometimes confuse verbs with words that are similar in spelling, pronunciation, or meaning—for example, *affect/effect, lie/lay, imply/infer.* Regardless of the source of confusion, you can solve the problem by looking up a troublesome verb in a dictionary. There you will find the principal parts, the meaning, and sometimes notes on usage. Furthermore, the following pairs of words are discussed in the Glossary of Usage.

accept, except	ensure, insure
advice, advise	hanged, hung
affect, effect	imply, infer
aggravate, irritate	lay, lie
bring, take	lend, loan
burst, bust	lose, loose
censor, censure	orient, orientate
complement, compliment	precede, proceed
comprise, compose	prosecute, persecute
convince, persuade	raise, rise
device, devise	set, sit
emigrate, immigrate	use, utilize

12

PRONOUN REFERENCE

A pronoun's antecedent is the person, thing, or idea to which the pronoun refers. Normally, a pronoun takes its meaning from its antecedent.

> The French flag is called the "Tricolor" because it has three vertical bands of different colors. [The pronoun *it* stands for the antecedent *the French flag.*]

> Nathaniel Currier issued his first two prints in 1835. [The pronoun *his* stands for the antecedent *Nathaniel Currier.*]

When you revise, make sure that the antecedent of each pronoun is absolutely clear. The following discussion covers the common problems of **pronoun reference.**

12a IMPLIED REFERENCE

A pronoun's antecedent must be stated, not merely implied. In the following sentence, the appropriate antecedent of *one* is *horse,* but *horse* does not appear.

IMPLIED REFERENCE: At first, horseback riding scared me because I had never been on one.

To avoid implied reference, you can provide a clear antecedent or remove the pronoun.

CLEAR ANTECEDENT: At first, I was scared to ride a horse because I had never been on one.

REMOVAL OF PRONOUN: At first, horseback riding scared me because I had never ridden before.

In the next sentence, the possessive *Homer's* is functioning as a modifier, not as a noun, and therefore cannot serve as the antecedent of *he.*

IMPLIED REFERENCE: In Homer's poems, he recounts the events of the Trojan War.

The antecedent *Homer* can be provided, or *he* can be eliminated.

CLEAR ANTECEDENT: In his poems, Homer recounts the events of the Trojan War.

REMOVAL OF PRONOUN: Homer's poems recount the events of the Trojan War.

12b BROAD REFERENCE

In broad reference, a pronoun has no antecedent and stands instead for an idea or ideas expressed in the preceding discussion. Although readers can sometimes understand broad reference, it is usually not clear and should be avoided. For example, in the following passage, a reader cannot be sure what the writer means by the pronoun *this.*

BROAD: The space above the spout of a boiling kettle of water is filled with an invisible gas called "water vapor," or "steam." The visible cloud above this space is not steam but droplets of water formed when the gas cools. This is called "condensation."

To avoid this kind of broad reference, you can supply a noun or noun phrase that describes the idea referred to.

REVISED: The space above the spout of a boiling kettle of water is filled with an invisible gas called "water vapor," or "steam." The visible cloud above this space is not steam but droplets of water formed when the gas cools. This droplet formation is called "condensation."

Another kind of broad reference involves a dependent clause that begins with *which*.

**ref
12c**

BROAD: Next semester, personal computers can be connected to the university system, which will reduce the amount of equipment students will need to work at home.

The pronoun *which* seems to refer to *university system* but, in fact, refers to the entire idea expressed by the preceding clause: "Next semester, personal computers can be connected to the university system." The sentence should be revised to provide a clear antecedent for *which* or to remove the pronoun.

CLEAR ANTECEDENT: Next semester, personal computers can be connected to the university system—an arrangement which will reduce the amount of equipment students will need to work at home.

REMOVAL OF PRONOUN: Next semester, personal computers can be connected to the university system, reducing the amount of equipment students will need to work at home.

12c   INDEFINITE *YOU, THEY,* AND *IT*

In conversation, speakers frequently use *you, they,* and *it* indefinitely—that is, to refer to people or things in general. This kind of reference, however, is not acceptable in formal writing.

INDEFINITE *YOU:*   You can inherit certain diseases.

REVISED: People can inherit certain diseases.

INDEFINITE *THEY:*   In Houston they have thousands of acres of parks.

REVISED: Houston has thousands of acres of parks.

INDEFINITE *IT:*   It states in the Declaration of Independence that everyone is created equal.

REVISED: The Declaration of Independence states that everyone is created equal.

12d AMBIGUOUS REFERENCE

A pronoun should refer unmistakably to one antecedent. If a
pronoun seems to refer to more than one, the meaning is ambiguous. Consequently, readers cannot immediately identify which
possible antecedent is meant. For example, in the following sentence, *they* can refer to *fire fighters,* to *city council members,* or
to both.

**ref
12e**

> AMBIGUOUS REFERENCE: When the fire fighters met with the city coun-
> cil members, they outlined the problems.

The sentence must be revised to eliminate the ambiguity.

> REVISED: The fire fighters, who outlined the problems, met with the
> city council members.

> REVISED: The fire fighters met with the city council members, who out-
> lined the problems.

> REVISED: At the meeting, the fire fighters and the council members out-
> lined the problems.

12e MIXED USES OF *IT*

The word *it* can be used as a personal pronoun, an expletive, or a
predicate substitute.

> I wanted the Corvette as soon as I saw it. [The pronoun *it* refers to
> the noun phrase, *the Corvette.*]

> It is dangerous to sleep in the sun. [The expletive *it* begins the sen-
> tence and delays the subject, *to sleep in the sun.*]

> If you really want to major in music, you should do it. [*Do it* substi-
> tutes for part of the predicate, *major in music.*]

When *it* is used in different ways in the same sentence or sequential
sentences, the result can be confusing and awkward. In the following passage, for example, *it* appears first as a pronoun, second as an
expletive, and third as a predicate substitute.

**ref
12g**

MIXED USE

>   Our financial adviser suggests that we sell our house since it has become a drain on our budget. It is hard, however, to let go of a place with beautiful memories; and we really don't want to do it.

For clarity's sake, the passage should be rewritten to eliminate mixed use of *it*. In the following revised version, *it* is used twice as a personal pronoun, referring to *house*.

REVISED

>   Our financial adviser suggests that we sell our house since it has become a drain on our budget. The house is so full of beautiful memories, however, that we don't want to give it up.

12f   REMOTE REFERENCE

A pronoun must be close enough to its antecedent to make the reference instantly clear. For example, in the following passage, a sentence intervenes between the pronoun *they* and its antecedent, *fairies*.

REMOTE ANTECEDENT

>   Fairies—small, magical creatures—appear in most of the folklore of the Middle Ages. During that time, belief in magic exerted a strong influence on human behavior. They might be mischievous, helpful, or fearsome; but always they interfered in the daily lives of the folk.

The pronouns are so remote from their antecedent that the reference is unclear. Repeating the noun antecedent solves the problem.

REVISED

>   Fairies—small, magical creatures—appear in most of the folklore of the Middle Ages. During that time, belief in magic exerted a strong influence on human behavior. Fairies might be mischievous, helpful, or fearsome; but always they interfered in the daily lives of the folk.

12g   TITLES AND HEADINGS AS ANTECEDENTS

Titles of papers and headings in the text cannot be the antecedents of pronouns.

No Antecedent

Glaciers

They are rivers of ice, with movement measured in inches per day instead of miles per hour. . . .

ref
12g

Revised

Glaciers

Glaciers are rivers of ice, with movement measured in inches per day instead of miles per hour. . . .

13

PRONOUN-ANTECEDENT AGREEMENT

A pronoun must agree in number with its antecedent—that is, the noun or noun phrase to which the pronoun refers. A singular antecedent requires a singular pronoun; a plural antecedent, a plural pronoun.

SINGULAR ANTECEDENT/SINGULAR PRONOUN: The <u>amethyst</u> is usually purple or bluish-violet; <u>it</u> is a semiprecious stone made from a variety of quartz.

PLURAL ANTECEDENT/PLURAL PRONOUN: <u>Amethysts</u> are usually purple or bluish-violet; <u>they</u> are semiprecious stones made from a variety of quartz.

When revising, be sure of **pronoun-antecedent agreement.** In most cases, you simply find the antecedent and check to see whether it matches the pronoun in number. If the number of an antecedent is not obvious, the following guidelines will help you choose the appropriate pronoun.

13a ANTECEDENTS JOINED BY *AND*

Usually, antecedents joined by *and* require a plural pronoun.

PLURAL PRONOUN: The wombat and the bandicoot carry their young in pouches.

In two instances, however, antecedents joined by *and* require a singular pronoun.

- When the antecedents refer to a single person, place, thing, or idea

SINGULAR PRONOUN: The judge and executioner eyes his victim impassively.

SINGULAR PRONOUN: The candidate loudly supports law and order—as though it were debatable.

- When *each* or *every* precedes the compound

SINGULAR PRONOUN: Each hot spell and each rainstorm took its toll on my dwindling vegetable garden.

SINGULAR PRONOUN: Every retired bronc rider and calf roper in the Southwest had paid his entry fee.

13b ANTECEDENTS JOINED BY *OR/NOR*

When singular antecedents are joined by *or/nor,* use a singular pronoun. When plural antecedents are joined by *or/nor,* use a plural pronoun.

SINGULAR PRONOUN: The field judge or the back judge blew his whistle.

PLURAL PRONOUN: Neither the Russians nor the Chinese sent their delegations.

When one antecedent is singular and the other plural, the pronoun agrees with the nearer antecedent. To avoid an awkward sentence, place the plural antecedent nearer the pronoun.

AWKWARD: Neither my grandparents nor my mother would sign her name to the petition.

REVISED: Neither my mother nor my grandparents would sign their names to the petition.

13c INDEFINITE PRONOUNS AND SEXIST LANGUAGE

A common problem in pronoun-antecedent agreement occurs with indefinite pronouns that can refer to people: *anybody, anyone, each, either, everybody, everyone, neither, nobody, no one,* and *none.* In casual conversation, speakers often use the plural pronoun *their* with these indefinites:

INFORMAL: Everyone in the auto-repair clinic provides their own tools.

This construction, however, is not acceptable in formal prose. *Everyone* is singular and requires not only a singular verb but also a singular pronoun. In the past, writers used *he, him,* or *his* to refer to both males and females.

OUTDATED: Everyone in the auto-repair clinic provides his own tools.

Today, the use of a masculine pronoun for both men and women is often considered sexist language and should be avoided if feasible. (See 32e.) One alternative is to change the antecedent, the verb, and the pronoun to the plural.

PLURAL CONSTRUCTION: Participants in the auto-repair clinic provide their own tools.

Another alternative is to use both a masculine and a feminine pronoun.

SINGULAR CONSTRUCTION: Everyone in the auto-repair clinic provides his or her own tools.

Remember, however, that frequent use of both masculine and feminine pronouns is awkward and wearisome. If you do not want to switch to the plural, you should eliminate pronouns where possible.

AWKWARD: Everyone in the auto-repair clinic provides his or her tools so that he or she can work individually with instructors. The clinic, however, furnishes the vehicles needed by everyone for his or her hands-on training.

REVISED: Everyone in the auto-repair clinic provides the tools for working individually with instructors. The clinic, however, furnishes the vehicles needed for hands-on training.

13d   GENERIC NOUNS AND SEXIST LANGUAGE

Sexist language can be a problem when nouns are used generically to refer to all members of a group—*the astronaut* can refer to all astronauts, *the writer* to all writers, *the swimmer* to all swimmers, *the police officer* to all police officers. Even though these generic nouns refer to more than one person, they require singular pronouns. Formerly, writers used *he, him, his,* which were supposed to refer to both sexes. Today, the use of masculine pronouns to refer to both males and females is often thought unacceptable. (See 32e.)

OUTDATED: The astronaut must begin his training long before a flight.

You can make such a sentence acceptable by including both the feminine and the masculine pronoun or by rewriting the sentence with plural nouns and pronouns. Or you can eliminate the pronoun altogether.

SINGULAR PRONOUNS: The astronaut must begin his or her training long before a flight.

PLURAL PRONOUN: Astronauts must begin their training long before flights.

NO PRONOUN: The astronaut must begin training long before a flight.

13e   COLLECTIVE NOUNS AS ANTECEDENTS

Collective nouns—such as *audience, jury, orchestra, committee, family*—are singular when they refer to a group as a unit and plural when they refer to the individual members in the group. Therefore, depending on their meanings, collective nouns may require singular or plural pronouns.

GROUP AS A UNIT: The family incorporated itself for tax purposes.

INDIVIDUAL MEMBERS: The family are squabbling over their grandfather's estate.

If *the family are* sounds peculiar to you—as it does to many people—you can always supply a subject that is clearly plural.

PLURAL SUBJECT: The members of the family are squabbling over their grandfather's estate.

14

CASE OF NOUNS AND PRONOUNS

Nouns and pronouns have **case,** that is, different forms for different functions. Most pronouns and all nouns change form only in the possessive—the case that expresses such ideas as ownership (*your phone*), authorship (*Ann's poetry*), measurement (*week's pay*), and source (*president's power*). A few pronouns have three cases.

Subjective	*Objective*	*Possessive*
I	me	my/mine
he	him	his
she	her	her/hers
we	us	our/ours
they	them	their/theirs
who	whom	whose
whoever	whomever	

The subjective forms of these pronouns are used as subjects and subject complements, sometimes called *predicate nominatives.*

> <u>We</u> fed the animals a high-protein diet. [subject]

> The first guest to arrive was <u>she</u>. [subject complement]

The objective forms are used as objects and as subjects and objects of infinitives.

> The voters will never elect <u>him</u>. [direct object]

> The new hospital gave <u>them</u> hope. [indirect object]

85

I felt the painting looking at me. [object of preposition]

My manager wanted me to hire them. [subject and object of infinitive]

In addition to case, some pronouns have forms made with the suffixes -self and -selves: myself, yourself, himself, herself, itself, ourselves, yourselves, themselves. These forms are used in two ways.

- As reflexives: objects that rename subjects

  She corrected herself.

  The winners congratulated themselves.

  I was ashamed of myself.

- As emphatics: pronouns that repeat, for emphasis, the nouns or pronouns they refer to

  The owner himself waited on tables.

  You must write the letter yourself.

  They catered the party themselves.

Although use of incorrect pronoun case does not ordinarily mislead the reader, it is considered nonstandard. Therefore, when you revise your papers, check the case of pronouns carefully. The following guidelines should help you choose the appropriate forms.

14a CASE IN COMPOUND CONSTRUCTIONS

Compounding in no way affects the case of a pronoun. When in doubt about which case is appropriate, simply drop all other elements in the compound construction. Then you can readily determine the correct form.

The Senator hired Mary and (I or me). [You would write *The Senator hired me,* not *The Senator hired I.* Thus, the correct sentence is *The Senator hired Mary and me.*]

Both his brother and (he or him) attended Yale. [You would write *He attended Yale,* not *Him attended Yale.* Thus, the correct sentence is *Both his brother and he attended Yale.*]

In a compound appositive, pronoun case depends on the use of the word that the appositive renames. An appositive renaming a subject or subject complement is in the subjective case; an appositive renaming an object or object complement is in the objective case.

> The centers, Hackett and he, were benched for fighting. [*Hackett and he* renames the subject, *centers.* Thus, the pronoun is in the subjective case.]

> The cabin was built by three people—Craig, Ray, and me. [*Craig, Ray, and me* renames *people,* the object of the preposition *by.* Thus, the pronoun is in the objective case.]

Compounds that often cause mistakes contain pronouns in the first-person singular. Always use *me* as the object of any preposition, regardless of the context.

NONSTANDARD: Just between you and I, the credit union is in financial trouble.

CORRECT: Just between you and me, the credit union is in financial trouble.

Use the pronoun *myself* only as a reflexive or an emphatic. Never use *myself* when the subjective or objective case is called for.

NONSTANDARD: Brett and myself had dinner at Antoine's.

CORRECT: Brett and I had dinner at Antoine's.

NONSTANDARD: The coach saw Lee and myself at the party.

CORRECT: The coach saw Lee and me at the party.

14b PRONOUN CASE AFTER *BE*

In conversational English, most people use pronouns in the objective case as complements of *be.*

INFORMAL: It's me.

INFORMAL: That's him.

Although the objective case is appropriate in conversation, the subjective case is required in formal writing.

FORMAL: The first dignitary presented at state occasions was always he.

FORMAL: The only medical doctor in the county was she.

14c *WHO/WHOM* AND *WHOEVER/WHOMEVER*

Although the form *whom* is not common in conversation, you should observe the case distinctions between *who/whoever* (subjective case) and *whom/whomever* (objective case) when you write or speak in formal English.

To use the forms correctly, you must determine the pronoun's use in its own clause—whether independent or dependent. You can make this determination by the following method.

1.   Isolate the pronoun's clause, and ignore the rest of the sentence.
2.   Put the parts of the isolated clause in normal sentence order (subject + verb + other elements).
3.   Substitute pronouns to see which fits. If you would normally use *he, she,* or *they,* choose *who* or *whoever.* If you would normally use *him, her,* or *them,* choose, *whom* or *whomever.*

A few sample sentences will illustrate the method.

(Who/whom) did you contact?

You did contact who/whom?

You did contact him.

Whom did you contact?

These are the recruits (who/whom) we think will go to OCS.

Who/whom will go to OCS?

They will go to OCS.

These are the recruits who we think will go to OCS.

The newspaper always attacks (whoever/whomever) the governor appoints.

The governor appoints whoever/whomever.

The governor appoints her.

The newspaper always attacks whomever the governor appoints.

14d   CASE IN ELLIPTICAL CLAUSES

Dependent clauses introduced by *than* or *as* are often elliptical—
that is, some parts are not stated but understood (7d). When an elliptical clause contains a pronoun, you might have to fill in the
missing parts to determine the pronoun's case. For example, suppose you were trying to decide which pronoun to use in the following sentence: *Her parents seemed younger than (she/her.)*
Completing the sentence will reveal the correct form.

ELLIPTICAL: Her parents seemed younger than she.

COMPLETE: Her parents seemed younger than she seemed.

In some elliptical clauses, either subjective or objective case is
possible. Be sure to choose the pronoun form that conveys the
intended meaning.

ELLIPTICAL: The skiing lessons helped Joan more than I.

COMPLETE: The skiing lessons helped Joan more than I helped Joan.

ELLIPTICAL: The skiing lessons helped Joan more than me.

COMPLETE: The skiing lessons helped Joan more than they helped me.

ELLIPTICAL: Her friends annoy me as much as she.

COMPLETE: Her friends annoy me as much as she annoys me.

ELLIPTICAL: Her friends annoy me as much as her.

COMPLETE: Her friends annoy me as much as they annoy her.

14e   POSSESSIVE CASE WITH GERUNDS

A gerund is the *-ing* of a verb functioning as a noun (5c). In formal
prose, nouns and pronouns acting as determiners for gerunds must

be in the possessive case: *my singing, Frank's passing, their whispering.* In conversation, you might say, "I don't mind him spending the money." But you should write, "The public objected to his spending money on state dinners"—because it is the spending that the public objects to, not him. *His* identifies whose spending it was.

case 14e

INFORMAL: The listeners quickly tired of the <u>candidate</u> evading the issue.

FORMAL: The listeners quickly tired of the <u>candidate's</u> evading the issue.

INFORMAL: The security office objected to <u>them</u> parking in the fire lanes.

FORMAL: The security office objected to <u>their</u> parking in the fire lanes.

15

NONSTANDARD ADJECTIVE AND ADVERB FORMS

Adjectives and adverbs are modifiers—that is, they describe and qualify other elements of sentences. Adjectives modify nouns and pronouns. Adverbs modify verbs, adjectives, other adverbs, and whole clauses. (See Chapter 3.) Many adjectives and adverbs have characteristic forms. Confusion or misuse will produce **nonstandard adjective and adverb forms.**

15a CONFUSION OF ADJECTIVES AND ADVERBS

Be careful not to substitute adjectives for adverbs. A few adjectives and adverbs (such as *fast, early, late*) share identical forms. However, the adjective and adverb forms of most modifiers are different. In fact, many adverbs are formed by adding *-ly* to adjectives. For example, *serious* and *perfect* are adjectives; *seriously* and *perfectly* are adverbs.

ADJECTIVE SUBSTITUTED FOR ADVERB: We talked <u>serious</u> about our future.

REVISED: We talked <u>seriously</u> about our future. [adverb modifying *talked*]

91

REVISED: We had a serious conversation about our future. [adjective modifying *conversation*]

ADJECTIVE SUBSTITUTED FOR ADVERB: He recited the speech perfect.

REVISED: He recited the speech perfectly. [adverb modifying *recited*]

REVISED: His speech was perfect. [adjective modifying *speech*]

You probably have little difficulty with modifiers such as *serious/seriously* and *perfect/perfectly*. However, because of a conflict between conversational and written English, a few pairs of modifiers are particularly troublesome.

awful/awfully   most/almost

bad/badly   real/really

good/well

The adjective forms of these modifiers should be used after linking verbs such as *feel, taste, sound,* and *smell*. (See 7a.3.)

ADVERB SUBSTITUTED FOR ADJECTIVE: I feel badly.

REVISED: I feel bad.

If you have problems with any of these troublesome modifiers, look them up in the Glossary of Usage at the end of this book. There they are defined, and their appropriate uses are discussed and illustrated.

15b   INAPPROPRIATE COMPARATIVE AND SUPERLATIVE FORMS

Most adjectives and adverbs have three forms, or degrees. The positive form is the simple form of the modifier. The comparative form (expressed by *-er, more,* or *less*) is used to compare two items. The superlative form (expressed by *-est, most,* or *least*) is used to compare more than two items. (See 3c for discussion and examples.)

Do not use the comparative form to refer to more than two items or the superlative to refer to only two.

INAPPROPRIATE COMPARATIVE:	Jones is the <u>more interesting</u> of all the lecturers.
REVISED:	Jones is the <u>most interesting</u> of all the lecturers.
INAPPROPRIATE SUPERLATIVE:	We should buy the <u>fastest</u> of the two printers.
REVISED:	We should buy the <u>faster</u> of the two printers.

Avoid double comparisons—the use of *more* or *most* with another comparative or superlative modifier. Sentences containing double comparisons are nonstandard.

DOUBLE COMPARISON:	This summer is <u>more hotter</u> than the last.
REVISED:	This summer is <u>hotter</u> than the last.
DOUBLE COMPARISON:	The <u>most unusualest</u> piece in the collection was an ebony necklace.
REVISED:	The <u>most unusual</u> piece in the collection was an ebony necklace.

Some adjectives, called *absolutes,* cannot logically express degree. For example, one thing cannot be more first than another nor more infinite: something is either first or not, either finite or infinite. About other adjectives, however, there is disagreement. Some people claim that perfection, uniqueness, and correctness can be approximated. Thus, one thing can be more perfect, more unique, or more correct than another. Other people apply strict logic: something is either perfect or imperfect, unique or not unique, correct or incorrect.

Because many readers disapprove of the comparison of absolutes, you can always insert *more nearly* before the adjective.

QUESTIONABLE COMPARISON:	The second portrait is a <u>more perfect</u> likeness than the first.

REVISED: The second portrait is a more nearly perfect likeness than the first.

15c INAPPROPRIATE DEMONSTRATIVES

The demonstratives (*this, that, these,* and *those*) can function not only as pronouns but also as determiners—*this concept, that tablet, these entries, those mistakes.* Only two problems are usually associated with these modifiers.

- The use of *them* in place of *these* or *those*

    NONSTANDARD: Them shoes were half price.

    REVISED: Those shoes were half price.

- The use of *these* instead of *this* before a singular noun like *kind, sort,* or *type*

    NONSTANDARD: These kind of flowers bloom twice a year.

    REVISED: This kind of flower blooms twice a year.

    REVISED: These kinds of flowers bloom twice a year.

16

DANGLING AND MISPLACED MODIFIERS

The function of modifiers is to describe other words—to qualify, limit, intensify, or explain them. Thus, modifiers and the words they describe form a close relationship, which must be immediately clear to readers. When a modifier is not clearly related to any other word in its sentence, it is called **dangling.**

DANGLING PHRASE: To have a successful camping trip, the right equipment must be packed.

REVISED: To have a successful trip, campers must pack the right equipment.

DANGLING CLAUSE: When covered with a fine white ash, the chicken should be placed on the grill.

REVISED: When the coals are covered with a fine white ash, the chicken should be placed on the grill.

When a modifier seems to relate to the wrong element in a sentence, it is called **misplaced.**

95

MISPLACED PHRASE: He led me to a corner table <u>with a sneer.</u>

REVISED: <u>With a sneer,</u> he led me to a corner table.

MISPLACED CLAUSE: We cooked fresh vegetables on an old wood stove <u>that we had picked that morning.</u>

REVISED: On an old wood stove, we cooked fresh vegetables <u>that we had picked that morning.</u>

Both types of faulty modification can create awkward and confusing constructions. Therefore, when you revise your writing be sure to eliminate dangling and misplaced modifiers.

16a DANGLING MODIFIERS

Although any modifier can dangle, the problem occurs most commonly with verbal phrases and elliptical clauses. (See Chapter 5 and 7d.)

(1) Dangling verbals: participles, infinitives, and gerunds

When a verbal phrase modifier begins a sentence, the verbal should refer to the subject of the following clause. Without this logical connection between the verbal and the subject, the modifier dangles. To revise an introductory dangling verbal, you can make the logical connection between verbal and subject, or you can eliminate the verbal.

DANGLING PARTICIPLE: <u>Scoring a touchdown in the last seconds,</u> the game was won 6-0.

REVISED: <u>Scoring a touchdown in the last seconds,</u> the team won the game 6-0.

REVISED: The team won the game 6-0 with a touchdown in the last four seconds.

DANGLING INFINITIVE: <u>To restore the damaged wood,</u> a special chemical was used.

REVISED:	To restore the damaged wood, they used a ~~special chemical.~~

REVISED:	A special chemical restored the damaged wood.
DANGLING GERUND:	In deciding the case, illegally obtained evidence was used.
REVISED:	In deciding the case, the judge used illegally obtained evidence.
REVISED:	The judge's decision was based partially on illegally obtained evidence.

Less common is a dangling modifier in the middle or at the end of a sentence. If the relationship between actor and action is not immediately clear, the sentence will be weak or confusing. To revise this kind of dangling structure, you can make a clear connection between the verbal and a preceding noun or pronoun, or you can eliminate the verbal.

DANGLING GERUND:	My dexterity improved by practicing the piano.
REVISED:	I improved my dexterity by practicing the piano.
REVISED:	Piano practice improved my dexterity.
DANGLING PARTICIPLE:	The evidence showed an increase in the water-pollution level, concluding that the habitat might endanger waterfowl.
REVISED:	The evidence showed an increase in the water-pollution level, suggesting that the habitat might endanger waterfowl.
REVISED:	Because the evidence showed an increase in the water-pollution level, researchers concluded that the habitat might endanger waterfowl.

A few verbals do not dangle, even though they do not modify a specific noun. These include nominative absolutes (5d) as well as common expressions that modify whole sentences (*considering, assuming, to conclude, to tell the truth,* and so forth).

NOMINATIVE ABSOLUTE:	The swing set finally assembled, Father lay down in complete exhaustion.
COMMON EXPRESSION:	Considering the expense, the trip isn't worth it.
COMMON EXPRESSION:	To tell the truth, an independent candidate would have a good chance.

(2) Dangling elliptical clauses

In an elliptical clause (7d), the subject and a form of the verb *be* are sometimes omitted. If an elliptical dependent clause is correctly constructed, its omitted subject is the same as the subject of the main clause.

| ELLIPTICAL: | While attending Radcliffe, she began her autobiography. [*She was* is omitted after *while*.] |
| ELLIPTICAL: | Although responsible for the crash, the air controller refuses to accept any blame. [*The air controller is* is omitted after *although*.] |

An elliptical clause dangles when the omitted subject is not the same as the subject of the main clause. To correct a dangling clause, you can make the subject of the main clause the same as the omitted subject of the elliptical clause. Or you can rewrite the sentence to avoid the ellipsis.

DANGLING CLAUSE:	While living in Tahiti, rich, tropical settings were painted by Gauguin.
REVISED:	While living in Tahiti, Gauguin painted rich, tropical settings.
REVISED:	In Tahiti, Gauguin painted rich, tropical settings.
DANGLING CLAUSE:	If dissatisfied with a product, a complaint should be made.
REVISED:	If dissatisfied with a product, the consumer should complain.
REVISED:	The consumer who is dissatisfied with a product should complain.

16b   MISPLACED MODIFIERS

A modifier can be positioned so that it seems to modify the wrong word or phrase. It is possible to misplace any sort of modifier—a word, a phrase, or a clause.

(1)   Misplaced words

The most commonly misplaced words are "qualifiers" such as *only, nearly, simply, almost, even,* and *just.* In speech, these words usually occur before the verb, regardless of what they modify. In written English, however, you should place qualifiers immediately before (or as near as possible to) the words they modify.

MISPLACED: He only died yesterday.

REVISED: He died only yesterday.

MISPLACED: The students just pay one-third of the cost.

REVISED: The students pay just one-third of the cost.

Misplacement of words other than qualifiers often leads to ambiguity.

AMBIGUOUS: Follow the instructions for installing the antenna carefully. [*Carefully* can modify either *follow* or *installing.*]

REVISED: Follow carefully the instructions for installing the antenna. [*Carefully* modifies *follow.*]

REVISED: Follow the instructions for carefully installing the antenna. [*Carefully* modifies *installing.*]

(2)   Misplaced prepositional phrases

You should place prepositional phrases as near as possible to the words or elements they modify because placement affects the meaning of sentences.

The researchers studied aggressive behavior in Washington. [*In Washington* modifies *behavior.*]

The researchers in Washington studied aggressive behavior. [*In Washington* modifies *researchers.*]

Misplacing a prepositional phrase can produce a sentence that is unclear or even silly.

MISPLACED: The computer contained the voting statistics we had collected on the hard disk.

REVISED: On the hard disk, the computer contained the voting statistics we had collected.

MISPLACED: Heinrich planned to conquer France on his deathbed.

REVISED: On his deathbed, Heinrich planned to conquer France.

(3) Misplaced clauses

Dependent clauses should refer clearly and logically to the words that they modify. In some sentences, you can move misplaced dependent clauses near the words they modify. In other sentences, you may have to rewrite to eliminate the misplaced clauses.

MISPLACED: The archeologists found at the site a ceramic pot they had been digging in for two years. [Clause modifies *pot.*]

CLAUSE MOVED: The archeologists found a ceramic pot at the site they had been digging in for two years. [Clause modifies *site.*]

MISPLACED: Because of his allergies, he could not drive a tractor in a hayfield that was not air-conditioned. [Clause modifies *hayfield.*]

CLAUSE ELIMINATED: Because of his allergies, he could not drive an un-air-conditioned tractor in a hayfield. [*Un-air-conditioned* modifies *tractor.*]

(4) Squinting modifiers

"Squinting" modifiers are misplaced in such a way that they can modify either the preceding or the following elements.

SQUINTING: The courses he teaches <u>frequently</u> have been cancelled. [*Frequently* modifies either *teaches* or *have been cancelled.*]

dm/
mm
16b

REVISED: The courses he <u>frequently</u> teaches have been cancelled. [*Frequently* modifies *teaches.*]

REVISED: The courses he teaches have been cancelled <u>frequently</u>. [*Frequently* modifies *have been cancelled.*]

SQUINTING: They told him <u>after the meeting</u> to submit a proposal. [*After the meeting* can modify *told* or *to submit.*]

REVISED: <u>After the meeting,</u> they told him to submit a proposal. [*After the meeting* modifies *told.*]

REVISED: They told him to submit a proposal <u>after the meeting</u>. [*After the meeting* modifies *to submit.*]

17

SHIFTS

A **shift** is any unnecessary change from one pattern to another. In all writing, readers anticipate certain patterns. For example, in a single sentence, they expect a verb to follow a subject and an object to follow a transitive verb. In a passage, they are puzzled if past time shifts to the present without a reason or if the same noun shifts from singular to plural.

An illogical shift hampers communication; it moves the readers' attention away from your message. Therefore, while revising, watch for shifts. They are easy to make in early drafts when you are concentrating on ideas rather than on grammatical structure.

17a SHIFTS IN TENSE SEQUENCE

In a passage of prose and even within a single sentence, the verb forms should follow a consistent and logical pattern—usually called tense sequence. This sequence involves not only the verb tenses but also very often the modal auxiliaries *can, could, will,* and *would.* (For a more complete discussion of tense and modal auxiliaries, see 4b, 4c, and 4d.)

(1) Simple tenses

Tense establishes the time frame of a verb. The simple present usually indicates that an activity always or normally happens, while the simple present progressive indicates that an activity is currently happening. The simple past indicates that an activity is already complete, while the simple past progressive indicates a past activity in progress. Obviously, when the time frame changes from present to past or past to present, so do the verb forms. On the other hand, when the time does not change, neither should the verb forms.

shft 17a

PRESENT TIME: Convertibles always sell [present] best in the spring when the weather is [present] warm.

PRESENT TIME: Convertibles are selling [present progressive] well this spring because the weather is [present] unusually warm.

PAST TIME: Convertibles sold [past] well last spring after interest rates fell [past].

PAST TIME: Convertibles sold [past] well last spring when interest rates were falling [past progressive].

(2)   Perfect tenses

The perfect tenses can indicate a "layering" of time; that is, they establish a relationship between one time and another. The present perfect (*have/has* + past participle) can say that an activity began in the past and continues into the present. The past perfect (*had* + past participle) can say that one past activity was completed before another specified time in the past. In general, follow these guidelines for sequencing the perfect tenses:

- Use present perfect with present tense or time.

- Use past perfect with past tense or time.

PRESENT TIME: I take [present] scuba diving from a woman who has taught [present perfect] for ten years.

PAST TIME: I took [past] scuba diving from a woman who had taught [past perfect] for ten years.

(3)   Modal auxiliaries

Modal auxiliaries are words like *can, could, will, would, should, might, must.* (See 4b.3.) Instead of time, these words express ideas like ability, possibility, recommendation, and requirement. When sequencing verbs, pay special attention to *can/could* and *will/would.* Conversational English allows a rather careless and unsystematic use of these four modals. In written English, however, the conventions are stricter.

- Use *can* with *will* and *could* with *would.*

- Use *can* and *will* with present tense and time.

- Use *could* and *would* with past tense and time.

Illogical shifts in verb sequence will result from mismatching modals, tenses, and times. So, remember to observe the conventions not only within single sentences but also throughout passages.

SHIFTED: If you can predict market trends, you would make a fortune.

SHIFTED: If you could predict market trends, you will make a fortune.

CONSISTENT: If you can predict market trends, you will make a fortune.

CONSISTENT: If you could predict market trends, you would make a fortune.

SHIFTED: She thought she can sell real estate.

SHIFTED: She thinks she could sell real estate.

CONSISTENT: She thinks she can sell real estate.

CONSISTENT: She thought she could sell real estate.

SHIFTED: The gym is spacious and well arranged. For example, the free weights are in a large, mirrored room by themselves. Therefore, you can concentrate on your form, and you would not bump into people who were using the Nautilus machines.

CONSISTENT PRESENT: The gym is spacious and well arranged. For example, the free weights are in a large, mirrored room by themselves. Therefore, you can concentrate

on your form, and you will not bump into people
who are using the Nautilus machines.

CONSISTENT PAST: The gym was spacious and well arranged. For example, the free weights were in a large, mirrored
room by themselves. Therefore, you could concentrate on your form, and you would not bump into
people who were using the Nautilus machines.

(4)   Historical present

When discussing literature, use the "historical present." In other
words, no matter when the work is set, describe the action as though
it were currently taking place. For example, Sinclair Lewis's novel
Main Street takes place in the first half of the twentieth century, but
you use present time to report the activities of the characters.

> The conflict in *Main Street* is between Carol and the town. The
> citizens of Gopher Prairie are self-satisfied; Carol is bored and bewil-
> dered by their complacency.

When you want to show layers of time, you can use the perfect verb
forms. The present perfect indicates that one action began before
another and still continues. For example, the following sentence
shows two different time frames: first Carol *marries* and later she
realizes, but she is still married.

> Carol realizes that she has married a man who shares their
> complacency.

The past perfect indicates than one action occurred before another
and no longer continues. For example, the next sentence shows
these two time frames: first Carol *dreams* and later she *proves,* but
she no longer dreams.

> In college, she had dreamed of doing something important: "I'll get
> my hands on one of those prairie towns and make it beautiful." But
> once in a real prairie town, Carol proves to be an ineffectual reformer.

17b   SHIFTS IN INFINITIVES AND PARTICIPLES

In addition to main verbs and auxiliaries, prose usually contains
infinitives and participles, often called *verbals* (see Chapter 5).

Although verbals function as nouns and modifiers, they are still verb forms and therefore must be consistent with the time frame of a sentence or passage.

**shft
17b**

(1) Infinitives

The choice of infinitive form depends upon the main verb in the clause. In general, follow these guidelines.

- To express a time the same as the main verb or later than the main verb, use the present infinitive (*to* + base form).

  They <u>are trying</u> <u>to repair</u> the old bridge. [Both times are present.]

  They <u>tried</u> <u>to repair</u> the old bridge. [Both times are past.]

  The university <u>plans</u> <u>to host</u> the conference. [Hosting comes later than planning.]

- To express a time earlier than the main verb, use the perfect infinitive (*to* + *have* + past participle).

  I <u>would like</u> <u>to have completed</u> my course work before this year. [Completing comes earlier than liking.]

(2) Participles

As with infinitives, the choice of participle form depends upon the main verb in the clause. In general, follow these guidelines.

- To express a time the same as the main verb or later than the main verb, use the present participle (*looking, going*).

  By <u>thinning</u> the trees, we <u>ensure</u> better growth. [Both times are present.]

  <u>Bolting</u> out of the gate, the horse <u>threw</u> its jockey. [Both times are past.]

- To express a time earlier than the main verb, use the past participle (*looked, gone*) or the perfect participle (*having looked, having gone*).

Tired of the silly argument, Scott left the meeting. [Tiring came earlier than leaving.]

Having tired of the silly argument, Scott left the meeting. [Tiring came earlier than leaving.]

17c SHIFTS IN MOOD

The indicative is the verb mood most common in prose. But sometimes, for special meanings, you use the imperative or the subjunctive mood. (See 4f.) You can mix moods when the logic of a passage demands the shift, but an unnecessary or illogical shift results in awkward prose.

SHIFTED: If I were [subjunctive] an honor student and I was [indicative] ready to graduate, I would apply to a medical school.

CONSISTENT: If I were [subjunctive] an honor student and I were [subjunctive] ready to graduate, I would apply to a medical school.

SHIFTED: In one day, eat [imperative] no more than 30 milligrams of cholesterol, and you should drink [indicative] no more than 4 ounces of alcohol.

CONSISTENT: In one day, eat [imperative] no more than 30 milligrams of cholesterol, and drink [imperative] no more than 4 ounces of alcohol.

CONSISTENT: In one day, you should eat [indicative] no more than 30 milligrams of cholesterol, and you should drink [indicative] no more than 4 ounces of alcohol.

17d SHIFTS IN VOICE

The term *voice* refers to whether the subject of a sentence performs the action (active voice) or receives the action (passive voice). (See 4e.) You should not shift, without good reason, between active and passive voice—particularly within a sentence. A shift in voice usually results in an awkward and cumbersome sentence.

SHIFTED: In the eighteenth century, Noah Webster set out [active] to make American English independent from British English; and through his books, great influence was exerted [passive] on the language.

CONSISTENT: In the eighteenth century, Noah Webster set out to make American English independent from British English; and through his books, he exerted great influence on the language.

17e SHIFTS IN NUMBER

The term *number* refers to singular (one) and plural (more than one). You should not shift carelessly between singular and plural nouns that should have the same number.

SHIFTED: Beekeepers wear protective veils over their face.

REVISED: Beekeepers wear protective veils over their faces.

SHIFTED: Frequently, a person exercises to relieve stress. As a result, people sometimes become psychologically dependent on excessive exercising.

REVISED: Frequently, people exercise to relieve stress and, as a result, sometimes become psychologically dependent on excessive exercising.

17f SHIFTS IN PERSON

The term *person* refers to first person (*I, we*), second person (*you*), and third person (all other pronouns and all nouns). Shifts in person usually involve *you* and a noun. If you are directly addressing your reader, you can revise these shifts by using *you* consistently. However, if you are referring to a group of people in general, revising in the third person is the better solution.

SHIFTED: Off-campus students should use the bus system because you get frustrated trying to park every day.

REVISED IN SECOND PERSON:	If you live off campus, you should use the bus system because you will get frustrated trying to park every day.
REVISED IN THIRD PERSON:	Off-campus students should use the but system because they get frustrated trying to park every day.

**shft
17h**

17g   SHIFTS BETWEEN DIRECT AND INDIRECT DISCOURSE

In direct discourse, the exact words of a speaker or writer appear in quotation marks: *Truman said, "If you can't convince them, confuse them."* In indirect discourse, the words of the speaker or writer are not reported exactly, and the quotation marks are omitted: *Truman said that if you can't convince people, you should try to confuse them.* A shift from one type of discourse to the other can create an awkward, unbalanced sentence.

SHIFTED:	The reporter said, "I would rather write about steeplechases than football games," but that his editor would not approve.

The reporter's words should be stated in either direct or indirect discourse.

DIRECT DISCOURSE:	The reporter said, "I would rather write about steeplechases than football games, but my editor wouldn't approve."
INDIRECT DISCOURSE:	The reporter said that he preferred to write about steeplechases rather than football games but that his editor would not approve.

17h   MIXED CONSTRUCTIONS OR FAULTY PREDICATIONS

When the structure of a sentence shifts so that the elements in the subject and predicate do not fit together, the result is a mixed construction, also called a *faulty predication*. The various ways that structures can be mismatched are not entirely predictable;

nevertheless, the problem lies either in the grammar of the sentence or in the logic.

shft 17h

(1)   Ungrammatical shifts

One common ungrammatical shift occurs when a writer tries to express a reason or a definition with a pattern such as *the reason is because, something is when, a place is where.* When *be* is the main verb in a sentence expressing a reason or definition, the structure of the sentence should be *noun = noun.* In other words, the subject is a noun (or noun equivalent); therefore, the complement in the predicate should also be a noun (or noun equivalent). The conjunctions *because, when,* and *where* introduce adverb clauses, which are not noun equivalents. In the following revisions, the complements are changed from adverb constructions to noun constructions.

SHIFTED: The reason tuition increased was because enrollment dropped. [adverb clause introduced with *because*]

REVISED: The reason tuition increased was that enrollment dropped. [noun clause introduced with *that*]

SHIFTED: A malapropism is when a person humorously misuses a word. [adverb clause introduced with *when*]

REVISED: A malapropism is the humorous misuse of a word. [noun phrase]

SHIFTED: Farm teams are where players train for the major leagues. [adverb clause introduced by *where*]

REVISED: Farm teams are training grounds for the major leagues. [noun phrase]

Another way to remove a shift from noun to adverb complement is to rewrite the sentence without using *be.*

REVISED: Tuition increased because enrollment dropped. [adverb clause modifying *increased*]

REVISED: A malapropism results when a person humorously misuses a word. [adverb clause modifying *results*]

REVISED: At farm clubs, players train for the major leagues. [adverb phrase modifying *train*]

(2) Illogical shifts

In another kind of mixed construction, the subject and predicate do not fit together logically. For example, in the following shifted sentences, the subjects cannot perform the action of the verbs. The revised sentences make a logical connection between the parts.

SHIFTED: The use of some plastics can melt in microwave ovens. [The use cannot melt.]

REVISED: Some plastics can melt in microwave ovens. [Some plastics can melt.]

SHIFTED: Tanning lotions have changed their sales efforts to appeal to our fear of skin cancer. [Lotions cannot change sales efforts.]

REVISED: Manufacturers of tanning lotions have changed their sales efforts to appeal to our fear of skin cancer. [Manufacturers can change sales efforts.]

SHIFTED: The desk clerk's attitude was filled with arrogance and indifference. [An attitude cannot be filled.]

REVISED: The desk clerk was arrogant and indifferent. [A clerk can be arrogant.]

18

SPLIT

CONSTRUCTIONS

A grammatical construction consists of closely related items—for example, subject and predicate, auxiliary verb and main verb, verb and object. In a **split construction,** the items are separated by an interruptive element, such as a modifier or parenthetical remark. No rule forbids the splitting of a construction, but you should be cautious. Some splits blur meaning and sound awkward.

18a SPLIT SUBJECTS AND VERBS

Subjects and verbs do not always appear next to each other; modifiers or other elements may interrupt the construction. Be sure, however, that the interruption is not so long that it distracts a reader or creates a cumbersome structure. You can often revise a sentence with a split subject and predicate by moving the intervening element.

> SPLIT: The language, with a simple sound system of only five vowels and seven consonants, is easy to learn.

> REVISED: With a simple sound system of only five vowels and seven consonants, the language is easy to learn.

In some cases, you can restructure the sentence to position the subject and verb closer together. In the following sentence, for example, the long interruptive element can be rewritten as the predicate.

SPLIT: Our campus <u>newspaper</u>, which caricatures such groups as ~~graduate students, athletes, sorority and fraternity members,~~ and independents, <u>is edited</u> by two promising comedy writers.

REVISED: Our campus <u>newspaper</u>, edited by two promising comedy writers, <u>caricatures</u> such groups as graduate students, athletes, sorority and fraternity members, and independents.

Another possible solution is to divide a cumbersome construction into two separate sentences.

SPLIT: Shopping <u>malls</u>, which have grown from clusters of shops to elaborate structures with fountains, exotic plants, restaurants, and theaters, <u>have led</u> the American consumer to associate buying with entertainment.

REVISED: Shopping <u>malls</u> <u>have grown</u> from clusters of shops to elaborate structures with fountains, exotic plants, theaters, and restaurants. These extravagant <u>centers</u> <u>have led</u> the American consumer to associate buying with entertainment.

18b   SPLIT VERBS AND COMPLEMENTS

Sometimes a modifier separates a verb from its direct object or subject complement—elements that complete the verb's meaning. When a verb and its completer are separated unnecessarily, the interruptive element should be moved to another place in the sentence.

SPLIT: The marathoner <u>injured</u>, during the last race, his left <u>foot</u>.

REVISED: The marathoner <u>injured</u> his <u>foot</u> during the last race.

SPLIT: No one <u>knows</u>, although some historians estimate about 5,000, <u>exactly how many</u> soldiers the Germans lost on D-Day.

REVISED: Although some historians estimate about 5,000, no one <u>knows</u> exactly how many soldiers the Germans lost on D-Day.

18c   SPLIT VERBS

The verbs in many sentences are not single words but phrases: *would improve, will be moving, has been profiteering, could have been defined.* Frequently adverbs occur between the parts of a verb phrase. In fact, sometimes the natural place for an adverb seems to be within, rather than before or after, a verb phrase.

> The issue was hotly debated.

> Experts are now predicting a rise in prices.

> The new drug will not produce any side effects.

Nevertheless, you should not split a verb phrase awkwardly with a long modifier, especially a prepositional phrase or a clause.

> SPLIT: The insurance company is, regardless of the number of people involved in an accident, required to pay each one.

> REVISED: Regardless of the number of people involved in an accident, the insurance company is required to pay each one.

> SPLIT: A conversion will, when the plates are in metric measurement, give the needed dimensions.

> REVISED: A conversion will give the needed dimensions when the plates are in metric measurement.

18d   SPLIT INFINITIVES

An infinitive is the *to* form of a verb: *to go, to understand, to be.* In a split infinitive, the *to* is separated from the verb itself: *to sometimes go, to not so clearly understand, to soon be.* In general, you should avoid splitting infinitives—particularly with long modifiers—since the split can create awkward constructions.

> SPLIT INFINITIVE: The robot's three-pronged finger arrangement allows it to with a great deal of accuracy pick up objects.

> REVISED: The robot's three-pronged finger arrangement allows it to pick up objects with a great deal of accuracy.

Even splitting an infinitive with a short modifier can sometimes create an awkward rhythm.

> SPLIT INFINITIVE: Don Knotts' portrayal of Deputy Barney Fife seems to never lose popularity.

REVISED: Don Knotts' portrayal of Deputy Barney Fife seems ~~never to lose popularity.~~

Of course, you cannot always avoid splitting an infinitive because of the normal patterns of the language. In the following sentence, for example, *more than* cannot be moved.

NORMAL SPLIT: We expect our profits to more than double next year.

Other times, you may want to split an infinitive to ensure your intended meaning or to avoid an awkward sentence rhythm. For instance, the following split infinitive is acceptable.

ACCEPTABLE SPLIT: The task force met to quickly assess the extent of the
                              oil spill.

If you try to avoid the split by placing *quickly* in front of *to,* you change the meaning of the sentence.

CHANGED MEANING: The task force met quickly to assess the extent of
                              the oil spill.

If you place *quickly* after *assess,* you create an awkward structure.

AWKWARD STRUCTURE: The task force met to assess quickly the extent of
                              the oil spill.

19

INCOMPLETE
CONSTRUCTIONS

In some sentences, a word or words needed for grammatical completeness may not appear. The omission does not always detract from the meaning. For example, the following sentences would be perfectly clear even if the words in brackets were omitted.

> Did you think [that] we weren't coming?

> The police made the arrest while [they were] on a routine inspection.

> Zombies have always frightened me more than werewolves [have frightened me].

Sometimes, however, an omission makes a sentence confusing.

CONFUSING:	She writes more often to her representative than you.
POSSIBLE MEANING:	She writes more often to her representative than you do.
POSSIBLE MEANING:	She writes more often to her representative than she does to you.

When a reader doesn't know exactly what the writer has left out, the construction is not acceptable. You can easily correct **incomplete constructions** by adding the necessary words.

19a   OMISSIONS IN COMPOUND CONSTRUCTIONS

Make sure that the omission of a necessary part of a compound expression does not obscure structure or meaning.

OMISSION OF DETERMINER:	My teacher and counselor advised me to study physics. [*My teacher and counselor* could refer to one person or two.]
REVISED TO MEAN ONE PERSON:	My teacher counseled me to study physics.
REVISED TO MEAN TWO PEOPLE:	My teacher and my counselor advised me to study physics.
OMISSION OF PART OF VERB:	I have never and will never be interested in the stock market. [*Been* must follow *have*.]
REVISED:	I have never been and will never be interested in the stock market.
OMISSION OF PART OF IDIOM:	The bright lights detract and ruin the effect of the display. [*From* must follow *detract*.]
REVISED:	The bright lights detract from and ruin the effect of the display.

19b   OMITTED *THAT*

Frequently, the word *that* can be omitted from the beginning of a noun clause without any loss of meaning.

The players believed [that] they would win.

In some sentences, however, the omission will cause the main clause and the noun clause to fuse. Readers cannot tell where one clause ends and the other begins. For instance, in the following sentence, the subject of the second clause looks like the object of the first clause.

**inc
19c**

OMISSION OF *THAT:*   He noticed the mistake worried me.

REVISED: He noticed that the mistake worried me.

19c   INCOMPLETE COMPARISONS

Omissions frequently occur in comparisons, and usually a reader can fill in the missing word or words with no difficulty.

This route is as long as that one [is long].

The copies from this machine are darker than those [copies are dark].

The weather is hotter this week than [it was] last [week].

In some comparative constructions, however, the omissions cause the comparison to be incomplete. For example, in clauses beginning with *than* or *as,* an omission can create ambiguity. A reader cannot with certainty fill in the missing word or words.

INCOMPLETE: Stray dogs are friendlier to me than my roommate.

POSSIBLE MEANING: Stray dogs are friendlier to me than my roommate is.

POSSIBLE MEANING: Stray dogs are friendlier to me than they are to my roommate.

Also, in *than* or *as* clauses, the omission of *other* may cause something to be illogically compared to itself. For example, in the following sentence, the omission suggests that Texas is not a state.

INCOMPLETE: Texas produces more oil than any state.

REVISED: Texas produces more oil than any other state.

A double comparison requires the three conjunctions *as . . . as . . . than*—for example, "The pig is *as* smart *as,* if not smarter *than,* the dog." The omission of the second *as* makes the first comparison incomplete.

INCOMPLETE: Aiken's autobiography is as successful, if not more successful than, Adam's.

REVISED: Aiken's autobiography is as successful as, if not more suc-
~~cessful than,~~ Adam's.

Incomplete comparisons may also result from unexplained
modifiers. Modifiers like *best, worst, cutest,* or *sweetest* should be
completed.

INCOMPLETE: *Gone with the Wind* is the best movie.

POSSIBLE MEANING: *Gone with the Wind* is the best movie ever made.

POSSIBLE MEANING: *Gone with the Wind* is the best movie I have ever
seen.

In informal conversation, a speaker sometimes uses *so, such,* or *too*
as an intensifier without explaining results—*so nice, too hard.* In
formal English, however, these modifiers signal comparisons or
measurements, and the omitted explanation leaves the idea incomplete. A writer, therefore, must either complete the comparison or
use a true intensifier like *very* or *extremely.*

INCOMPLETE: The noise of the plane was so loud.

REVISED: The noise of the plane was so loud that we could not hear
what was said.

REVISED: The noise of the plane was extremely loud.

In addition, an omission may cause the illogical comparison of
two different classes of entities. For example, in the following sentence, the writer has compared a technique to a contender.

INCOMPLETE: His technique for throwing the discus is unlike any other
contender.

REVISED: His technique for throwing the discus is unlike any other
contender's.

REVISED: His technique for throwing the discus is unlike that of any
other contender.

20

PARALLELISM

Sentences frequently contain lists of two or more items. Such items in a sequence must be parallel; that is, they must have the same grammatical structure. The following examples illustrate parallel sequence.

2 NOUN PHRASES:	The best beer has both <u>natural ingredients</u> and <u>natural fermentation</u>.
3 PREPOSITIONAL PHRASES:	The Shakespeare company has traveled not only <u>to city theaters</u> and <u>to college campuses</u> but also <u>to small communities</u>.
4 VERB FORMS:	"Uncooperative" computers have been <u>rid-dled</u> with bullets, <u>burned up</u> with gasoline, <u>stabbed</u> with screwdrivers, and <u>hammered</u> with shoes.
3 NOUN CLAUSES:	We now know <u>that sleep has at least four depths</u>, <u>that dreaming is most intense in the period of rapid eye movement</u>, and <u>that sleep deprivation is dangerous</u>.

Be sure to make items parallel in a compound structure, a series, a list, or an outline. A mixture of grammatical structures lacks logic and symmetry.

20a PARALLELISM IN COMPOUND STRUCTURES

/ /
20a

The two items in a compound structure must be grammatically the same: *pencil* and *paper, working* and *playing, to search* and *to find, when they read* and *when they listen.* Although the two items are most often linked by *and,* there are several other ways to connect them.

(1) Compounding with coordinating conjunctions *(and, but, or, nor, yet)*

The elements on either side of a coordinating conjunction must be the same grammatical construction.

NOT PARALLEL:	The heat wave will increase the demand for electricity and causing power outages. [*And* joins a verb phrase to a participial phrase.]
REVISED WITH 2 VERB PHRASES:	The heat wave will increase the demand for electricity and will cause power outages.
NOT PARALLEL:	The bicycle path should be located along Route 234 or to follow the Pendleton River. [*Or* joins a prepositional phrase to an infinitive phrase.]
REVISED WITH 2 PREPOSITIONAL PHRASES:	The bicycle path should be located along Route 234 or beside the Pendleton River.

(2) Compounding with correlative conjunctions *(not only . . . but also, not . . . but, either . . . or, neither . . . nor, both . . . and)*

Whatever grammatical element follows the first part of a correlative conjunction must also follow the second part.

/ /
20a

NOT PARALLEL:	I will either leave from National Airport or from Dulles. [*Either* is followed by a verb; *or* is followed by a prepositional phrase.]
REVISED WITH 2 PREPOSITIONAL PHRASES:	I will leave either from National Airport or from Dulles.
NOT PARALLEL:	The reporter wondered both what the lawyer had meant and the need for reporting the remark. [*Both* is followed by a noun clause; *and* is followed by a noun phrase.]
REVISED WITH 2 NOUN CLAUSES:	The reporter wondered both what the lawyer had meant and whether the remark should be reported.
NOT PARALLEL:	We not only want to visit the Corcoran Gallery but also the Hirshhorn Museum. [*Not only* is followed by a verb; *but also* is followed by a noun.]
REVISED WITH 2 NOUN PHRASES:	We want to visit not only the Corcoran Gallery but also the Hirshhorn Museum.

(3) Compounding with other connecting words (*not, as well as, rather than, less than, more than, from . . . to, instead of*)

Some words and phrases create compound structures in the same manner as the coordinating conjunctions: they must join elements with the same grammatical structure.

NOT PARALLEL:	We should advertise the car wash rather than to be overlooked by poten-

tial customers. [*Rather than* joins a verb phrase to an infinitive phrase.]

REVISED WITH 2 VERB PHRASES: We should advertise the car wash rather than be overlooked by potential customers.

NOT PARALLEL: The reporter has covered the trial from the swearing in of the jury to when the judge sentenced the murderer. [*From . . . to* joins a noun phrase to a subordinate clause.]

REVISED WITH 2 NOUN PHRASES: The reporter has covered the trial from the swearing in of the jury to the sentencing by the judge.

NOT PARALLEL: My history teacher is guilty of telling about past events instead of an explanation of them. [*Instead of* joins a gerund phrase and a noun phrase.]

REVISED WITH 2 GERUND PHRASES: My history teacher is guilty of telling about past events instead of explaining them.

20b PARALLELISM IN SERIES, LISTS, AND OUTLINES

A sequence of more than two items may appear within a sentence or in a list with one item under the other. All the items, no matter how many, must have the same grammatical structure.

NOT PARALLEL: The students go to the clinic to get vitamins for anemia, for aspirins for headaches, or just counseling. [The series contains an infinitive phrase, a prepositional phrase, and a noun phrase.]

REVISED WITH 3 NOUN PHRASES: The students go to the clinic to get vitamins for anemia, aspirins for headaches,

/ /
20b

or counseling for their emotional problems.

NOT PARALLEL: I asked the curator whether the museum was well funded, about the style of paintings it featured, and to supply the names of its patrons. [The series contains a noun clause, a prepositional phrase, and an infinitive phrase.]

REVISED WITH 3 CLAUSES: I asked the curator whether the museum was well funded, what style of paintings it featured, and if he would supply the names of its patrons.

NOT PARALLEL: The members decided to fulfill these responsibilities:
1. Meet with parents and guardians
2. Meet with interested citizens
3. Answers to questions from the media
4. A record of responses to telephone calls

[The list contains two verb phrases and two noun phrases.]

REVISED WITH 4 VERB PHRASES: The members decided to fulfill these responsibilities:
1. Meet with parents and guardians
2. Meet with interested citizens
3. Answer questions from the media
4. Record responses to telephone calls

NOT PARALLEL: Slang: Its Useful Purposes
I. Slang used to identify social groups
II. To enliven language
III. Slang gives us new names
IV. Euphemisms for things that are unpleasant or offensive

[The outline contains a noun phrase, an infinitive phrase, an independent clause, and a noun phrase.]

REVISED WITH 4 SENTENCES:

Slang's Useful Purposes

// **20b**

I. Social groups use slang as a sign of identification.
II. Slang develops to enliven language, to eliminate monotony.
III. Slang gives us names for new things, such as physical objects or social movements.
IV. Slang supplies euphemisms for unpleasant or offensive actions and places.

REVISED WITH SERIES OF NOUNS:

The Usefulness of Slang

I. In-group identification
II. Variety
III. Names for new things
IV. Euphemisms

III

PUNCTUATION AND MECHANICS

Punctuation and mechanics are signals that work together with words and structures to create meaning. With the aid of these signals, readers anticipate, link, separate, stress, de-emphasize, and characterize ideas according to a writer's wishes. In fact, readers rely so heavily on these marks that their misuse can distort or obscure intended meaning. Therefore, to communicate clearly, you must use punctuation marks and mechanics according to standard practice.

21

COMMAS

The most versatile of all punctuation marks, **commas** enclose, separate, and set off information. Because commas indicate sentence structure and meaning, their use is essential to clear writing.

21a COMMAS BETWEEN INDEPENDENT CLAUSES JOINED BY COORDINATING CONJUNCTIONS

One way to join two independent clauses is with a comma and a coordinating conjunction (*and, but, or, nor, for, so,* and *yet*).

> The Vice President will arrive at 9:30, and the commissioning of the battleship will begin at 10:00.

> The regular edition of the dictionary is twelve volumes, but the compact edition is only two.

> I have to maintain a C average, or my parents will make me pay for my own courses.

> All the dormitories were full, so we were housed temporarily in local motels and hotels.

You may omit the comma when the independent clauses are very short and parallel in structure and when the conjunction is *and, but, or,* or *nor.*

The lights are off <u>and</u> the door is locked.

You should, however, always include the comma when the conjunction is *for, so,* and *yet.* Because these conjunctions can function as other parts of speech, the comma prevents misreading. For example, in the first sentence of the following pair, *for* seems to be a preposition; in the second, the comma makes clear that *for* is a conjunction.

MISLEADING: They went back home for their roots were there.

CLEAR: They went back home, for their roots were there.

In the first sentence of the next pair, *yet* seems to be an adverb of time; in the second, *yet* is clearly a conjunction.

MISLEADING: We didn't want to go yet we thought it was our duty.

CLEAR: We didn't want to go, yet we thought it was our duty.

NOTE: When independent clauses are long or contain internal punctuation, you may prefer to join them with a semicolon and a coordinating conjunction to show the major break in the sentence. (See 22c.)

If you approach the colt slowly, talking in a calm voice, you can gain his confidence; but if you move abruptly or speak sharply, he will bolt.

21b COMMAS AFTER INTRODUCTORY PREPOSITIONAL PHRASES, VERBALS, AND DEPENDENT CLAUSES

An introductory or dependent clause appears at the beginning of a sentence or another clause—either independent or dependent. For a discussion of verbals, dependent clauses, and independent clauses, see Chapter 5 and Chapter 7.

(1)   Introductory prepositional phrases

A comma usually follows a long introductory prepositional phrase (a preposition and its object) or a combination of phrases.

INTRODUCING A SENTENCE:	At yesterday's press conference, the coach denied the NCAA charges of recruiting violations.
INTRODUCING A DEPENDENT CLAUSE:	The local television station announced that <u>as a result of a recent campaign,</u> the city government had agreed to improve the public bus service.
INTRODUCING A SENTENCE:	<u>After a bizarre wedding ceremony in the health spa,</u> the couple jogged off into the sunset.
INTRODUCING A SECOND INDEPENDENT CLAUSE:	The well-known *couturiers* once catered to the idle rich, <u>but with so many women now in the business world,</u> designers are taking a more practical approach to fashion.

If a prepositional phrase is short and does not interfere with ease of reading, you can omit the comma.

<u>By 1862</u> the pony express no longer existed.

<u>At twilight</u> we always heard the whippoorwill.

(2) Introductory verbals and verbal phrases

You should place a comma after an introductory verbal (participle, infinitive, or gerund) or verbal phrase, regardless of its length. (See Chapter 5.)

PARTICIPIAL PHRASE INTRODUCING A SENTENCE:	<u>Built in 1752,</u> Connecticut Hall is the oldest building on the Yale campus.
PARTICIPIAL PHRASE INTRODUCING A SECOND INDEPENDENT CLAUSE:	He swung the door open; <u>then realizing his error,</u> he stammered and backed from the room.
INFINITIVE PHRASE INTRODUCING A SENTENCE:	<u>To avoid the crowds,</u> I did my Christmas shopping in September.

GERUND PHRASE INTRODUCING A SENTENCE:	By encroaching on the dense woods, ~~we have greatly reduced the wild~~ turkey population.

Use a comma even after a single introductory participle or infinitive.

, 21b

PARTICIPLE INTRODUCING A SENTENCE:	Exhausted, she fell asleep on the chair.
INFINITIVES INTRODUCING A FIRST AND SECOND INDEPENDENT CLAUSE:	To jitterbug, you must tense your arm muscles, but to waltz, you must relax them.

(3) Introductory adverb clauses

Most introductory clauses are adverb clauses, introduced by subordinate conjunctions such as *after, although, as soon as, because, before, even though, if, once, since, unless, when, where, while.* (See 7c.1.) Usually, a comma should separate an introductory adverb clause from the rest of the sentence.

> Although hypnosis now has a recognized place in medicine, the technique has its opponents.

> Unless the student newspaper can generate more advertising, readers will have to pay fifty cents per issue.

> When a tuning fork is struck, the tone remains always the same.

A comma should also follow an adverb clause that introduces a subsequent clause in a sentence.

> A baby is born with the language center in the left side of the brain, but if he or she suffers brain injury very early in infancy, the language center can shift to the right side.

> The power went out because when I plugged in the coffeepot, I overloaded the circuit.

After a short introductory clause that does not interfere with ease of reading, you can omit the comma. Nevertheless, the comma is always appropriate.

CORRECT: When it snows I get depressed.

CORRECT: When it snows, I get depressed.

(4)   Introductory noun clauses

Normally, a noun clause used as an object or complement follows the verb and should not be separated from the rest of the sentence with a comma. (See 7c.3.)

COMPLEMENT: People can be whatever they want to be.

DIRECT OBJECT: The group automatically oppose whomever labor supports.

When the normal order is reversed and the noun clause is introductory, it should be followed by a comma.

INTRODUCTORY COMPLEMENT: Whatever people want to be, they can be.

INTRODUCTORY OBJECT: Whomever labor supports, the group automatically opposes.

NOTE: A noun clause that functions as the subject of a sentence should not be followed by a comma.

Whatever you prefer is acceptable to me.

21c   COMMAS TO SET OFF NONRESTRICTIVE ELEMENTS

The terms *nonrestrictive* and *restrictive* usually refer to adjective clauses, verbals and verbal phrases, and appositives (words and phrases that rename or restate). A nonrestrictive element is not essential to the meaning of its sentence. In other words, readers do not need the element to identify the word or phrase it follows. By setting off a nonrestrictive element with commas, you point to its nonessential role in the construction.

NONRESTRICTIVE CLAUSE: A widely cultivated fruit is the strawberry, which belongs to the rose family.

NONRESTRICTIVE VERBAL PHRASE:	Pompeii, covered by volcanic ash, was sealed for almost 1,700 years.
NONRESTRICTIVE APPOSITIVE:	Lister, a physician at Glasgow University, founded antiseptic surgery.

In contrast, a restrictive element is essential to the meaning of its sentence. Readers use the element to identify the word or phrase it follows. The absence of commas around a restrictive element points to its essential role in the construction.

21c

RESTRICTIVE CLAUSE:	The rose that I prefer is the edible strawberry.
RESTRICTIVE VERBAL PHRASE:	The volcanic ash covering Pompeii sealed the city for almost 1,700 years.
RESTRICTIVE APPOSITIVE:	Antiseptic surgery was founded by the physician Lister.

Several techniques will help you determine whether an element is restrictive or nonrestrictive.

- **Look for the introductory words in clauses.**

  A clause that begins with *that* is restrictive.

  The Warren Report summarizes the events that relate to John F. Kennedy's assassination.

  Athletes should eat foods that are high in complex carbohydrates.

  A clause with no introductory word is restrictive.

  The lands Alexander conquered stretched from Greece to northwestern India. [*That* is understood before *Alexander.*]

  The artists we admire usually startle or amuse us. [*Whom* or *that* is understood before *we.*]

  A clause that begins with *which* is usually nonrestrictive.

  The area is famous for its pink grapefruit, which is unusually sweet.

  Her hobbies, which included rock climbing and camping, led to her career as a forest ranger.

- **Look for proper nouns.**

  An element following a proper noun is usually nonrestrictive.

One of Europe's most effective monarchs was Elizabeth I, who successfully overcame religious strife, a bankrupt treasury, war with France, and the Spanish Armada.

The Dalmatian, also called the coach dog, closely resembles a pointer.

The best known American clown was probably Emmett Kelly, the forlorn tramp.

- **Look for elements that can refer to only one possible person, place, or thing.**

Elements with only one possible referent are nonrestrictive.

My family hero is my mother's mother, who once rode a horse from Dallas to San Francisco.

His first car, purchased from a neighbor for $300, was a '58 Pontiac.

I was craving my favorite cold-weather food, vegetable soup.

- **Look for appositives introduced by *or*.**

Appositives introduced by *or* are nonrestrictive because they explain or define the nouns they follow. Without commas, the appositives will seem to be alternatives in *either/or* compounds. In the following sentence, for instance, *body language* defines *kinesis*. Were the comma removed, the sentence would erroneously suggest alternatives, *either body language or kinesis*.

The company trains all its personnel in kinesis, or body language.

- **Check intended meaning.**

Occasionally, an element can be either nonrestrictive or restrictive, depending on the writer's intent. In these cases, punctuation must indicate the meaning. For example, the first sentence below, with commas, means "All politicians sacrifice integrity for power, and all are dangerous." In contrast, the second sentence, without commas, means "Some politicians sacrifice integrity for power, and those particular politicians are dangerous."

NONRESTRICTIVE: Politicians, who sacrifice integrity for power, are dangerous.

RESTRICTIVE:	Politicians who sacrifice integrity for power are dangerous.

Similarly, different punctuation in the next two sentences produces different meanings. The writer of the first sentence has only one daughter; the writer of the second, more than one daughter.

NONRESTRICTIVE:	I spent Christmas with my daughter, who lives in Miami.
RESTRICTIVE:	I spent Christmas with my daughter who lives in Miami.

'
21d

21d COMMAS BETWEEN ITEMS IN A SERIES AND BETWEEN COORDINATE ADJECTIVES

Without commas, parallel items in a sentence can run together and obscure meaning. Commas separate the items and make the meaning clear.

(1) Items in a series

A series is a list of three or more parallel structures—three or more nouns, adjectives, verb phrases, prepositional phrases, dependent clauses, independent clauses, and so on. Ordinarily, you should use commas to separate items in a series. (If the series items themselves contain commas, use semicolons. See 22d.)

ADJECTIVES:	We are looking for someone reliable, efficient, and versatile.
NOUN PHRASES:	When in doubt about the procedure, consult the lab manual, the operational instructions, or the student assistant.
DEPENDENT CLAUSES:	When I returned to my room, I found that my roommate had eaten lunch on my bed, that one of his friends had spilled coffee on my history notes, and that another friend had borrowed my sports jacket.

INDEPENDENT CLAUSES: The roots absorb the water from the soil, the sapwood carries the water to the leaves, and the leaves make food for the tree.

Some writers, particularly journalists, omit the comma before the conjunction and the last element in the series. However, omission of this comma can sometimes cause misreading.

21d

UNCLEAR: The Grievance Committee met with three petitioners, two students and a faculty member.

The reader cannot know whether the committee met with six people or with three. But proper punctuation can make the meaning clear.

CLEAR: The Grievance Committee met with three petitioners, two students, and a faculty member. [six people, listed as items in a series]

CLEAR: The Grievance Committee met with three petitioners: two students and a faculty member. [three people, presented as an appositive following a colon]

(2) Coordinate adjectives

Coordinate adjectives can be rearranged and can be logically connected by *and.* In the absence of *and,* commas should separate coordinate adjectives.

COORDINATE: He liked to play tennis on a shady, secluded court.

REARRANGED: He liked to play tennis on a secluded, shady court.

CONNECTED WITH *AND:* He liked to play tennis on a shady and secluded court.

Noncoordinate adjectives, which can be neither rearranged nor connected with *and,* should not be separated by commas.

NONCOORDINATE:	He liked to play tennis on an old clay court.
IMPOSSIBLE:	He like to play tennis on a clay old court.
IMPOSSIBLE:	He liked to play tennis on an old and clay court.

When an adjective phrase contains both coordinate and non-coordinate adjectives, the same principle applies: commas should appear in positions where *and* could be inserted.

COORDINATE AND NONCOORDINATE:	I was met at the door by two large, shaggy, playful Irish setters.
POSSIBLE:	I was met at the door by two large and shaggy and playful Irish setters.
IMPOSSIBLE:	I was met at the door by two and large and shaggy and playful and Irish setters.

21e COMMAS IN PLACE OF OMITTED WORDS

When consecutive clauses have parallel structure and common vocabulary, a comma can replace the verb or part of the predicate.

Rankin received 312 votes; Jenkins, 117. [The comma replaces *received.*]

The older sister wanted to be an actress, and the younger sister, a doctor. [The comma replaces *wanted to be.*]

The first question was on the prose of the eighteenth century; the second, on the poetry; and the third, on the drama. [The commas replace *was.*]

21f COMMAS TO SET OFF PARENTHETICAL, TRANSITIONAL, AND CONTRASTIVE ELEMENTS

Commas set off parenthetical, transitional, and contrastive elements to show that these structures are added to an otherwise complete sentence.

(1) Parenthetical elements

A parenthetical element is a structure that could be enclosed in parentheses without changing the meaning of the sentence. The element can occur within a sentence and interrupt the structure abruptly, or it can appear at the end of a sentence and serve as a concluding remark. In either case, use a comma or commas to set off the element from the rest of the sentence.

INTERRUPTING THE SUBJECT AND VERB:	The coach, <u>according to informed sources,</u> intends to leave after this season.
INTERRUPTING THE VERB AND OBJECT:	The bank officers said, <u>believe it or not,</u> that they had accurately reported the assets.
INTERRUPTING THE VERB PHRASE:	She was not, <u>strictly speaking,</u> managing the estate.
CONCLUDING REMARK:	Salaries have not improved at all during the past three years, <u>at least not as far as the clerical staff is concerned.</u>

(2) Transitional expressions

Transitional expressions, or conjunctive adverbs, are words and phrases such as *however, therefore, for example, in conclusion, accordingly, nevertheless, in addition,* and so on. For a complete list, see *Transitional Expression* in the Glossary of Terms. You should set off these expressions with commas.

Houseplants available at nurseries can be expensive and, <u>in addition,</u> difficult to grow. <u>Therefore,</u> people without green thumbs are often reluctant to spend money to watch their purchases wither and die. There is, <u>however,</u> a solution for people who want to grow plants with little expense or effort—the avocado.

The seed of a well-ripened avocado planted in porous soil will sprout and produce a good-sized plant in a few weeks. An avocado plant grown in the house will not, <u>of course,</u> flower or bear fruit.

Nevertheless, it will provide inexpensive, luxurious, and trouble-free greenery.

(3)   Contrastive elements

Elements that contrast with whatever has preceded usually begin with words like *not, never, but, unlike,* and *rather than.* Normally, you should set these elements off with commas.

> It was the beginning, not the end, of the social upheaval.

> Our codes of conduct in those days were dictated by our peers, never by our parents.

You may omit the commas when the contrastive elements are not abrupt. To emphasize the elements, however, always include the commas.

> NOT EMPHATIC: The speech was informative but tedious.

> EMPHATIC: The speech was informative, but tedious.

21g   COMMAS TO SET OFF INTERJECTIONS, WORDS IN DIRECT ADDRESS, AND TAG QUESTIONS

Interjections, words in direct address, and tag questions are all elements loosely connected to a basic clause. Use commas to set off these elements from the rest of the sentence.

(1)   Interjections

An interjection is an exclamation with no grammatical connection to the rest of the sentence. You may punctuate an interjection as a separate sentence with a period or an exclamation point. Or you may punctuate it as part of another sentence by setting it off with a comma or commas.

> Well, the time has finally come to act.

> His costume was, no kidding, a shower curtain.

(2) Words in direct address

You should always set off words in direct address, which name whomever or whatever is spoken to.

Excuse me, sir, is this the plane to Denver?

Sit and beg, Butch.

(3) Tag questions

Tag questions appear at the end of statements and ask for verification. Always set these questions off with commas.

The budget was balanced, wasn't it?

She did not ask for a second opinion, did she?

21h COMMAS IN SPECIAL CONTEXTS: IN DATES, PLACES, ADDRESSES; IN NUMBERS; WITH TITLES OF INDIVIDUALS; WITH QUOTATION MARKS

When you position commas in special constructions such as dates and addresses, you should follow current conventions and practices.

(1) Dates, places, and addresses

The commas in dates, places, and addresses serve to isolate each item for the reader.

- Pattern: Month day, year,

  She graduated on May 22, 1986, from Loyola University. [commas before and after the year when the day is given]

- Pattern: Day month year

  She graduated 22 May 1986 from Loyola University. [no commas when the day precedes the month]

- Pattern: Month year

> She graduated in May 1986 from Loyola University. [no commas when the day is unspecified]

- Pattern: City, state,

> We surveyed the voters in St. Louis, Missouri, two weeks before the election. [commas before and after the names of states]

- Pattern: Street address, city, state zip code,

> Ship the package to 1110 East Marina Road, Dallas, TX 75201, within ten days. [comma between street address and city; comma between city and state; no comma between state and zip code; comma between zip code and material that follows]

(2)   Numbers expressing amounts

Commas indicate thousands and millions in numbers of five or more digits. Many people also prefer commas in four-digit numbers.

> Last year the company sold 2,165 records; this year they sold 1,926,021.

(3)   Titles of individuals

A title following a name should be set off with commas.

> Applications for the summer co-op program should be sent to Kathryn McLeod, travel director, or to Carl Jenkins, personnel director.

Usually, *Jr.* or *Sr.* following a name is set off with commas. Some people, however, prefer to omit the commas, and you should honor that preference.

> Mr. and Mrs. James W. Marcott, Jr., hosted the reception.

> James Hillery Godbold Sr. donated the funds.

(4)   Direct quotations

Commas should set off a grammatically independent quotation from the words that identify its source. When a comma and a closing quotation mark occur together, the comma comes first.

"You can't expect to hit the jackpot," said Flip Wilson, "if you don't put a few nickels in the machine."

"The results of the tests are insignificant," according to Dr. Landrum.

"It was a perfect title," Dixon thought, "in that it crystallized the article's niggling mindlessness, its funereal parade of yawn-enforcing facts, the pseudo-light it threw upon non-problems." (Kingsley Amis)

21j

A comma is not appropriate when a quotation is an integral part of the sentence structure.

Ayn Rand defined civilization as "the progress toward a society of privacy."

Who said that for every credibility gap, there is a "gullibility fill"?

21i COMMAS TO ENSURE INTENDED READING

In some instances, commas are necessary simply to prevent misreading. For example, in the following sentence, the comma indicates that *can try* is not a unit.

CONFUSING: Employees who can try to carpool twice a week.

CLEAR: Employees who can, try to carpool twice a week.

In other instances, commas create stylistic effects. For example, the commas in the next two sentences are not grammatically necessary; instead, they indicate pauses and create a reading different from the usual.

"There is no safety in numbers, or in anything else." (James Thurber)

The child had never had a guardian, and never had a friend.

21j INAPPROPRIATE COMMAS

Commas are inappropriate in the following situations, except when necessary to ensure proper reading.

• Between major sentence elements—such as subject and predicate, verb and object, items in a verb phrase

INAPPROPRIATE: Several people on horseback, suddenly appeared at the
~~bridge. [separation of subject and predicate]~~

REVISED: Several people on horseback suddenly appeared at the
bridge.

INAPPROPRIATE: Conner realized, that he wanted to go home. [separation of verb and object]

REVISED: Conner realized that he wanted to go home.

,
21j

- Between two items joined by a coordinating conjunction or correlative conjunctions unless those items are independent clauses

INAPPROPRIATE: The road began at the edge of the field, and ended abruptly in the middle. [separation of two verbs]

REVISED: The road began at the edge of the field and ended abruptly in the middle.

INAPPROPRIATE: We hoped the commission would prohibit not only channelization, but also the planting of kudzu. [separation of two objects]

REVISED: We hoped the commission would prohibit not only channelization but also the planting of kudzu.

INAPPROPRIATE: Most critics agreed that the plot relied too heavily on coincidence, and the director relied too heavily on special effects. [separation of two dependent clauses, with *that* understood after *and*]

REVISED: Most critics agreed that the plot relied too heavily on coincidence and the director relied too heavily on special effects.

- After the final adjective in a series

INAPPROPRIATE: He wore a cheap, shabby, and ill-fitting, suit.

REVISED: He wore a cheap, shabby, and ill-fitting suit.

- After a coordinating or a subordinating conjunction

<table>
<tr><td>INAPPROPRIATE:</td><td>We ate at a terrible restaurant that featured waffles and, fried seafood.</td></tr>
<tr><td>REVISED:</td><td>We ate at a terrible restaurant that featured waffles and fried seafood.</td></tr>
<tr><td>INAPPROPRIATE:</td><td>Nothing grows in that section of the yard because, there is too much lime in the soil.</td></tr>
<tr><td>REVISED:</td><td>Nothing grows in that section of the yard because there is too much lime in the soil.</td></tr>
</table>

21j

- Between an indirect quotation and the rest of the sentence

INAPPROPRIATE: The author said, that the historical data had been carefully researched.

REVISED: The author said that the historical data had been carefully researched.

22

SEMICOLONS

Semicolons are marks of punctuation weaker than periods but stronger than commas. Basically, there are two positions for semicolons: between independent clauses and between items in a series that contain commas. In each position, the semicolon occurs between coordinate elements—that is, elements of the same grammatical construction.

22a SEMICOLONS BETWEEN INDEPENDENT CLAUSES NOT JOINED BY COORDINATING CONJUNCTIONS

Independent clauses can be joined in a variety of ways, depending on the ideas expressed. (See 33a.1.) The semicolon is a logical choice when the ideas in each clause seem fairly equal and balanced. For example, in the three sentences that follow, the semicolon functions like the conjunction *and.*

> The left brain controls the right side of the body; the right brain controls the left side.

> Shakespeare's vocabulary included about 20,000 words; Milton's included about 11,000.

> Lights went out; elevators stopped; traffic stood still.

The semicolon is also an option when none of the coordinating conjunctions (*and, but, or, for, nor, so, yet*) seems to express the appropriate relationship.

> The bus was a bizarre sight; it lurched, swayed, and heaved itself forward like a drunk.

> Their motive was not money; it was something far more interesting than that.

> Benjamin Franklin carried out a number of experiments with lightning; in one of them, he passed an electric current through a chain of six men.

Semicolons should not be overused within a single passage. They are more noticeable than commas and thus should be used sparingly, lest they lose their effect.

> OVERUSED: Bluegrass is an old-timey sound from Virginia, Tennessee, and Kentucky; it is the most traditional form of country music. Now the bluegrass festival has become a popular entertainment; families pack picnic lunches to spend the day listening to professionals and amateurs play. Some fans listen to the performances on the stage; others wander about enjoying the impromptu sessions on the grounds.

> REVISED: An old-timey sound from Virginia, Tennessee, and Kentucky, bluegrass is the most traditional form of country music. Now the bluegrass festival has become a popular entertainment. Families pack picnic lunches to spend the day listening to professionals and amateurs play. Some fans listen to the performances on the stage; others wander about enjoying the impromptu sessions on the grounds.

22b SEMICOLONS BETWEEN INDEPENDENT CLAUSES JOINED BY TRANSITIONAL EXPRESSIONS

When two independent clauses are joined, their relationship is often signalled by a transitional expression, such as *however, therefore, also, nevertheless, for example, consequently,* or *instead.* (For a more complete list, see *Transitional Expression* in the Glos-

;
22b

sary of Terms.) These expressions are not grammatical conjunctions but adverbs modifying the entire clause. Thus, in the absence of a true conjunction, the semicolon joins the clauses.

> People under stress report long, complex dreams; <u>however</u>, people with placid lives report dreams that are uneventful and usually uninteresting.

> Each year the group publishes a list of words and phrases that should be banned from the language; <u>for example</u>, one year it listed "at this point in time" and "have a nice day."

;
22c

The difference between a transitional expression and a conjunction can be illustrated very simply: a transitional expression can be moved about in a clause; a conjunction cannot.

POSSIBLE: We feared that computers would increase unemployment; <u>instead</u>, they have created more jobs.

POSSIBLE: We feared that computers would increase unemployment; they have, <u>instead</u>, created more jobs.

POSSIBLE: We feared that computers would increase unemployment, <u>but</u> they have created more jobs.

IMPOSSIBLE: We feared that computers would increase unemployment, they have, <u>but</u>, created more jobs.

22c   SEMICOLONS BETWEEN INDEPENDENT CLAUSES JOINED BY COORDINATING CONJUNCTIONS

Ordinarily a comma appears between two independent clauses joined by a coordinating conjunction (*and, but, or, nor, for, so, yet*). However, when the first independent clause contains commas, a semicolon clarifies the structure.

UNCLEAR: Of the 11,000 men who encamped at Valley Forge, only 8,000 came with shoes, and only 8,000 survived.

REVISED: Of the 11,000 men who encamped at Valley Forge, only 8,000 came with shoes; and only 8,000 survived.

> UNCLEAR: The books effectively deal with systems and languages such as UNIX, BASIC, PASCAL, C, COBOL, but these books cost approximately twenty dollars each.
>
> REVISED: The books effectively deal with systems and languages such as UNIX, BASIC, PASCAL, C, COBOL; but these books cost approximately twenty dollars each.

When only one comma occurs in the first independent clause, you can use a comma or a semicolon with the conjunction. Either of the following versions is appropriate.

> By purchasing a month-long pass for the train, travelers can save five dollars; but a year-long pass will save ninety dollars.

> By purchasing a month-long pass for the train, travelers can save five dollars, but a year-long pass will save ninety dollars.

22d SEMICOLONS BETWEEN ITEMS IN A SERIES WITH INTERNAL PUNCTUATION

Ordinarily commas separate items in a series.

> We subscribe to *Time, Newsweek,* and *Harper's.*

If, however, the items themselves contain commas, semicolons are required to mark the separation.

> UNCLEAR: The train stops in Birmingham, Alabama, Atlanta, Georgia, Charlotte, North Carolina, and Charlottesville, Virginia.
>
> REVISED: The train stops in Birmingham, Alabama; Atlanta, Georgia; Charlotte, North Carolina; and Charlottesville, Virginia.

> UNCLEAR: The most significant dates of the Civil War were April 12, 1861, July 3, 1863, and April 9, 1865.
>
> REVISED: The most significant dates of the Civil War were April 12, 1861; July 3, 1863; and April 9, 1865.

> UNCLEAR: The participants in the exhibit are Judi Parker, who paints in watercolor, Simon Rogers, who is a potter, and Peter Mondavian, who sculpts in transparent plastic.

REVISED: The participants in the exhibit are Judi Parker, who paints in watercolor; Simon Rogers, who is a potter; and Peter Mondavian, who sculpts in transparent plastic.

22e INAPPROPRIATE SEMICOLONS

Avoid semicolons in these positions:

● **Between elements that are not coordinate**

INAPPROPRIATE: Only 7 plays by Sophocles now exist; even though he supposedly wrote 124.

REVISED: Only 7 plays by Sophocles now exist, even though he supposedly wrote 124.

● **Before a list**

INAPPROPRIATE: I have checked the following sources; encyclopedias, almanacs, indexes, and abstracts.

REVISED: I have checked the following sources: encyclopedias, almanacs, indexes, and abstracts.

REVISED: I have checked the following sources—encyclopedias, almanacs, indexes, and abstracts.

CHAPTER

23

COLONS

Although the **colon** is used in diverse constructions, it has only two basic purposes: to point ahead and to separate. No matter what its purpose, the colon has a formal and official tone.

23a COLONS BEFORE LISTS

A colon sometimes announces that a list will follow. Usually, the list is written not as a tabulation but as a continuation of the sentence. However, in scientific, technical, and business writing, the list is often separated from the sentence and itemized down the page.

NONTECHNICAL WRITING: Several American writers have died young without completing work they had started: F. Scott Fitzgerald, Nathanael West, and James Agee.

TECHNICAL WRITING: According to sports psychologists, athletes can improve their performances by several techniques:
1. goal setting
2. mental practice
3. relaxation

Most experts agree that a complete sentence should precede a colon. In fact, writers often precede a list with an expression like *the following* or *as follows* in order to avoid splitting elements, such as a verb or preposition from its object.

SPLIT: We visited: Athens, Kusadasi, Rhodes, and Heraklion.

REVISED: We visited the following places: Athens, Kusadasi, Rhodes, and Heraklion.

SPLIT: The root *carn* appears in: *incarnation, carnage,* and *carnival.*

REVISED: The root *carn* appears in the following words: *incarnation, carnage,* and *carnival.*

:
23c

23b COLONS BEFORE APPOSITIVES THAT END SENTENCES

An appositive renames and identifies another sentence element, as *pitcher* renames *Satchel Paige* in the following example.

Satchel Paige, a great pitcher, entered the major leagues at the age of 42.

When an appositive appears at the end of a sentence, an introductory colon creates drama or emphasis.

Seventy years after the hoax of the Piltdown Man, a surprising new suspect has been found: Sir Arthur Conan Doyle.

All the evidence points to the same conclusion: that a vast source of oil exists in the area.

23c COLONS BETWEEN INDEPENDENT CLAUSES

Usually, two independent clauses are joined with a comma and a co-ordinating conjunction or with a semicolon. On occasion, however, the second clause explains or illustrates the first clause or some part of it. A colon between the two clauses can indicate this special relationship. If the second clause is a formal statement or principle, you may capitalize the first word.

Galileo discovered that Copernicus was correct: Earth was not the center of the universe.

The most exciting shot in volleyball is the spike: one team tries to drive the ball across the net at up to 110 miles an hour.

23d COLONS BEFORE GRAMMATICALLY INDEPENDENT QUOTATIONS

A grammatically independent quotation is a complete sentence or several complete sentences. Ordinarily a comma separates the quotation from the rest of the sentence, but when the quotation is especially long and when the tone is formal, a colon may separate the two.

In a radio address on April 7, 1932, Roosevelt made a statement that still seems modern: "These unhappy times call for the building of plans . . . that build from the bottom up and not from the top down, that put their faith once more in the forgotten man at the bottom of the economic pyramid."

In 1945 Einstein wrote optimistically: "I do not believe that civilization will be wiped out in a war fought with the atomic bomb. Perhaps two-thirds of the people of the Earth might be killed, but enough men capable of thinking, and enough books, would be left to start again, and civilization could be restored."

23e COLONS BETWEEN TITLES AND SUBTITLES

A colon separates a title from a subtitle.

The Masks of God: Creative Mythology

Famine on the Wind: Plant Diseases and Human History

"Boomerang: The Stick That Returns"

"*Timon of Athens*: A Reconsideration"

23f COLONS IN CORRESPONDENCE

Several elements in business correspondence contain colons.

- Salutation

    Dear Ms. Plavin:

- Attention or subject line

    Attention: Dr. Grace Fortune

    Subject: Reassignment of Duties

- Headings in memoranda

    To: Part-Time Employees

    From: Milton Greenberg, Personnel Director

    Date: May 3, 1993

23g   COLONS WITH NUMERICAL ELEMENTS

In several types of numerical sequences, colons separate the parts—hours from minutes, chapters from verses, and numbers in ratios.

    5:30 P.M.   Psalms 29:2

    10:00 A.M.   4:3

23h   INAPPROPRIATE COLONS

Do not use a colon between the following elements.

- An independent and a dependent clause or phrase

    INAPPROPRIATE: I have received only one response to my letters: al-
                     though I wrote to twenty companies.

        REVISED: I have received only one response to my letters, al-
                     though I wrote to twenty companies.

- The parts of a phrase—for example, a verb and its complement, a preposition and its object, or *to* and the rest of the infinitive

INAPPROPRIATE: Is acid rain ruining: our gardens, our lakes, our farms?

REVISED: Is acid rain ruining our gardens, our lakes, our farms?

INAPPROPRIATE: Please send catalogues to: Carolyn Hacker and Stephen Hastings.

REVISED: Please send catalogues to Carolyn Hacker and Stephen Hastings.

INAPPROPRIATE: They are planning to: secure funds and send out a request for bids.

REVISED: They are planning to secure funds and send out a request for bids.

24

DASHES, PARENTHESES, AND BRACKETS

Dashes, parentheses, and **brackets** primarily enclose information, isolating it from the rest of a sentence. But the effect of these three marks of punctuation is somewhat different. Dashes emphasize the elements they enclose. Parentheses de-emphasize interrupters and nonessential elements. Brackets usually enclose clarifications, especially in direct quotations.

DASHES

24a DASHES TO SET OFF APPOSITIVES CONTAINING COMMAS

An appositive is a word or phrase that renames or restates. Dashes set off an appositive containing commas so that a reader can see where it begins and ends. As the examples show, an appositive may appear in the middle of a sentence, at the end, or at the beginning.

CONFUSING: A number of the Founding Fathers, Jefferson, Madison, Adams, Hamilton, were extremely intellectual.

REVISED: A number of the Founding Fathers—Jefferson, Madison, Adams, Hamilton—were extremely intellectual.

CONFUSING: The pitcher can throw a variety of breaking pitches, curves, screwballs, and knuckleballs.

REVISED: The pitcher can throw a variety of breaking pitches—curves, screwballs, and knuckleballs.

CONFUSING: A poet, dramatist, novelist, essayist, historian, Voltaire has been an influential figure in the history of thought.

REVISED: A poet, dramatist, novelist, essayist, historian—Voltaire has been an influential figure in the history of thought.

24b DASHES TO SET OFF NONRESTRICTIVE MODIFIERS CONTAINING COMMAS

Ordinarily commas set off a nonrestrictive modifier, whether a clause or a phrase. (See 21c.) When the modifier itself contains commas, however, dashes can make its boundaries clear.

Jules Feiffer—who has produced cartoons, novels, plays, and screenplays—uses humor to reflect human folly.

By the eighteenth century, riddles—written, at least—were becoming less suggestive and vulgar.

24c DASHES TO EMPHASIZE SENTENCE ELEMENTS

Dashes can emphasize any kind of construction (a word, a phrase, or a clause) that can be set off or separated from the rest of the sentence.

We have noticed a persistent quality in the lives of famous people—confidence.

They were stealing—via computer—hundreds of thousands of dollars ~~in goods and services.~~

In *Walden,* Thoreau tells how he built his cabin—down to the cost of the nails.

Most people who read food magazines never cook anything by the recipes—they're too difficult.

24d   DASHES WITH INTERRUPTERS

Dashes effectively set off an element that interrupts the continuity of prose, separates the essential parts of a sentence pattern, or breaks a piece of dialogue.

The author was sitting—slouching, really—on the sofa.

"I never knew—well, I don't suppose it matters now."

"But not—I really wouldn't call the move a mistake."

PARENTHESES

24e   PARENTHESES TO ENCLOSE INTERRUPTERS

Parentheses isolate and de-emphasize elements that interrupt a sentence or passage. Interrupters may be explanations, illustrations, or clarifications. They may be single words, phrases, or even whole sentences.

Since 1603, the royal arms of Britain have been supported by the English lion (dexter) and the Scottish unicorn (sinister).

KYB CHG (Keyboard Change) allows an operator to change the keyboard arrangement.

Monticello (pronounced *Montichel'lo* in the Italian way) was built on a Virginia hilltop Jefferson's father had left him.

When one whole sentence interrupts another, the interrupter neither begins with a capital letter nor ends with a period.

> After the Civil War, gangs of homeless burglars (they called themselves "yeggs") rode the freight trains, robbing and stealing along the way.

When a whole sentence is inserted between sentences, the interrupter begins with a capital letter and ends with a period. The final parenthesis follows the period.

> In his early youth Wordsworth was an enthusiast for the French Revolution. (He had been influenced by the ideas of Rousseau.) But as he grew older, he became increasingly conservative.

24f PARENTHESES FOR REFERENCES TO PAGES, FIGURES, TABLES, AND CHAPTERS

Parentheses can enclose references to specific pages, to relevant figures or tables, or to different chapters. The following examples illustrate the two ways to make these references: inside a sentence or as a separate sentence.

> A map of the river shows where each aquatic plant still grows (45).

> James McNeill Whistler is considered the forerunner of abstract art. (See pp. 52–76.)

> The inertial reel makes seat belts lock up automatically (see the accompanying diagram).

> Safes fall into two types: fire-resistant safes for records and burglar-resistant safes for money. (See figs., p. 167.)

BRACKETS

24g BRACKETS AROUND INSERTIONS IN DIRECT QUOTATIONS

Exact quotations taken out of context often contain pronouns without clear references, terms needing explanation, or names without identification. In such situations, you can insert clarifications in brackets after the unclear word or phrase. Or you may replace the unclear word or phrase with the bracketed clarification.

> De Tocqueville wrote, "They [the Americans] have all a lively faith in the perfectibility of man."

or

> De Tocqueville wrote, "[The Americans] have all a lively faith in the perfectibility of man."

> The author points out, "The Countess of Lovelace [Byron's daughter] met Babbage and soon became the first computer programmer."

or

> The author points out, "[Byron's daughter] met Babbage and soon became the first computer programmer."

You may also use brackets to insert corrections in direct quotations.

> Harry Truman wrote a letter to his daughter on March 19, 1956, saying, "If you don't trust the people you love . . . you'll be the unhappiest and [most] frustrated person alive."

Instead of adding a correction, a writer can insert *sic* in brackets following the error to show that it appeared "thus" in the source.

> From Hyeres, Fitzgerald wrote Thomas Boyd: "The moon is an absolutely *au fait* Mediteraenean [sic] moon with a blurred silver linnen [sic] cap . . . we're both a little tight and very happily drunk."

To emphasize an element in the source being quoted, you may italicize (or underline) the element and insert an explanation in brackets.

> According to the article, "As a society, we need to grapple with the *real* problem—which is the lack of consensus—not about public education, but over what public education should be about [italics mine]."

24h BRACKETS FOR PARENTHESES INSIDE PARENTHESES

On the very rare occasions when parentheses are required inside parentheses, brackets replace the inner set.

> Most psychologists believe that phobias are stress related. (But a recent study [1994] suggests that agoraphobia may have biological origins.)

25

PERIODS, QUESTION MARKS, AND EXCLAMATION POINTS

Periods, question marks, and **exclamation points** are called end (or terminal) marks because they appear primarily at the ends of complete sentences. The period most commonly occurs after sentences and abbreviations. The question mark occurs mainly after a direct question. Exclamation points are common only after statements in advertising copy, warnings in instructions, and emotional speeches in dialogue.

PERIODS

25a   PERIODS AS END PUNCTUATION

Periods follow several types of complete sentences.

.
25b

STATEMENTS:	Mardi Gras is the last day before Lent.
COMMANDS:	Use linseed oil on saddles and bridles.
INDIRECT QUESTIONS:	He asked whether we had a reservation.

After polite requests, usually in correspondence, you may use either a period or a question mark.

Would you please send me your brochure on wildflowers.

Would you please send me your brochure on wildflowers?

To set off a mild interjection, you may use either a period or a comma (21g.1).

Well. Hindsight is always 20-20.

Well, hindsight is always 20-20.

25b   PERIODS IN OUTLINES AND DISPLAYED LISTS

Periods follow numbers and letters in displayed lists, unless the numbers and letters are enclosed in parentheses.

Cathedrals
  I. Types of Cathedrals
    A. Palace Churches
    B. Abbeys
  II. Famous Cathedrals
    A. French Cathedrals
    B. English Cathedrals
    C. Italian Cathedrals

The report should include the following:
1. Abstract
2. Introduction

3. Procedure
4. Discussion
5. Conclusions and recommendations

25c INAPPROPRIATE PERIODS

25d

Do not use periods in the following situations.

- After a period marking the end of an abbreviation

INAPPROPRIATE: The ceremony began at 3:00 P.M..

REVISED: The ceremony began at 3:00 P.M.

- After words and phrases in displayed lists

INAPPROPRIATE
Improperly canned foods can spoil for four reasons:
1. growth of yeasts and molds.
2. growth of bacteria.
3. presence of enzymes.
4. process of oxidation.

REVISED
Improperly canned foods can spoil for four reasons:
1. growth of yeasts and molds
2. growth of bacteria
3. presence of enzymes
4. process of oxidation

QUESTION MARKS

25d QUESTION MARKS AS END PUNCTUATION

The question mark is used as end punctuation in several different constructions.

- After direct questions

  When is the off-season in Florida?

- After sentences with tag questions

  September is unusually hot, isn't it?

- After elliptical questions in a series

  Should politicians be required to reveal all the details of their private lives? Why? And to whom?

25e

25e QUESTION MARKS WITHIN SENTENCES

Direct questions usually appear alone.

  What will be won?

On rare occasions a direct question appears, not alone, but as the subject of a sentence.

  What will be won? was on their minds.

In this case, the question mark emphasizes the question. Be careful, however, to avoid using a question mark if the question is indirect and cannot appear separately.

INAPPROPRIATE:	What we can gain by further negotiation? is the first question.
REVISED:	What we can gain by further negotiation is the first question.
REVISED:	What can we gain by further negotiation? is the first question.

  A question mark can also express doubt about a fact such as a date, a place, a statistic, and the like.

  The first edition of the novel (1918?) was banned in the United States.

  The most famous of the Cleopatras (VII?) lived from 69 to 30 B.C.

EXCLAMATION POINTS

25f   EXCLAMATION POINTS IN DIALOGUE

An exclamation point is used in dialogue to indicate that the speaker is shouting or expressing intense feelings.

> "Stop!" the engineer shouted. "There is a unicorn on the tracks!"

> "Shut up!" she said between clenched teeth. "Just shut up!"

25g   EXCLAMATION POINTS WITH INTERJECTIONS

Interjections are expressions of emotion, such as *well, goodness, oh,* and *whew.* You can punctuate a mild interjection with a period or a comma.

> Well. I suppose we could reconsider the matter.

> Oh, he does not understand.

When the interjection expresses strong emotion, however, you can use an exclamation point.

> Well! You've said quite enough.

> Whew! That car barely missed me!

25h   EXCLAMATION POINTS FOR EMPHASIS

Exclamation points are often used in warnings to catch the reader's attention and help prevent accidents.

> WARNING! DO NOT USE NEAR OPEN FLAME!

In prose, exclamation points can emphasize something astonishing or ironic.

> New pesticides arrive at the rate of five hundred a year!

> If we are lucky, we will have to battle only mosquitoes and ignorance!

You should, however, use exclamation points for emphasis very, very sparingly. When overused, they lose their dramatic effect.

Inexperienced writers sometimes try to convey enthusiasm by using exclamation points and vague words such as *great, wonderful, marvelous,* and *perfect.* Specific details, however, are more convincing than exclamation points, as the following two passages illustrate.

25h

INEFFECTIVE: My favorite place to visit in winter is Rancho Mirage in the California desert. The scenery is marvelous! And the weather is great!

REVISED: My favorite place to visit in winter is Rancho Mirage in the California desert. The town is set in a lush oasis surrounded by a stark desert and rugged mountains. The temperature gets up to about 80 degrees during the day and down to about 60 degrees at night.

Another ineffective use of the exclamation point is to stress the importance of an idea. A better technique is to use words and phrases that express more specifically the degree of the idea's importance. Compare these sentences.

VAGUE: We must revise the nursing curriculum!

REVISED: One of our major goals should be to revise the nursing curriculum.

REVISED: Our primary concern should be the revision of the nursing curriculum.

REVISED: Until we revise the nursing curriculum, we can make no progress at all.

CHAPTER

26

APOSTROPHES

Apostrophes have three functions to form possessives, to allow contractions, and in a few contexts to precede *s* in plurals. By far the most common of the three, however, is to indicate possession.

26a APOSTROPHES TO INDICATE POSSESSION

The grammatical term *possession* refers to such relationships as ownership, origin, and measurement *Claudia s house, the professor s approval, a week s vacation.* Some pronouns have special possessive forms: *my/mine, our/ours, your/yours, his, her/hers, its, their/theirs, whose.* Nouns and all other pronouns are made possessive by the addition of an apostrophe plus *s* or simply an apostrophe.

The general rules for showing possession with apostrophes follow.

- Add **s** to most singular nouns and to singular indefinite pronouns.

    doctor → doctor's diagnosis

    novel → novel's plot

    Don Quixote → Don Quixote's quest

    Ross → Ross's boat

Ms. Jones → Ms. Jones's office

everybody → everybody's responsibility

someone → someone's parking space

neither → neither's fault

- Add ' to singular proper names when the addition of another -*s* would make pronunciation peculiar or difficult.

Jesus → Jesus' teachings

Moses → Moses' leadership

Aristophanes → Aristophanes' plays

Xerxes → Xerxes' conquests

- Add ' to plural nouns that end in *s*.

teachers → teachers' pay

divers → divers' training school

six months → six months' pay

trees → trees' roots

- Add '*s* to plural nouns that do not end in *s*.

oxen → oxen's yokes

children → children's art

bacteria → bacteria's behavior

alumni → alumni's involvement

sheep → sheep's pasture

- Add '*s* or ' to the last word of a compound noun or pronoun.

editor in chief → editor in chief's opinion

attorney generals → attorney generals' decisions

no one else → no one else's business

- Add '*s* or ' to the last name only to indicate joint possession.

Lebanon and Syria → Lebanon and Syria's disagreement

Crick and Watson → Crick and Watson's discovery

juniors and misses → juniors and misses' department

- Add **'s** or **'** to each name to indicate individual possession of more than one noun.

the mayor and governor → the mayor's and governor's policies

the Falcons and Saints → the Falcons' and Saints' schedules

26b APOSTROPHES TO CREATE CONTRACTIONS

In contractions, the apostrophe takes the place of omitted letters, numbers, or words.

it's = it is, it has	goin' (dialect) = going
who's = who is, who has	don't = do not
they're = they are	won't = will not
I'll = I will	would've = would have
'65 = 1965	we'd = we would
rock'n'roll = rock and roll	o'clock = of the clock

Remember that *till, though,* and *round* are all words, not contractions. Do not write *'till, 'though,* and *'round.*

26c APOSTROPHES TO INDICATE PLURALS OF LETTERS AND WORDS USED AS WORDS

Whenever possible, form the plurals of letters or words used as such in the usual way—by adding an *s*. Sometimes, however, the *s* alone is not clear; then you should add an apostrophe plus the *s*. The apostrophe prevents the *s* from looking like a part of a letter or word.

Unclear Plural: She writes her *m*s and *n*s alike.

| CLEAR PLURAL: | She writes her *m*'s and *n*'s alike. |

| UNCLEAR PLURAL: | You have used too many *and*s. |
| CLEAR PLURAL: | You have used too many *and*'s. |

Notice that the problem occurs only with lowercase letters, not with capitals (*GIs, YMCAs, CEOs*).

26d

26d INAPPROPRIATE APOSTROPHES

Do not use apostrophes in the following situations.

- Within a word, even though the word itself ends in *s*

NONSTANDARD	REVISED
Charle's	Charles's
Jone's	Jones's
the Raider's	the Raiders'

- In the plural of an ordinary word

NONSTANDARD	REVISED
tomato's	tomatoes
price's	prices

- In the plural form of numerals. Although once considered standard, the apostrophes are no longer necessary.

NOT CURRENT	REVISED
5's	5s
10's and 1,000's	10s and 1,000s
1960's	1960s

- In the possessive forms of personal pronouns and in the possessive form of *who*. All personal pronouns and the pronoun *who* form possessives without the apostrophe.

NONSTANDARD	REVISED
it's/its'	its
her's/hers'	hers
your's/yours'	yours
our's/ours'	ours
their's/theirs'	theirs
who's	whose

26d

NOTE: Readers are especially confused by the incorrect use of *it's* and *who's* as possessives. Remember that *it's* and *who's* are contractions for *it is* or *it has* and *who is* or *who has;* they are never possessives.

NONSTANDARD: Do not buy the album; it's lyrics are not worth hearing more than once.

REVISED: Do not buy the album; its lyrics are not worth hearing more than once.

NONSTANDARD: They discussed Planet 10, who's existence has been suggested by irregularities in the orbits of Uranus and Neptune.

REVISED: They discussed Planet 10, whose existence has been suggested by irregularities in the orbits of Uranus and Neptune.

27

QUOTATION MARKS AND ELLIPSIS MARKS

Although quotation marks and ellipsis marks have several uses, these marks appear most often in quotations, reproductions of someone s exact words. **Quotation marks** show the beginning and end of the citation. **Ellipsis marks** indicate where a part or parts of the original statement have been deleted.

QUOTATION MARKS

27a QUOTATION MARKS TO ENCLOSE DIRECT QUOTATIONS

Direct quotations of a few sentences or lines should be enclosed in quotation marks. The identifying expressions, such as *the source said* or *according to the source,* appear at the beginning, middle, or end of the quotation and should not be enclosed inside the quotation marks.

According to George Marshall, "The refusal of the British and Russian peoples to accept what appeared to be inevitable defeat was the great factor in the salvage of our civilization."

"The refusal of the British and Russian peoples to accept what appeared to be inevitable defeat was," George Marshall maintained, "the great factor in the salvage of our civilization."

"The refusal of the British and Russian peoples to accept what appeared to be inevitable defeat was the great factor in the salvage of our civilization," George Marshall reported in 1945.

Quotation marks also should enclose a part of a quoted statement.

George Marshall reported that Britain's and Russia's refusal to accept defeat in World War II was "the great factor in the salvage of our civilization."

George Marshall pointed out that Britain's and Russia's refusal to accept "inevitable defeat" in World War II saved civilization.

You should not use quotation marks when a quoted passage is long, that is, more than four typed lines or more than forty words. Instead, you should set up the passage as a "block," separate from the text, with each line indented. (See 40i.1.)

Also, do not use quotation marks with an indirect quotation, one in which the source is paraphrased.

George Marshall pointed out that in World War II Britain and Russia saved civilization by refusing to give up.

On some occasions, a quoted passage may itself contain a quotation. If a quoted passage already contains quotation marks, double marks (". . .") surround the whole passage, and single marks ('. . .') surround the inside quotation. On a keyboard, make the single quotation marks with the apostrophe key.

ORIGINAL: His situation reminds one of a line, a plea really, from Maurice Sendak's harrowing slapstick fantasy *Higglety Pigglety Pop!:* "There must be more to life than having everything." (Leonard Marcus)

QUOTATION: Marcus points out that the child's situation reminds him of a "plea . . . from Maurice Sendak's harrowing slapstick fantasy *Higglety Pigglety Pop!:* 'There must be more to life than having everything!'"

27b   QUOTATION MARKS WITH OTHER PUNCTUATION MARKS

When closing quotation marks appear with other marks of punctuation, strict conventions govern the order.

(1)   Quotation marks with the period and the comma

A closing quotation mark should follow a period or comma. This rule applies even when closing quotation marks are both single and double.

> The judge who handled the case referred to the problem that "most defendants are indigents without easy access to assistance."

> "I've never seen a 3-D movie," she insisted.

> After finishing "The Headless Cupid," he read "The Famous Stanley Kidnapping Case."

> The book pointed out that "Japan is creating enormous research and industrial centers called 'technopolises.'"

EXCEPTION: When a parenthetical citation intervenes, the quotation mark should precede the citation, and the period should follow.

> Stendhal conducts "the rites of initiation into the nineteenth century" (Levin 149).

(2)   Quotation marks with the semicolon and the colon

A closing quotation mark should always precede a semicolon or colon.

> Many people in business and government use jargon and "acronymese"; in fact, they often leave ordinary people totally in the dark.

> He said, "The work must be finished on time"; and he meant it.

The sign listed the scheduled performances of "Mostly Mozart": July 19, July 27, and August 2.

According to the report, "Japan is shifting to a basic research phase": no longer will Japan be dependent on borrowed findings.

(3) Quotation marks with the question mark, exclamation point, and dash

The quotation mark should follow a question mark, exclamation point, or dash that punctuates the quoted material.

The advertisement asked, "Why give the common, when you can give the preferred?"

At the end of the game, the happy fan shouted, "Time to celebrate, man!"

He said, "No—" and was immediately interrupted.

A closing quotation mark should precede a question mark, exclamation point, or dash that punctuates the unquoted part of the sentence.

Which character says, "I am a feather for each wind that blows"?

Don't ever write an antiquated expression like "heretofore"!

"These"—he pointed to a tray of snails—"are delicious."

Sometimes both the quoted and unquoted material in a sentence are questions. In these cases, the closing quotation mark should follow the question mark.

What poem asks, "And by what way shall I go back?"

Did you ask, "Was H. L. Mencken from Baltimore?"

On rare occasions, a sequence may include a single quotation mark, a double quotation mark, and a question mark.

The professor asked the class, "Who wrote 'Ozymandias'?"

In this example, the single quotation mark should go first because the title it encloses is not a question; the question mark should go next because the quoted material, not the unquoted, is the question; and the double quotation mark should go last to conclude the quote.

27c QUOTATION MARKS IN DIALOGUE

When a dialogue with two or more speakers is represented on paper, the exact words of the speakers are placed inside quotation marks. Ordinarily the spoken words are interrupted with comments that set the scenes, identify the speakers, and create the tone. You must separate these comments from the spoken dialogue, as in the following excerpt from Joseph Conrad's "An Outpost of Progress."

" "
27d

> "Is this your revolver?" asked Makola, getting up.
> "Yes," said Kayerts; then he added very quickly, "He ran after me to shoot me—you saw!"
> "Yes, I saw," said Makola. "There is only one revolver; where's his?"
> "Don't know," whispered Kayerts in a voice that had become suddenly very faint.

You indicate every change of speaker by a new paragraph with quotation marks before and after the speech. To show that one speaker continues for more than one paragraph, place a quotation mark before each paragraph, but place the closing quotation mark only after the last paragraph. The following example includes two paragraphs containing the words of one speaker. Notice the omission of the quotation mark at the end of the first paragraph.

> The professor gave us instructions before we began to dig for dinosaur remains: "In digging for bones, you will excavate in one small area, moving earth bit by bit with an ice pick. If you are not careful, you could accidentally sweep away bones.
> "Always remember that dinosaurs deserve this care. They roamed the earth for 140 million years. Humans have so far only survived 4 million."

27d QUOTATION MARKS IN TITLES

Ordinarily, the way a title is marked tells a reader whether the title refers to a whole work or to only part of a larger work. Titles of collections and long works, such as anthologies and novels, appear in italics (or underlining). Titles of short works, such as short stories and poems, appear in quotation marks. In general, italicize titles found on the covers of published works, and enclose in quotation marks titles found within the covers. (For a complete discussion of italics, see 28a.)

SHORT STORY:	"Her Sweet Jerome," from *In Love and Trouble*
SHORT POEM:	"Terrence, This Is Stupid Stuff," from *A Shropshire Lad*
ESSAY:	"Sootfall and Fallout," from *Essays of E. B. White*
ARTICLE:	"The Mystery of Tears," from *Smithsonian*
EDITORIAL:	"Facts and Figures for the President," from the *Fort Wayne News-Sentinel*
CHAPTER:	"Velikovsky in Collision," from *Ever Since Darwin*
TV EPISODE:	"A Sound of Dolphins," from *The Undersea World of Jacques Cousteau*
SONG:	"It Ain't Necessarily So," from *Porgy and Bess*

27e QUOTATION MARKS AROUND WORDS USED IN SPECIAL WAYS

Quotation marks can show that words have been used in a special sense—for an ironic effect, with a twist of meaning, or as words. Make sure, however, that an enclosed word is indeed used in a special way. If it is not, the quotation marks will mislead readers.

> She insisted that the graduates from "her" school would never do such a thing.

> The report contained the "facts" of the case.

> When people talk about the movie, they use words like "strange," "haunting," and "weird."

27f INAPPROPRIATE QUOTATION MARKS

Avoid quotation marks in the following instances.

- Around the title of a composition when it appears on a title page or on the first page of a manuscript

INAPPROPRIATE:	"A Hero for Today"
REVISED:	A Hero for Today

- Around a nickname used in place of a name

INAPPROPRIATE:	In the 1950s, "Fats" Domino was one of the big names in rock and roll.
REVISED:	In the 1950s, Fats Domino was one of the big names in rock and roll.

" "
27g

- Around a slang or a trite expression used for lack of a more effective one

INAPPROPRIATE:	"Last but not least," we must consider the endangered species.
REVISED:	Finally, we must consider the endangered species.

- Around *yes* and *no* unless you are writing dialogue

INAPPROPRIATE:	Answer "yes" or "no."
REVISED:	Answer yes or no.

ELLIPSIS MARKS

27g   ELLIPSIS MARKS TO SHOW OMISSIONS

Ellipsis marks are a sequence of spaced periods that indicate an omission in a direct quotation. The number of periods you use depends on what has been omitted.

(1)   Omission within a single sentence

To show an omission within a single sentence, use three periods with a space before, between, and after each period.

ORIGINAL QUOTATION

"For the root of genius is in the unconscious, not the conscious, mind." (Dorothea Brande, *Becoming a Writer*)

QUOTATION WITH ELLIPSIS MARKS

Dorothea Brande wrote, "For the root of genius is in the unconscious . . . mind."

(2)   Omission at the end of a sentence

To show an omission at the end of a sentence, use a sentence period followed by three spaced periods.

ORIGINAL QUOTATION

"Most people who bother with the matter at all would admit that the English language is in a bad way, but it is generally assumed that we cannot by conscious action do anything about it." (George Orwell, "Politics and the English Language")

QUOTATION WITH ELLIPSIS MARKS

According to Orwell, "Most people who bother with the matter at all would admit that the English language is in a bad way. . . ."

NOTE: When the quotation is obviously a fragment of the whole, you do not use ellipsis marks at the end.

QUOTATION WITHOUT ELLIPSIS MARKS

Orwell comments that most people concerned about English think it's "in a bad way."

(3)   Omission of a whole sentence or several sentences

If an omission involves a whole sentence or several sentences, use four periods—the period of the last sentence quoted plus the three spaced periods showing ellipsis.

ORIGINAL QUOTATION

"Children are a relatively modern invention. Until a few hundred years ago they did not exist. In medieval and Renaissance painting you see pint-size men and women, wearing grown-up clothes and grown-up expressions, performing grown-up tasks." (Shana Alexander, "Kid's Country")

QUOTATION WITH ELLIPSIS MARKS

As Shana Alexander points out, "Children are a relatively modern invention. . . . In medieval and Renaissance painting you see pint-size men and women, wearing grown-up clothes and grown-up expressions, performing grown-up tasks."

(4) Omission at the beginning of a quotation

Do not use ellipsis marks to show an omission at the beginning of a quotation; instead, work the quoted words into your own syntax. The absence of an initial capital letter shows that the whole passage is not included. Also, when the quotation is obviously a fragment of the whole, you do not use ellipsis marks at the end.

ORIGINAL QUOTATION

"America's group of republics is merged in one, in the eyes of the world; and, for some purposes, in reality: but this involves no obligation to make them all alike in their produce and occupations." (Harriet Martineau, *Society in America*)

QUOTATION WITHOUT ELLIPSIS MARKS

Martineau wrote in 1834 that the merging of America's republics "involves no obligation to make them all alike."

(5) Omission of a line or lines of poetry

Use a line of spaced periods to show the omission of one or more lines of poetry. Remember that when you quote several lines of a poem, you should show them indented and formatted as in the original, without quotation marks.

ORIGINAL QUOTATION

Power, like a desolating pestilence,
Pollutes whate'er it touches; and obedience,
Bane of all genius, virtue, freedome, truth,
Makes slaves of men, and, of the human frame
A mechanized automaton.

QUOTATION WITH ELLIPSIS MARKS

Shelley writes in "Queen Mab":

Power, like a desolating pestilence,
Pollutes whate'er it touches; and obedience,

. . . .

Makes slaves of men, and, of the human frame
A mechanized automaton.

27h ELLIPSIS MARKS TO SHOW INTERRUPTION IN DIALOGUE

In dialogue, ellipsis marks can show interruption of a thought or statement.

"Well, Judge, I don't know . . ." and whatever he meant to say trailed off into silence.

"That car costs forty thousand . . . uh . . . forget it."

28

ITALICS/ UNDERLINING

Italic type is a slanted typeface used in printing and word process-ing to distinguish titles, foreign words, and words used in other spe-cial ways. When italic type is not available, **underlining** is the appropriate substitute. In fact, most style guides (including those of the Modern Language Association and the American Psychological Association) require underlining for manuscripts, even though ital-ics will appear in typeset copy.

28a ITALICS/UNDERLINING IN TITLES

Titles are marked either with quotation marks (27d) or with italics. As a general rule, italics are used for complete works; quotation marks, for parts of works. If you underline to represent italics, do not break the line. An unbroken line displays the title as a single unit and facilitates reading.

Although publishers do not always agree about when to use italics and when to use quotation marks, it is common practice to italicize the following kinds of titles.

- Books and book-length poems

    The Red Badge of Courage

    The Short Stories of Saki

Four Screen Plays of Ingmar Bergman

Don Juan

- Plays and movies

  Othello

  Crimes of the Heart

  Dr. Strangelove

- Reports and long pamphlets

  Handbook of Utilization of Aquatic Plants

  A Nation at Risk: The Imperative for Educational Reform

- Newspapers, magazines, and journals

  Predominant practice is not to italicize *the* beginning a title.

  the *Washington Post*

  the *New Republic*

  Art in America

  Journal of Dental Research

- Operas, ballets, albums

  Verdi's *Rigoletto*

  Bach's *Well-Tempered Clavier*

  Horowitz at the Met

  Paul Simon's *There Goes Rhymin' Simon*

- Television and radio series

  The Shadow

  The Jack Benny Show

  Star Trek

  Masterpiece Theatre

- Paintings and sculpture

  Absinthe Drinkers by Degas

  Guernica by Picasso

  Sky Cathedral by Louise Nevelson

  Three Way Piece No. 2 by Henry Moore

NOTE: Remember to consider the punctuation following a title.

Italicize or underline punctuation that is part of a title.

  They are acting in Who's Afraid of Virginia Woolf?

Do not italicize or underline sentence punctuation following a title.

  Have you ever read Babbitt?

Do not italicize an apostrophe or an apostrophe plus an *s* that is added to a title.

  The Counterfeiters' plot

  Time's editorial

EXCEPTIONS: Do not italicize the following titles.

- Names of standard dictionaries and encyclopedias unless referred to by their formal names

  Webster's Dictionary (Webster's Third New International Dictionary)

  Random House Dictionary (The Random House Dictionary of the English Language)

  Americana (Encyclopedia Americana)

- Names of standard religious books

  Bible

  Koran

  Talmud

- Directories and catalogs

  Atlanta Telephone Directory

  JC Penney Catalog

- The title of a composition when it appears on a title page or at the top of the first page of a manuscript

  The Trouble with Television

  The Unforgettable Miss Sternberger

28b ITALICS/UNDERLINING FOR WORDS, NUMBERS, AND LETTERS USED AS SUCH

When a word, letter, or number refers to itself rather than to its usual meaning, italics alert readers to this special use. Compare, for example, the following two sentences. In the first, *dog* has its usual meaning of canine animal; in the second, it refers to the word *dog*.

  The dog barked.

  Dog comes from Anglo-Saxon.

Compare the use of *225* in the next two sentences. In the first, *225* refers to a quantity; in the second, it refers to the number itself.

  We planted 225 tulip bulbs in front of the courthouse.

  Someone had written 225 in the wet cement.

Often this special use is signalled by the insertion of "the word," "the letter," "the number," or some other appropriate description.

  In a legal document, the word said refers to something or someone previously mentioned.

  His shirts are monogrammed with the letters HCC.

Even when the signal is not present, it can be easily supplied.

  He says you know after every sentence.

  He says [the words] you know after every sentence.

  Southerners sometimes drop a final r.

  Southerners sometimes drop a final r [sound].

  The British put two e's in judgment.

  The British put two [letter] e's in [the word] judgment.

NOTE: Words that refer to themselves can appear in quotation marks instead of italics. (See 27e.)

28c ITALICS/UNDERLINING FOR SOUNDS

Italicize sounds that are represented by words or combinations of letters.

> The music had a recurrent ta ta ta tum refrain.

> With a woosh-thump, the golf club sent the white ball over the fair-way.

28d ITALICS/UNDERLINING FOR FOREIGN WORDS

Italicize foreign names of the scientific genus and species of animals and plants.

> The new threat to the marsh is Hydrilla verticillata, which can choke out all other life.

Italicize foreign words that are not considered part of the vocabulary of English.

> People assume that movies with gladiators, casts of thousands, and elaborate costumes must ipso facto be bad.

> On the ship we ate in the tourist-class salle à manger.

Some foreign words are in such common use that they are now considered English. For example, words such as *ex officio, ballet, connoisseur,* and *debut,* though originally Latin and French, no longer need italicizing. When you are sure a word of foreign origin is familiar to your audience, you need not italicize it.

28e ITALICS/UNDERLINING FOR VEHICLES DESIGNATED BY PROPER NAMES

Italicize the proper names of ships, aircraft, and spacecraft.

> U.S.S. Iowa

> Challenger

28f ITALICS/UNDERLINING FOR EMPHASIS

You can italicize words for emphasis, but you should use this device in moderation. Overuse negates its impact.

The department's expenditures are edging toward the 300-billion-dollar mark.

She works all day as a secretary, and she still likes to type.

29

HYPHENS AND SLASHES

Unlike other punctuation marks such as commas and semicolons, **hyphens** and **slashes** never signal sentence structure. Instead they function on the word level hyphens to create compound words and slashes to show alternatives and make combinations.

HYPHENS

29a HYPHENS IN COMPOUND NOUNS AND VERBS

Compound nouns and verbs appear in three forms. Some are separated (*safe house*); others are hyphenated (*safe-conduct*); and still others are written together (*safeguard*). Often the hyphens distinguish between a noun and verb form, but even so, you cannot be sure which form contains the hyphen.

has-been (noun)	has been (verb)
send-off (noun)	send off (verb)
single-space (verb)	single space (noun)
black-market (verb)	black market (noun)

There is one fairly consistent tradition: hyphenated nouns can show the dual nature of jobs and roles.

actor-director	secretary-treasurer
player-coach	city-state
clerk-typist	restaurant-lounge

29b

Otherwise, your only guide for hyphenating nouns and verbs is an up-to-date dictionary. Although all dictionaries do not agree, they at least provide authority for whatever practice you follow.

29b HYPHENS IN COMPOUND MODIFIERS

You should hyphenate a compound modifier preceding a noun so that readers will immediately understand that the modifier forms a single unit and a single concept. For example, *30-gallon cans* refers to cans that hold 30 gallons, whereas *30 gallon cans* refers to 30 cans that hold one gallon. Compare the meanings of the following pairs.

four-glass sets	four glass sets
man-eating clams	man eating clams
above-mentioned facts	above mentioned facts
long-remembered story	long remembered story

If a compound modifier does not appear before a noun, omit the hyphen or hyphens.

HYPHENATED:	Fire destroyed the sixteenth-century building.
NOT HYPHENATED:	The architecture was sixteenth century.
HYPHENATED:	The machine registers only low-frequency sounds.
NOT HYPHENATED:	The sounds should be low frequency.
HYPHENATED:	I own a one-and-a-half-year-old beagle.
NOT HYPHENATED:	The beagle is one and a half years old.

A few compound modifiers preceding nouns are exceptions to this practice. You should not hyphenate a modifier made of an *-ly* adverb plus another word.

carefully written paper

highly successful restaurant

badly designed building

Also, do not use hyphens when a compound modifier is obviously a unit, as in the case of a modifier made from a proper noun, a foreign expression, or a standard compound noun.

Red Cross office

prima facie evidence

child welfare payment

When two compound modifiers have a word in common (*three-column and five-column charts*), the common word need not appear but once (*three- and five-column charts*). Notice, however, that you should retain the hyphen in each piece of the compound.

whole- or half-year lease

forty- or fifty-thousand dollars

10-, 12-, and 15-pitch typefaces

American-bred, -owned, and -trained colt

29C   HYPHENS WITH SOME PREFIXES

Most prefixes are attached directly to the base word, but *self-* and *ex-* are attached with hyphens.

self-defense	ex-champion
self-education	ex-clerk
self-conscious	ex-husband

Use a hyphen when a prefix is attached to a proper noun (easily identified by its capital letter).

29c

non-European	pre-Columbian
mid-Atlantic	anti-Communist
neo-Platonic	un-American

Sometimes a hyphen is necessary to distinguish words that would otherwise be identical.

recover	re-cover	reform	re-form
prejudicial	pre-judicial	extraordinary	extra-ordinary

When reading is complicated by a repeated letter or by two vowels in a row, use a hyphen to separate the prefix from the base.

non-nuclear	pro-union
anti-inflation	semi-independent

Many words with repeated letters that were once hyphenated are now written solid—for example, *preempt* and *reentry.* A current dictionary will usually illustrate acceptable spelling.

29d   HYPHENS IN NUMBERS

Use a hyphen with the following numbers.

- Spelled-out numbers from twenty-one to ninety-nine, whether they appear alone or as part of a larger number

    Alexander the Great died when he was only thirty-two.

    Thirty-two hundred of the automobiles were recalled.

- Spelled-out fractions, unless either the numerator or denominator already contains a hyphen

    One-fourth of those surveyed had voted.

    The arrow missed by two thirty-seconds of an inch.

- A range of numbers

During the years 1975–1981, the building served as the library.

See pages 25–96.

29e HYPHENS FOR WORD DIVISIONS AT THE ENDS OF LINES

Writers sometimes hyphenate words at the ends of lines in order to align the right margin. Words split between two lines, however, usually distract readers and slow down their reading pace. In addition, frequent hyphenation makes a paper look messy. If you must hyphenate, follow these guidelines.

- Divide words only between syllables. If you are not sure of the divisions, either do not divide the word, or look for the correct syllabication in the main entry of a dictionary.

- Consider pronunciation. *Chemotherapy* makes more sense divided *chemo·therapy* than *chem·otherapy; fra·ternity* seems preferable to *frater·nity.*

- Do not leave one letter on a line by itself. For example, *a·like* and *tax·i* should not be divided.

- Do not divide the last word on a page. It is inconvenient to turn the page to find the rest of the word.

SLASHES

29f SLASHES BETWEEN ALTERNATIVES

A slash between words can show alternatives—*and/or, he/she, pass/fail.* The mark replaces the *or* that would otherwise be needed to separate the alternatives.

radio/television

A.M./P.M.

animal/vegetable

In informal or technical papers, the slash is acceptable; in formal or nontechnical papers, the *or* is preferred.

29g SLASHES FOR MAKING COMBINATIONS

Combinations of words or numbers in compounds and sequences sometimes contain slashes.

Dallas/Fort Worth

The MacNeil/Lehrer News Hour

20/20 vision

4/21/81

1984/85

poet/critic/scholar

29h SLASHES BETWEEN LINES OF POETRY

Two or three lines of poetry can be quoted in their original form or in prose form (incorporated into a sentence, from margin to margin). When the prose form is used, slashes show the poetic line divisions.

Byron writes in *Don Juan,* "'Tis strange, but true; for truth is always strange;/ Stranger than fiction: if it could be told,/ How much would novels gain by the exchange!"

29i SLASHES FOR FRACTIONS

When a fraction is written in numerals, a slash separates the numerator from the denominator: *1/3, 3/5, 5/12.*

30

ABBREVIATIONS AND NUMBERS

The appropriate use of **abbreviations** and **numbers** depends in large part on their context. Abbreviations are appropriate in some circumstances; full words, in others. Sometimes, numbers should be expressed in words: other times, numerals are required. The following discussion outlines the conventions and describes the contexts that govern them.

ABBREVIATIONS

30a ABBREVIATIONS VS. FULL WORDS

Some abbreviations are so standard that the full form almost never appears. Others, however, may be used only in certain instances.

- Titles and ranks

  Use the abbreviations *Mr., Mrs.,* and *Ms.* when they appear before names. (*Miss* is not an abbreviation and is not followed by a period.)

  Use the abbreviations *Jr.* and *Sr.* when they appear as part of a name: *Joseph W. Alsop, Jr.* The full words are appropriate only on formal invitations.

You may abbreviate *doctor* when the title appears before a name: *Dr. Williams.*

You may abbreviate civil and military titles when they appear before a full name but not before a last name alone.

ACCEPTABLE:	Lt. Gov. John Bird, Col. Betty Morden
ACCEPTABLE:	Lieutenant Governor Bird, Colonel Morden
UNACCEPTABLE:	Lt. Gov. Bird, Col. Morden

You may abbreviate *Reverend* and *Honorable* when they precede a full name and do not follow *the.* Do not, however, abbreviate these titles when they precede a last name alone or when they follow *the.*

ACCEPTABLE:	Rev. Donald Yanella, Hon. Ann Lott
ACCEPTABLE:	Reverend Yanella, the Honorable Ann Lott
UNACCEPTABLE:	Rev. Yanella, the Hon. Lott

- Degrees and certifications

  You may abbreviate scholarly degrees (*B.A., M.S., Ph.D.*). Remember that when a degree follows a name, no other title should precede the name.

ACCEPTABLE:	Alice M. Cotton, Ph.D.
UNACCEPTABLE:	Dr. Alice M. Cotton, Ph.D.

- Time, days, and months

  Abbreviate time designations, such as *A.M., P.M., EST, CDT, A.D., B.C.* Remember that *A.D.* precedes a year and *B.C.* follows.

ACCEPTABLE:	The Han dynasty lasted from 202 B.C. to A.D. 220.
UNACCEPTABLE:	The Han dynasty lasted from 202 B.C. to 220 A.D.

In prose, always write out the names of days and months.

ACCEPTABLE: The ship sails on Friday, January 13.

UNACCEPTABLE: The ship sails on Fri., Jan. 13.

- Latin Expressions

  Except in extremely formal papers, use abbreviations for Latin expressions such as *i.e., e.g., vs.,* and so forth.

  abbr 30a

- Acronyms and familiar initials

  The full forms of initials pronounced as words (acronyms) are almost never written out: *sonar, ZIP, COBOL, Alcoa, NASA, snafu.* Neither are the full forms of many familiar initials: *UFO, ESP, IQ, ID, R.S.V.P., IBM, FBI, NBC.*

- Reference notations

  Abbreviate words such as *page(s), figure, edition,* and *volume* when they appear in bibliographies and documentation: *pp. 13-26, fig. 4, 3rd ed., Vol. 1.*

- Geographical Locations

  In general, do not abbreviate geographical locations except in addresses. In any context, however, you may write *Washington, D.C.,* or *U.S.* when it is used as an adjective but not as a noun.

  ACCEPTABLE: U.S. currency

  ACCEPTABLE: currency in the United States

  UNACCEPTABLE: currency in the U.S.

- Addresses

  In formal letters, do not abbreviate words such as *street, avenue, road,* and *building.* Also, when a compass direction precedes a street name, it is part of the name and not abbreviated: *49 Northwest Farris Street.* When a compass direction follows a street name, it indicates a city's section and is abbreviated: *49 Farris Street, NW.*

  You have the option of abbreviating names of states and territories with the two-letter codes used by the U.S. Postal Service.

Alabama	AL	Florida	FL
Alaska	AK	Georgia	GA
Arizona	AZ	Guam	GU

Arkansas	AR	Hawaii	HI
California	CA	Idaho	ID
Canal Zone	CZ	Illinois	IL
Colorado	CO	Indiana	IN
Connecticut	CT	Iowa	IA
Delaware	DE	Kansas	KS
District		Kentucky	KY
of Columbia	DC	Louisiana	LA
Maine	ME	Oklahoma	OK
Maryland	MD	Oregon	OR
Massachusetts	MA	Pennsylvania	PA
Michigan	MI	Puerto Rico	PR
Minnesota	MN	Rhode Island	RI
Mississippi	MS	South Carolina	SC
Missouri	MO	South Dakota	SD
Montana	MT	Tennessee	TN
Nebraska	NE	Texas	TX
Nevada	NV	Utah	UT
New Hampshire	NH	Vermont	VT
New Jersey	NJ	Virgin Islands	VI
New Mexico	NM	Virginia	VA
New York	NY	Washington	WA
North Carolina	NC	West Virginia	WV
North Dakota	ND	Wisconsin	WI
Ohio	OH	Wyoming	WY

30b PUNCTUATION AND CAPITALIZATION IN ABBREVIATIONS

Because the use of periods with abbreviations changes from time to time, you should check current practice in an up-to-date dictionary. There you will find that some abbreviations contain periods (*Dist. Atty., Sept., R.S.V.P.*), some have optional periods (*ft.* or *ft, lb.* or *lb, E.S.T.* or *EST*), and some have none.

Chemical symbols: Cu, N, Zn, Au

Acronyms: NATO, UNESCO, CORE

Military terms: POW, USA, GI

Points of the compass: NE, NW, SE

States in Postal Service abbreviations: HI, OH, AZ, OK

In general, the capitalization of an abbreviation reflects that of the full word: *GOP* (*Grand Old Party*), *Ph.D.* (*Doctor of Philosophy*), *hwy.* (*highway*), *Btu* (*British thermal unit*). But capitalization of a few abbreviations cannot be predicted by the capitalization in the full words: *eV* (*electron volt*), *a.m.* or *A.M.* (*ante meridiem*), *A.D.* (*anno Domini*), *n.d.* or *N.D.* (*no date*). When you are unsure of capitalization, check a recent dictionary.

**abbr
30c**

NUMBERS

30c NUMBERS EXPRESSED IN NUMERALS

In any type of paper, use numerals for the following. (See 30d for the appropriate use of numbers expressed in words.)

- Numbers in dates and addresses

  On June 31, 1989, the couple moved to 520 State Street.

- Exact amounts of money

  Each participant is charged $7.50.

  The starting salary is $21,000.

- Sections of books and page numbers

  Chapter 2 ends on page 9.

- Numbers that accompany abbreviations and symbols

  The temperature was 8° F at 6:30 a.m.

  Less than 5% of the group successfully quit smoking.

- Measurements and statistics

  Only 6 percent of the applicants qualified for aid.

  This soup contains 9 grams of fat per serving.

- Fractions, decimals, ratios, and mathematical functions

    They had restored about 4/5 of the Indian mound.

    Multiply the result by 5.

    For other numbers, non-technical and technical writers generally follow different systems and use numerals for the following.

- In non-technical papers, most numbers that require more than two words (Hyphenated numbers such as *thirty-eight* are counted as one word.)

    In the OED, the meanings are illustrated by more than 83,000 quotations.

    The twenty stories were selected from more than 350 publications.

- In technical papers, all numbers 10 and above

    From a low of 21 in 1944, the whooping crane population topped 200 in the late 1980s.

    The four barrier islands have a total of 51 miles of beach.

30d NUMBERS EXPRESSED IN WORDS

Words are appropriate for the following numbers.

- In non-technical papers, numbers that can be stated in one or two words (The numbers in dates, addresses, measurements, etc., are always numerals, 30c.)

    About four hundred years ago, Christopher Marlowe, at the age of twenty-nine, was murdered in a bar fight.

    Supposedly, the Cult of Isis has over fifteen thousand followers in fifty countries.

- In technical papers, numbers from one to nine

    Only three red-cockaded woodpeckers have been seen in the area in the last eight years.

    The mutual fund's return for the last six months was 11.95%.

- EXCEPTION: In parallel structures, the numbers should be all numerals or all words depending on the clearest presentation and the style used in the rest of the paper.

  The garden contains two hundred varieties of bulbs and thirty shrubs.

  The museum has expanded its presentation from 85 paintings to 125. [clearer than *eighty-five* and *one hundred and twenty-five*]

  According to the responses, 5 people had never voted; 25 had voted occasionally; and 17 had voted in every election.

- In both non-technical and technical papers, numbers that begin sentences.

  One hundred and twenty-five pages into the book, readers finally learn the narrator's identity.

  Forty-five copies of the questionnaire were distributed, and 32 were returned.

30e MIXED NUMERALS AND WORDS

For clarity and ease of reading, use a combination of words and figures in two circumstances.

- Adjacent modifiers

  When two separate numbers make up adjacent modifiers, express one number in numerals and one in words.

  We need ten 12-foot planks.

  They bought 5,000 thirteen-cent stamps.

- Large rounded numbers

  Because *million* and *billion* require so many zeros when expressed in numerals, readers find it easier to comprehend a combination of numerals and words.

  We cannot expect a city government to accommodate 8 million people.

  The debt was an awesome 5 billion dollars.

31

CAPITAL LETTERS

Primarily, **capital letters** signal the beginnings of sentences and designate proper names and official titles. The practice of capitalizing the first word of a sentence is simple and stable. But the practice of capitalizing proper names and titles is more complex; authorities disagree, and conventions change. Furthermore, a word may be capitalized in one situation but not in another. The solution to most problems of capitalization, however, can be found in a standard up-to-date dictionary or a handbook like this one.

31a CAPITALIZATION OF FIRST WORDS

By capitalizing the first word in an element, you can alert readers to the start of something new for example, a complete sentence, a quotation, a line of poetry, or an item in a list. In some cases, capitalization is required; in other cases, it is optional.

(1) Required capitals

- The first word in a complete sentence

    Students broke the security of the computer system.

    Does Assateague Island have nude beaches?

EXCEPTION: You should not capitalize a sentence's first letter when the sentence appears inside parentheses within another sentence.

> The school's decision surprised everyone (he was, after all, a star player).

- The first word in a quotation that begins a new sentence

**cap
31a**

> Macbeth asks, "Will all great Neptune's ocean wash this blood clean from my hand?"

NOTE: When the quoted sentence is split, only the first word begins with a capital letter.

> "In a real dark night of the soul," Fitzgerald writes, "it is always three o'clock in the morning."

If the quotation does not begin a new sentence, the first word is not capitalized.

> Mussolini believed that only war put "the stamp of nobility upon the peoples who have the courage to face it."

- The first word in each line of a traditional poem

> But words are things and a small drop of ink,
> Falling like dew upon a thought, produces
> That which makes thousands, perhaps millions, think.
> From Byron's *Don Juan*

- The first word in each entry of an outline

> Japanese Military Operations in Indochina
>   I. Military reasons for the operations
> II. Entry of the Japanese
>   A. Occupation of Laos
>   B. Occupation of Vietnam
>   C. Occupation of Cambodia
> III. Japanese wartime bases
> IV. Surrender to the Allied forces

- The first word of a salutation and complimentary close

> My dear Sir: Yours truly,
>
> To whom it may concern: Sincerely yours,

(2) Optional capitals

- The first word in an elliptical question

    Does an office this small really need a copier? Two word processors? A switchboard?

    Is the book a novel? an autobiography? a travelogue?

- The first word in a formal statement after a colon

    The lesson we learned was this: Work helps keep juveniles out of trouble.

    Orson Welles' reputation is a mystery: he is considered a genius on the basis of one work—*Citizen Kane.*

- The first word of each item in a list

    The benefits include:

Life and medical insurance	Investment programs
Accident insurance	Retirement program

    The test determined the car's

(1) reliability	(3) performance
(2) comfort	(4) economy

31b CAPITALIZATION OF PROPER NAMES AND PROPER ADJECTIVES

Proper nouns are the names of specific persons, places, and things. In general, you should capitalize these nouns and the adjectives derived from them.

France	French culture
Colombia	Colombian coffee
Jefferson	Jeffersonian ideals
Henry James	Jamesian story

The following categories illustrate the kinds of words considered proper nouns and adjectives.

NAMES OF PEOPLE AND ANIMALS:	Gerry Wieland, Jean Kindelberger, Tom Sawyer, Trigger, Gargantua
PLACE NAMES:	Venus, Africa, Potomac River, Montpelier, Union Station, Statue of Liberty
ORGANIZATIONS:	Department of State, Committee for Economic Development, Milwaukee Chamber of Commerce, National Council of Churches
HISTORICAL NAMES:	Elizabethan Age, Tonkin Resolution, Truman Doctrine, Battle of Wounded Knee, Renaissance
RELIGIOUS TERMS:	God; He, His, Him [referring to God in a religious context]; Buddhism; Shinto; Palm Sunday, Ramadan
NAMES IN EDUCATION:	California Polytechnic State University, Basic Wiring II, World History 101, Rhodes Scholarship, Scholastic Aptitude Test
AWARDS:	National Book Award, Pulitzer Prize, Good Conduct Medal, Medal of Honor
CALENDAR TERMS:	Monday, August, Veterans Day, Bastille Day
PRODUCT NAMES:	Renault Alliance, Ford Mustang, Soyuz T-5, Frigidaire, Ivory soap [The common term of a product's name is usually not capitalized.]
ETHNIC TERMS:	English, Japanese, Serbian, Sioux, Indo-European
BIOLOGICAL TERMS:	*Equidae, Bovidae, Canis rufus, Alligator mississippiensis* [Species are not capitalized.]

CHEMICAL ABBREVIATIONS: O [oxygen], Au [gold]

Also, you capitalize nicknames or substitutes for proper names.

OFFICIAL NAMES	SUBSTITUTES
New York City	Big Apple
Missouri	Show Me State
Earl Hines	Fatha Hines
William Warren	Grandfather (but *my grandfather*)
Mayor Stone	Mayor

cap
31c

Some words derived from proper nouns, however, are no longer capitalized; others are capitalized at times. For example, the word *maverick* (derived from the name of Senator Samuel A. Maverick of Texas) is not capitalized; the word *draconian* (derived from the Athenean lawgiver Draco) is sometimes capitalized and sometimes not. Check current practice in an up-to-date dictionary.

NO LONGER CAPITALIZED

boycott (after C. C. Boycott)

bourbon (after Bourbon County, Kentucky)

quixotic (after Don Quixote)

SOMETIMES CAPITALIZED, SOMETIMES LOWERCASE

Platonic/platonic (after Plato)

Scotch/scotch (after Scotland)

Herculean/herculean (after Hercules)

31c CAPITALIZATION OF TITLES OF HONOR OR RANK

Always capitalize titles of honor or rank—governmental, military, ecclesiastical, royal, or professional—when they precede names. When these titles do not precede names, you usually do not capitalize them.

CAPITAL:	In Texas, <u>Governor</u> Miriam A. "Ma" Ferguson served from ~~1925–27 and from 1933–35.~~
NO CAPITAL:	Miriam A. "Ma" Ferguson of Texas served as <u>governor</u> of Texas after her husband was impeached.
CAPITAL:	In 1863, <u>General</u> William S. Rosecrans fought at Chickamauga.
NO CAPITAL:	William S. Rosecrans, a <u>general</u> with the Union army, fought at Chickamauga.
CAPITAL:	After retiring, <u>Professor</u> Deutsch went into politics.
NO CAPITAL:	After retiring, Dr. Deutsch, a <u>professor</u> of American history, went into politics.

**cap
31d**

You may, however, capitalize a few titles even when they do not precede names: President, Vice President, and the titles of other important members of the government. Either capital or lowercase letters are correct, but be consistent throughout a composition.

Taft, the largest man ever to serve as <u>President</u> (or <u>president</u>), weighed over 300 pounds.

Elihu Root, <u>Secretary of State</u> (or <u>secretary of state</u>) under Theodore Roosevelt, won the 1912 Nobel peace prize.

Margaret Chase Smith, the <u>Senator</u> (or <u>senator</u>) from Maine, campaigned for the Republican presidential nomination in 1964.

31d   CAPITALIZATION OF ACADEMIC AND PROFESSIONAL DEGREES

Capitalize academic and professional degrees only when they appear immediately after a name or when they are abbreviated.

CAPITALS:	George Pratt, <u>Doctor of Laws</u>, died last year.
CAPITALS:	George Pratt, <u>LL.D.</u>, died last year.
NO CAPITALS:	George Pratt earned his <u>doctor of laws</u> degree in 1932.
CAPITALS:	Doris Leigh completed her <u>B.A.</u> degree in 1912.

No Capitals:	Doris Leigh completed her <u>bachelor of arts</u> degree in 1912.
Capitals:	Lee Wallerstein, <u>CPA</u>, made the audit.
No Capitals:	An independent <u>certified public accountant</u> made the audit.

**cap
31e**

31e CAPITALIZATION IN TITLES OF WRITTEN MATERIAL AND ARTISTIC WORKS

Although there are various styles for capitalization within titles, the Modern Language Association (MLA) calls for capitalizing these words:

- The first word [When *the* is the first word of a periodical, it is dropped from the title, e.g., *Washington Post,* not *The Washington Post.*]

- The last word

- Every noun, pronoun, verb, adjective, adverb, and subordinating conjunction

- Any word that follows a colon, dash, or question mark

The following words are not capitalized unless they are the first or last words of a title.

- Articles [*a, an, the*]

- Coordinating conjunctions and prepositions

- The infinitive marker [*to*]

When you use the MLA system, you must determine the part of speech of each word in a title. In the following examples, notice especially that *or* is a coordinating conjunction, *if* is a subordinating conjunction, *to* is an infinitive marker, and *with* is a preposition.

"Tall Talk: Half-Truth or Half-Lie"

"Well, If I Called the Wrong Number, Why Did You Answer the Phone?"

A World to Win

Still Life with Clay Pipe

A frequent variation of the MLA system is to capitalize subordinating conjunctions and prepositions that have four or more letters. If you prefer this variation, you would capitalize, for example, the subordinating conjunctions *when, unless,* and *because,* but not *if.* You would capitalize the prepositions *with, between,* and *toward,* but not *in, out,* and *of.*

31f CAPITALIZATION IN SOME ABBREVIATIONS

Times of day are written A.M. and P.M. or a.m. and p.m. In print, these abbreviations are usually in small capitals. A few other abbreviations are capitalized even though the terms they replace are not, for example *T.V.* or *TV* (for *television*), *B.A.* (for *bachelor of arts*), *R.R.* or *RR* (for *railroad*), *POW* (for *prisoner of war*), *NE* (for *northeast*), *O* (for *oxygen*), A.D. (for *anno Domini*).

31g CAPITALIZATION OF *I* AND *O*

The pronoun *I* is always capitalized, even when it is a part of a contraction—*I'm* or *I've.* The expression *O* is capitalized, except when spelled *ob.*

31h INAPPROPRIATE CAPITALS

You should not capitalize the following words.

- Common nouns, even when they appear in phrases that contain capitals

American history	Maxwell House coffee
Epson computer	French poodle

- Words referring to areas of study, unless they are titles of specific courses

CAPITALS	NO CAPITALS
Economics 302	economics
Algebra II	algebra
Studies in British Literature	literature
Introduction to Computing	computer science

cap 31h

NOTE: The names of languages are proper and are always capitalized: *French, English grammar, Chinese literature.*

- Words expressing family relationships, like *mother, father, aunt, uncle, grandmother,* and *grandfather,* unless they precede or substitute for names

CAPITAL: We learned to garden by helping Uncle Will.

NO CAPITAL: We learned to garden by helping our uncle.

CAPITAL: When she was sixty-five, Grandmother bought a Porsche.

NO CAPITAL: When she was sixty-five, my grandmother bought a Porsche.

- The words *north, south, southwest,* and so on when they refer to compass directions [These words are capitalized when they refer to regions.]

CAPITAL: The North won the Civil War.

NO CAPITAL: Drive north.

CAPITAL: The first Europeans to explore the Southwest were the Spaniards.

NO CAPITAL: The area lies southwest of here.

- Seasons, unless they are personified

CAPITAL: "Come, gentle Spring! ethereal Mildness! come."

NO CAPITAL: You plant the seeds in the spring.

- *Earth, moon,* and *sun* except when these words are used in connection with named planets (and without *the*)

CAPITAL:	Mercury and Venus are closer to the sun than Earth is.
NO CAPITAL:	The earth is the fifth largest planet.
CAPITAL:	The distance of Earth from Moon is 238,857 miles.
NO CAPITAL:	In an eclipse, the moon is too small to hide the sun.

**cap
31h**

IV

STYLE

A writing style results from a number of details: vocabulary, sentence length, sentence patterns, figures of speech, sound and rhythm. Often these details are spontaneous choices—a reflection of the writer's personality, education, and experience. But reliance on spontaneous decisions will not always produce effective writing. Developing a good prose style requires thoughtful choices of words and sentence structures.

32

WORD CHOICE

The English language has borrowed extensively from other languages. The result is an enormous vocabulary of some million words, many with similar meanings. *Roget's Thesaurus,* for example, lists almost 100 synonyms for *insane* and over 150 synonyms for *destroy.* From this abundance, writers choose the words that best fit intended meaning and individual styles.

32a LEVELS OF FORMALITY

Each time you write, you should decide whether to use a formal or an informal voice. The decision depends on your purpose and your audience. A formal voice is appropriate for business correspondence, reports, research papers, and articles in scholarly journals—documents in which writers distance themselves personally from readers. On the other hand, an informal voice is appropriate for purposes such as humorous writing, advertising, and articles in popular magazines—material in which writers try to establish a personal relationship with readers. Thus, you should use a formal style to establish a polite, professional relationship with a reader and an informal style to establish a friendly, conversational relationship.

The degree of formality or informality is established in large part by vocabulary. Words derived from Anglo-Saxon (Old English) seem more informal and conversational than words derived or borrowed from other languages. For example, the Anglo-Saxon derivatives *lucky, get, buy,* and *crazy* seem less formal than their synonyms derived from Greek and Latin: *fortunate, obtain, purchase,* and *demented.* Likewise, the English words *therefore* and *masterpiece* are less formal than their Latin counterparts *ergo* and *magnum opus.*

Clipped forms are more informal than full forms. For example, *pro, ad,* and *deli* are more informal than *professional, advertisement,* and *delicatessen.* Likewise, contractions (*can't, isn't, it's*) are more informal than uncontracted forms (*cannot, is not, it is*).

First person (*I, we*) and second person (*you*) are less formal than third (*one, the writer, the student*). If you are writing about yourself, *I* certainly seems more natural than *one* or *this writer.* If you are addressing the reader personally, *you* seems natural. Avoid, however, using *you* to mean people in general. (See 12c.)

wd style 32a

Slang is informal—sometimes, very informal—and its appearance in formal documents can reduce them to the absurd. Imagine, for example, coming upon this sentence in a university bulletin: *Students with wheels should boogie on over to the security office and get a decal.* On the other hand, a carefully chosen slang expression can make prose more interesting, vivid, or efficient. *Razzmatazz* is more interesting than *a flashy display. Bug a telephone* is more vivid than *equip a telephone with a microphone. Computer nerd* is certainly more efficient than *a person who forgets the social amenities in an obsession for computers.* Remember, however, that an abundance of slang will make prose seem silly. Furthermore, the meanings of slang expressions are frequently unstable, changing unpredictably from time to time and audience to audience.

Choosing a formal or informal voice is often arbitrary; in many circumstances, readers will accept either. But whichever you choose, you should maintain it consistently throughout a composition. Notice how the voice in the following passage seems to shift from formal to informal and back to formal. As a result, the reader gets mixed signals about the writer's attitude.

SHIFTED

If a person has no computer experience, shopping for a personal computer is very frustrating—primarily because the novice and the sales personnel do not use the same vocabulary. A salesperson will toss off a lot of stuff about memory, hard disks, and menus. And the novice will stand by nodding wisely but without a clue. This problem could be overcome if sales personnel were taught to explain in non-technical terms the capabilities of the equipment they sell.

A consistent voice—either informal or formal—makes clear the writer's attitude.

wd style 32b

INFORMAL

If you have no computer experience, shopping for a personal computer is a nightmare—primarily because the computer-impaired and the salespeople don't speak the same language. A salesperson will toss off a lot of stuff about memory, hard disks, and menus. And you will stand there nodding like an idiot but without a clue. This problem could be overcome if salespeople were taught to talk in plain English.

FORMAL

If a person has no computer experience, shopping for a personal computer is very frustrating—primarily because the novice and the sales personnel do not use the same vocabulary. A salesperson will casually discuss memory, hard disks, and menus. And the novice will stand by nodding wisely but understanding nothing. This problem could be overcome if sales personnel were taught to explain in non-technical terms the capabilities of the equipment they sell.

Remember that when you adopt a voice, you should maintain it consistently throughout a composition. Otherwise, your reader will not know how to react.

32b PRECISE PROSE

In conversation, you can be somewhat relaxed about the words you choose because a listener can stop you and ask for clarification. Furthermore, you can watch the listener for signs of confusion, and you can restate or clarify as you go along. But in writing, you have no such opportunities. Your language should be as precise as possible to ensure that your reader understands exactly what you mean. This precision rests primarily on vocabulary. To control the meaning of your prose, you should carefully consider the meanings of words—both their denotation and connotation. And you should try to strike the right balance between the general and the specific, between the abstract and the concrete.

(1) Denotation and connotation

The denotation of a word is the dictionary definition, the word's meaning devoid of any emotional association. The word *penguin* denotes a flightless marine bird; the word *piano* denotes a familiar keyboard instrument. If you want to use a word recently acquired or found in a thesaurus, make sure you know the word's denotation. Archie Bunker got laughs by saying, "You're invading the issue"; and Dizzy Dean was famous for remarks like "The players went back to their respectable bases." Except for an intentional comic effect, however, such mistakes (malapropisms) will ruin your credibility.

In addition to denotation, you should consider whether a word has connotation—that is, whether it evokes an emotional response. For example, to most readers, *home* seems more personal and secure than *house.* When we think of a house, we usually envision a building. But we think of home as more than a building: It is family, childhood memories, friends, and even an entire community. Consider the word *spy.* It evokes the image of an unsavory character, probably a traitor. But *secret agent* calls up James Bond, the dashing hero, using wit and muscle to overcome evil. The denotation of *suave* is "smoothly gracious or polite; polished." The connotation suggests a man—one who is perhaps continental. On the other hand, *sophisticated* suggests either a man or a woman—worldly wise and refined. *Peril* seems more serious and more imminent than *danger; zealot,* more fanatical than *enthusiast; naked,* more stark than *nude.*

Keep in mind that many words have emotional associations, and try to choose vocabulary that will convey exactly the meaning you intend.

(2) General and specific words

General words refer to classes or categories (*magazine*); specific words refer to particular members of a class or category (*Newsweek*). Whether a word is general or specific is sometimes relative. For example, *media* is more general than *magazine,* and *last week's Newsweek* is more specific than *Newsweek.* The following lists illustrate a gradual progression from general to specific.

When you write, you should try to balance the general with the specific because both are inherent in the way we think. In other words, we sometimes reason by induction—moving from specific instances to find a generalization. For example, a person who sneezes every time a cat appears will conclude that he or she is allergic to cats. At other times, we reason by deduction—applying a general principle to a specific instance. A person who has an established allergy to cats and who suddenly begins sneezing will deduce that there is a cat in the area.

As we think and reason, we move back and forth from induction to deduction, from specifics to generalities. If you use both general and specific words when you write, readers are more likely to follow your reasoning process and thus more readily grasp your meaning. Suppose, for example, that you want to make the point that children learn valuable social skills in kindergarten. Relying exclusively on either general or specific words will obscure the point.

TOO GENERAL: Kindergartens benefit children by allowing interaction in a social environment. In kindergarten, children lose some of their egocentric perspective and learn to tolerate the needs and feelings of others.

TOO SPECIFIC: In kindergartens, children must share blocks, desks, and coloring books. Therefore, children learn not to snatch a toy that someone else is playing with. They also learn to say "please" and "thank you."

A mixture of general and specific words can convey the general idea and clarify it with details.

MIXED USE: Kindergartens benefit children by teaching them valuable social skills. For example, they learn to share desks, toys, and the teacher's attention. They learn that saying "please" and "thank you" is more pleasant and productive behavior than fighting and crying.

When you write, use general words for summing up and explaining; use specific words for supporting and detailing. This way, readers will understand not only what your conclusions are but also how you arrived at them.

(3)   Abstract and concrete words

Abstract words denote ideas, qualities, feelings—anything that has no physical existence. Concrete words denote specific realities—anything that can be seen, touched, heard, smelled, or tasted. Although both kinds of words appear in most prose, an overreliance on abstract terms can mask meaning and bore readers. For example, suppose you were defining the abstract concept of frustration. You could clarify the concept and enliven the discussion with a description of frustrating incidents—a traffic jam, a computer that refuses to compute, a test unrelated to lectures or reading assignments.

A good way to see the difference between abstract and concrete terms is to pair the two in sentences like the following.

Happiness is a cancelled 8:00 class on a cold, rainy morning.

Luxury is the smell of leather upholstery in a new Ferrari.

Panic is realizing that next Wednesday's test is this Wednesday.

In each of these sentences, the quality of the abstract word is made real by the concrete and familiar example.

If your prose seems impersonal and vague, try adding concrete facts, instances, and examples that will enliven, enrich, and clarify your meaning.

32c   VIGOROUS PROSE

To put some vigor and energy into your writing, you must think honestly about your subject. Otherwise, you may be tempted to rely on tired expressions repeated so often that they have become meaningless. You may also be tempted to avoid speaking directly about an unpleasant or controversial subject and thus create dull and lifeless prose. You do not have to be a professional writer to express yourself with energy and directness. But you do have to think honestly and speak honestly.

(1) Clichés

Clichés are expressions, perhaps once vivid but now stale from overuse. A cliché conveys a superficial thought—if indeed it conveys any thought at all. In fact, it usually detracts from the point. To recognize clichés, question the effectiveness of overly familiar expressions, and look for certain clues. One clue is that clichés often contain repeated sounds.

tried and true	takes the cake
black and blue	no great shakes
worse for wear	rhyme or reason
betwixt and between	rise and shine
super duper	wishy-washy
hit the hay	eager beaver
fit and trim	

Another clue is that clichés are frequently comparisons, such as metaphors and similes. (See 33d.) But instead of being fresh and interesting, these comparisons have become overly familiar and boring.

out in left field	avoid like the plague
chip on his shoulder	open a can of worms
dropped like a hot potato	make no bones about it
as cool as a cucumber	pretty as a picture
like a bolt from the blue	busy as a beaver
right in there pitching	

Some clichés neither contain repeated sounds nor express comparisons. They are merely combinations that for some reason catch on and then are repeated again and again.

as luck would have it	crushing blow
last but not least	stifling heat
sick and tired	hardened criminal
make a long story short	not half bad
stark raving mad	cruel fate
better late than never	a bang-up job
sigh of relief	one in a million
more easily said than done	rude awakening
agonizing defeat	agree wholeheartedly

If you do not think honestly about a subject, you may find yourself relying on clichés. Consider, for example, this passage on holiday stress.

> To me, the Christmas holidays are stressful because I always wind up rushing around at the last minute trying to find the perfect gifts for friends and relatives. Between shopping, cooking, cleaning, and going to parties, I never find the time for rest and relaxation before I have to return to the hectic pace of school.

The writer has not really thought about the subject but has merely strung clichés together (*wind up, rushing around at the last minute, the perfect gifts, rest and relaxation, hectic pace*). As a result, the passage is lifeless. Avoiding the clichés would encourage the writer to say something more interesting and vigorous.

> I would like to go home for Christmas to a quiet house where I could recover from the constant pressure of school deadlines. Instead, I go home to chaos. I plunge into department stores crowded with tired, irritable shoppers and search for gifts among the overpriced junk. I spend hours helping my parents to cook rich, fatty foods and to clean greasy, gunk-encrusted pans. I try to find rest in a house filled with breakable decorations and visiting children. No wonder the holidays cause stress.

You can, of course, use a cliché that has exactly the right meaning. But you would be wise to follow the lead of William L. Shirer and let the reader know you are not using the expression naively. In his autobiography, *Twentieth Century Journey,* Shirer remarks of his adventures as a foreign correspondent, "To say that 'there is no substitute for experience' may be indulging in a stale cliché, but it has much truth in it."

wd
style
32c

(2) Euphemisms

The etymology of *euphemism* points to its meaning; in Greek *eu* means "good" and *pheme* means "speech." Thus, a euphemism is the substitution of a polite or inoffensive term for one that might be considered coarse or unpleasant. For example, you would probably be more comfortable writing *senior citizen* rather than *old person* or writing *disabled* rather than *crippled.* Many euphemisms like these result from a natural and well-intentioned motive—to make reality seem less harsh and cruel. But when euphemisms distort or glorify the ordinary, they can be dishonest and pretentious. A government that supports assassination might call it "neutralization"; a jeweler who sells rhinestones might advertise "faux diamonds"; a person who deals in pornography might describe the books and movies as "adult."

Dependence on euphemisms creates a weak style that evades the reality of its subject. For example, in the following passage, the subject is hidden behind indirect euphemisms (*peer pressure, experiment with artificial stimulants, social isolation, mental and physical disorders*).

> Students are constantly under peer pressure to experiment with artificial stimulants. Those who resist the pressure will often suffer social isolation. Those who succumb to the pressure, however, can suffer serious physical and mental disorders.

The euphemisms in the passage weaken the urgency of the problem. Without the euphemisms, the dangers become real, and the real has impact and vigor.

> Students are constantly pressured by their classmates to drink and take drugs. Those who resist the pressure will often lose friends and

invitations. Those who do not resist, however, can lose their minds or even their lives.

Whenever possible, avoid dishonest and evasive language. Use, instead, direct and vigorous expressions. The list that follows suggests possible substitutions for some common euphemisms.

EUPHEMISMS	DIRECT EXPRESSIONS
correctional facility	prison
previously owned cars	used cars
depopulate	kill
revenue enhancements	taxes
mobile manor	trailer park
interred	buried
nonpassing grade	failing grade
preneed arrangements	funeral arrangements
sanitary engineer	garbage collector
horticultural surgeon	tree trimmer

**wd
style
32d**

32d CLUTTERED PROSE

If you have ever tried to make sense out of tax instructions or an insurance policy, you know how frustrating cluttered prose can be. Readers should not have to sort through unnecessary words and confusing phrases, searching for meaning. Good writing is clear; the meaning comes through readily. So when you revise, remember to clear out the clutter that results from gobbledygook, surplus words, and dense noun phrases.

(1) Gobbledygook

There is a widespread movement in government and business to eliminate gobbledygook, also called *jargon, bureaucratic language, double-talk, officialese, federalese,* and *doublespeak.* This language is full of abstractions, indirect words, and convoluted constructions; it is devoid of humanity and sensitivity. You can recognize gobbledygook by its pomposity and wordiness.

GOBBLEDYGOOK:	The committee must implement the operationalizing of those mechanisms and modes of activity and strategies necessary to maintain the viability of the institution's fiscal management operations.
REVISED:	The committee must take measures to ensure the institution's financial security.

wd
style
32d

The success rate of the "plain English" movement is not impressive, probably because the causes of gobbledygook have not been eliminated (and possibly cannot be). Gobbledygook flourishes for a variety of reasons: its writers have nothing substantive to say; they do not fully understand their subjects; they try to protect themselves from criticism of their ideas; they do not really want anyone to understand what they say; they believe, rightly or wrongly, that the inflated prose impresses readers.

Some of the words and phrases popular in gobbledygook follow. You should avoid them and use instead their "plain" counterparts.

GOBBLEDYGOOK	PLAIN ENGLISH
initiate	begin
terminate	end
utilize	use
transmit	send
administrate	administer
notate	note
orientate	orient
summarization	summary
origination	origin
routinization	routine
pursuant to	according to

cognizant of	aware of
conversant with	familiar with
inoperative	broken
at this point in time	now
prior to	before
subsequent to	after
a majority of	most
a number of	many, some
of considerable magnitude	large
as a means of	for
as a result	so
at the rate of	at
due to the fact that	because
for the purpose of	for
in connection with	about
in the interest of	for
in such a manner as to	to
in the neighborhood of	about

**wd
style
32d**

When readers must struggle to glean sense from a passage, the consequences of gobbledygook are always annoyance and frustration. But when the struggle takes place in documents relating to business, medicine, insurance, and taxes, the consequences can endanger the economy and the public well-being. As William Zinsser comments in *On Writing Well,*

> What people want is plain talk. It's what the stockholder wants from his corporation, what the customer wants from his bank, what the widow wants from the Government office that is handling her Social Security. There is a yearning for human contact and a resentment of bombast. Any institution that won't take the trouble to be clear and personal will lose friends, customers and money.

(2)   Surplus words, or redundancies

Surplus words congest prose with redundancies and meaningless clutter. Without thinking, people often use phrases like these: *past history, blue in color, playground area.* Yet, some of the words in these phrases are unnecessary. History is always in the past; blue is a color; and a playground is an area. As the following passage demonstrates, surplus words add nothing to prose except flab.

SURPLUS WORDS: Our future plans are to add workshops in the areas of accounting, the method of maintaining automobiles, and the process of organic gardening. Instructors will begin with the basic fundamentals and then advance forward at a rate acceptable to individual persons enrolled. The end result will be a kind of class-directed learning technique.

Cutting the surplus away allows the ideas to emerge from the flab.

REVISED: We plan to add workshops in accounting, automobile maintenance, and organic gardening. Instructors will begin with the fundamentals and advance at a rate acceptable to the individuals enrolled. The result will be class-directed learning.

Listed are some familiar redundancies.

any and all	4:00 P.M. in the afternoon
basic fundamentals	free gift
completely finished	full and complete
consensus of opinion	future plans
crisis situation	important essentials
different individuals	in actual fact
each and every	modern world of today
educational process	personal friend

end result   reduce down

~~final outcome~~   ~~true facts~~

(3)   Dense noun phrases

The compounding of nouns has long been a tendency in English.
The language is full of such noun combinations as *tennis court,
china cup, lawn mower,* and *garden party.* These compounds are
more economic and sound more like English than *court for tennis,
cup made of china, mower for lawns,* and *party in a garden.*

**wd
style
32d**

Three or more nouns, however, may produce a compound so
"dense" that the reader has trouble deciding what modifies what.
For example, consider the noun phrase *campus sorority standards
board.* A reader must guess at the meaning: A standards board for
campus sororities? A sorority standards board located on campus? A
standards board made up of members of campus sororities? Adding
an adjective even further confounds readers: *new campus sorority
standards board.* What is new? The campus? The sorority? The
standards? The board?

You can sometimes clarify a dense phrase by the use of hyphens. Also, you can always rewrite part of the structure as a modifying phrase. The following examples demonstrate the two
techniques.

DENSE PHRASE:	new employee investment policy
CLARIFIED WITH HYPHEN:	new employee-investment policy
CLARIFIED WITH HYPHEN:	new-employee investment policy
DENSE PHRASE:	government industry regulations
CLARIFIED BY REWRITING:	government regulations for industries
CLARIFIED BY REWRITING:	regulations for government industries
DENSE PHRASE:	Nevada historical artifacts conference
CLARIFIED BY REWRITING:	conference in Nevada on historical artifacts
CLARIFIED BY REWRITING:	conference on historical artifacts found in Nevada

32e DISCRIMINATORY LANGUAGE

When editing your work, watch for discriminatory language, that is, language showing bias against any group. The appearance of ethnic, racial, sexual, or other biased terms will not only offend readers but also undermine your credibility and authority.

Of course, most writers do not deliberately choose to offend. Sometimes, however, discriminatory language is subtle and easily overlooked. The following guidelines can help ensure that you have not inadvertently included language that seems thoughtless or insensitive.

**wd
style
32e**

(1) Observing current usage

Try to use the terms currently preferred by the group you are discussing. Avoiding negative designations is usually easy; most people know which words demean or degrade deliberately. At times, however, the preferred terms are difficult to discover because preferences change. *Lunatic asylum,* for instance, gave way to *insane asylum,* in turn replaced by *mental hospital; slow students* became *students with a learning disability.* You may have to look to the news media, language authorities, or, when appropriate, the groups themselves for current designations.

(2) Avoiding irrelevant information

In general, avoid pointing out a person's race, age, gender, religion, ethnic background, or appearance, *unless* it is pertinent to the subject being discussed. For example, in an analysis of a skater's form and technique, a reference to the person's race or religion would ordinarily be out of place. In a discussion of a mayoral election, describing a candidate's hairstyle may make your opinions seem frivolous.

(3) Avoiding stereotypes

Stereotyping has no place in thoughtful writing. Informed, perceptive writers do not assume that certain groups of people have inher-

ent characteristics—that some groups are arrogant, some deferen-
tial, some lazy, some industrious, some smart, some stupid.

In general, try to avoid typecasting: the absent-minded professor; the jolly fat man; the prissy spinster librarian; the backward
South; the bland and boring Midwest; prudish New Englanders;
brusque Germans. These are not merely types; they are clichés.
Even if stereotypes do not insult your readers, they will certainly
bore them.

(4) Avoiding sexist categories

Unless you are writing specifically about male and female roles or
characteristics, you are wise not to generalize about these subjects.

- Avoid assumptions about professions. For example, executives,
  pilots, and doctors are not necessarily male; secretaries, flight at-
  tendants, and nurses are not necessarily female. As a rule, you
  should not point out the gender of a professional person: *a lady
  executive*, *a female pilot*, *a male nurse*, *a man secretary*.

- In the interest of fairness, use the same kind of language for the
  same characteristics in males and females. For example, do not
  call a male *angry*, and a female *upset* or a male *commanding* and
  a female with the same personality *bossy*. On the other hand, do
  not belittle a male's ego and praise a female's self-esteem.

- Use parallel terms to refer to males and females. *Man* is a parallel
  to *woman*, *boy* to *girl*, and *gentleman* to *lady*. A *man and his
  wife* is not parallel; *a husband and wife* or *a couple* is preferable. A man's given name and a woman's married name are not
  parallel. Instead of writing *Dan Blake and Mrs. Richard
  Mullins*, write *Dan Blake and Amy Mullins*.

(5) Using neutral terms

Nouns and pronouns that do not refer to gender are called "neutral."
In current usage, these words are preferred for groups that include
women as well as men. For example, *fire fighters* has replaced *fire-
men*. You need not go to the extreme of writing *huperson* for *human* or *freshperson* for *freshman*. Nevertheless, if a reasonable,
neutral term exists for a mixed-gender group, you may wish to use it.

- As the following list indicates, many masculine nouns have neutral substitutes.

EXAMPLE	NEUTRAL
manpower	personnel
policeman	police officer
mailman	mail carrier *or* postal worker
early man	early humans
Congressmen	members of Congress

- Unless you are sure you are writing to a man, do not use *Dear Sir* as the salutation of a business letter. Instead, write *Dear Sir or Madam*, use a personalized greeting, or write a simplified letter with no salutation and no complimentary close. The *Dear Sir* salutation reflects a male-dominated business world and could easily offend the very person being asked for a favor.

- Referring to males and females with the pronouns *he*, *him*, and *his* is viewed today as outdated. Often, you can substitute compounds like *he or she* and *her or him*, but repeated use of these compounds in a passage sounds unnatural. The following techniques can help you avoid awkward repetition.

     Make the noun anteccedent and the pronouns plural.

EXAMPLE: Each student must bring his own blue book.

NEUTRAL: All students must bring their own blue book.

     Change the masculine pronoun to an article (*a, an, the*).

EXAMPLE: Everyone was struggling with his assignment.

NEUTRAL: Everyone was struggling with the assignment.

     Change clauses to phrases.

EXAMPLE: When each contestant arrives, he will be given the rules.

NEUTRAL: After arriving, each contestant will be given the rules.

- Some writers prefer to avoid any mention of gender, even suffixes such as *-man* and *-ess*. As a result, *chair* or *chairperson* has become a substitute for *chairman*; *waitperson* or *waitron* for *waitress*; and so on. Many people, however, find this practice artificial. In fact, the U. S. Air Force decided to retain the term *airman*, since all substitutes sounded overly contrived.

If you object to a slavish search for unisex language, you can use more traditional terms. But remember your audience. When addressing women, for example, you may want to use the suffix *-woman* (as in *chairwoman* or *councilwoman*). In most instances, however, suffixes designating a female are unnecessary; the neutral words *aviator*, *executor*, and *poet* are preferable to the outdated words *aviatrix*, *executrix*, and *poetess*.

wd style 32e

(6) Maintaining objectivity

Try to maintain an objective view of all persons and groups. As a writer, you will probably address audiences that include white males; Anglo-Saxon protestants; and people with some degree of money, power, and social advantages. Therefore, avoid blanket assumptions about such groups as sorority and fraternity members, people who attend private schools, or men in civic organizations. Prejudice is unfair and offensive—even when directed against those felt to be privileged or powerful.

Avoiding discriminatory language is important. Just as important, however, is avoiding a witch hunt. Taken to extremes, "political correctness" will weaken your writing. *Middleman*, for example, is a perfectly legitimate term, widely understood. There is no point in confusing readers by substituting *distributional intermediary* merely to avoid the suffix *-man*. Little is gained by referring to a stripper as an *ecdysiast* when most readers will not recognize the euphemism. And no one is going to take seriously a writer who calls short people *vertically challenged*. Remember, the point of considerate language is to be fair and polite, not to be obscure or silly.

33

SENTENCE STYLE

A good prose style is smooth, clear, and interesting. These qualities rarely appear in a rough draft. Instead, they result from thoughtful revising from deliberate polishing of sentence structure to achieve variety, emphasis, and clarity; from heightening the effect with sound, rhythm, and figures of speech. In other words, good style requires finding clear and interesting structures to replace those that may be confusing or monotonous. The sections that follow offer some suggestions to help you revise prose by choosing structures that effectively express your ideas. Because many of the techniques require you to be familiar with phrase and clause structure, you may wish to review Chapter 5 and Chapter 7.

33a VARIETY

Although the number of possible sentences in English is infinite, the number of possible clause patterns is limited. (See 7a.) In fact, most sentences have the underlying pattern *subject* + *verb* + *object* or *complement.* If nothing is added to these basic patterns, the result is monotonous, choppy prose one short, simple sentence after another. In the following passage, for example, all the sentences are short and simple. To make things worse, they all begin in the same way, with the subject followed immediately by a verb.

CHOPPY: Wilson was born an aristocrat. He was brought up in a con-
          servative family. He was trained as a Hamiltonian. He became
          the greatest leader of the plain people since Lincoln.

The original version, in Morison and Commager's *The Growth of the American Republic,* is vastly superior.

ORIGINAL: Born an aristocrat, bred a conservative, trained a Hamilton-
            ian, he became the greatest leader of the plain people since
            Lincoln.

**sent
style
33a**

The basic pattern of this sentence is very simple: *he became leader* (subject + verb + complement). But the three introductory modifiers give the sentence an interesting structure and sound not found in the choppy passage.

Even a series of fairly long sentences can be as monotonous as choppy prose if the structures never vary. The following passage, for example, consists only of independent clauses joined by *and* or *but.* In addition, each clause begins with the subject and verb.

MONOTONOUS: George Pratt compared the horses' footfalls, and made
              an interesting discovery. The two horses seemed to run
              at the same speed, but Secretariat covered more dis-
              tance per stride. Secretariat covered 23.8 feet per
              stride, and Riva Ridge covered 23.2 feet.

Variations can eliminate the monotony. Notice that in the revised version, not only the structures but also the beginnings of the sentences are varied.

REVISED: By comparing the horses' footfalls, George Pratt made an in-
           teresting discovery. Although the two horses seemed to run
           at the same speed, Secretariat covered more distance per
           stride than Riva Ridge—23.8 feet versus 23.2 feet.

Variety in sentence structure, however, does not guarantee good writing. Even when sentence structure is varied, prose can sound monotonous if each sentence begins with the subject and verb of the main clause.

MONOTONOUS: Science recognizes a number of differences between men and women. Men are physically stronger, for example, whereas women have more physical stamina. Men have more genetic defects and weaker immune systems although women are more prone to phobias and depression. Neither sex should feel superior or inferior. The differences fit together like the pieces of a jigsaw puzzle, and they create the whole picture of human beings.

sent style 33a

The monotony can be eliminated by beginning some of the sentences with modifiers.

REVISED: Science recognizes a number of differences between men and women. For example, whereas men are physically stronger, women have more physical stamina. Although men have more genetic defects and weaker immune systems, women are more prone to phobias and depression. But neither sex should feel superior or inferior. Like the pieces of a jigsaw puzzle, the differences fit together to create the whole picture of human beings.

Coordination and subordination are two techniques for combining ideas and structures. Practicing these techniques will help you learn to manipulate—and thus to vary—sentence structure and sentence beginnings. With a knowledge of how to combine ideas in different ways, you can avoid simplistic and repetitious expression of thought.

(1) Combine independent clauses through coordination.

The most effective way to join two independent clauses depends on the relationship between the ideas expressed in the clauses. If the ideas have a kind of equality, you can simply connect one clause to the other with a comma and the conjunction *and* or with a semicolon.

SEPARATED: In the early 1900s, cocaine was used in many patent medicines. It was even present in the original formula of Coca-Cola.

COMBINED: In the early 1900s, cocaine was used in many patent medi-
~~cines, and it was even present in the original formula of~~
Coca-Cola.

COMBINED: In the early 1900s, cocaine was used in many patent medicines; it was even present in the original formula of Coca-
Cola.

Another way to show equality of ideas is to use the semicolon and a transitional expression such as *also, furthermore, in addition,* or *moreover.* The transitional expression can appear immediately after the semicolon or at some other appropriate place in the second clause.

SEPARATED: Pesticides have contaminated much of our groundwater.
They have left residues on much of the food we eat.

COMBINED: Pesticides have contaminated much of our groundwater; in
addition, they have left residues on much of the food we
eat.

COMBINED: Pesticides have contaminated much of our groundwater;
they have, in addition, left residues on much of the food
we eat.

When clauses have a cause/effect relationship, they can be joined with a comma and the coordinating conjunction *so* or *for* or with a semicolon and a transitional expression such as *therefore, consequently, as a result,* or *thus.*

SEPARATED: His two interests were medicine and children. He became a
pediatrician.

COMBINED: His two interests were medicine and children, so he became a pediatrician.

COMBINED: His two interests were medicine and children; consequently, he became a pediatrician.

Contrasting clauses can be joined with a comma and a coordinating conjunction *but, or, nor,* or *yet* or with a semicolon and a transitional expression such as *however, nevertheless,* or *on the other hand.*

SEPARATED: Augustus gave the Senate control of the peaceful provinces. He kept under his authority the unstable provinces of the frontier.

COMBINED: Augustus gave the Senate control of the peaceful provinces, but he kept under his authority the unstable provinces of the frontier.

COMBINED: Augustus gave the Senate control of the peaceful provinces; he kept under his authority, however, the unstable provinces of the frontier.

Other transitional expressions such as *for example, then,* and *in fact* link clauses. When clauses are joined with semicolons, these words can establish the relationship of the second clause to the first.

SEPARATED: An otherwise rational person often performs superstitious rituals. A baseball player may refuse to pitch without his favorite hat.

SECOND CLAUSE AS EXAMPLE: An otherwise rational person often performs superstitious rituals; a baseball player, for example, may refuse to pitch without his favorite hat.

SEPARATED: Her apartment was full of all sorts of animals. It seemed more like a pet store than a place to live.

SECOND CLAUSE AS REINFORCEMENT: Her apartment was full of all sorts of animals; in fact, it seemed more like a pet store than a place to live.

SEPARATED: To make the rock garden, cover the area with heavy plastic to keep out weeds. Add a layer of pea gravel for the base.

SECOND CLAUSE AS SECOND STEP: To make the rock garden, cover the area with heavy plastic to keep out weeds; then, add a layer of pea gravel for the base.

Alternatives can be emphasized by the correlative conjunctions *either . . . or* or *neither . . . nor.*

SEPARATED: The movies are getting sillier. Or I am getting more cynical.

COMBINED: <u>Either</u> the movies are getting sillier, <u>or</u> I am getting more cynical.

As the examples show, independent clauses are usually joined with conjunctions or with semicolons. Two less common devices are the colon and the dash. The colon indicates that the second clause explains or illustrates the first.

sent
style
33a

SEPARATED: The river was deceptively tranquil. Beneath the smooth, gently flowing surface were treacherous undertows.

SECOND CLAUSE AS EXPLANATION: The river was deceptively tranquil: beneath the smooth, gently flowing surface were treacherous undertows.

SEPARATED: The heat wave created a picnic atmosphere. Children played in the park fountains, while barefooted adults drank lemonade beneath shade trees.

SECOND CLAUSE AS ILLUSTRATION: The heat wave created a picnic atmosphere: children played in park fountains, while barefooted adults drank lemonade beneath shade trees.

Like the colon, the dash signals that the second clause explains the first or serves as an afterthought or addition to the first. Between independent clauses, the dash is a dramatic mark of punctuation, so you should use it sparingly. Overuse defeats the purpose.

SEPARATED: Cheerleaders are the most useless addition to football games. Their frantic efforts are almost totally ignored by the fans.

SECOND CLAUSE AS EXPLANATION:	Cheerleaders are the most useless addition to football games—their frantic efforts are almost totally ignored by the fans.
SEPARATED:	Ice cream doesn't taste as good as it did when I was a child. Spinach doesn't taste as bad either.
SECOND CLAUSE AS AFTERTHOUGHT:	Ice cream doesn't taste as good as it did when I was a child—spinach doesn't taste as bad either.

sent style 33a

The different techniques available for joining independent clauses allow you to clarify a relationship between ideas as well as to vary sentence structure. In choosing a technique, consider not only the need to avoid monotony but also the relationship you want to express.

(2) Combine shared elements through coordination.

When two or more sentences share elements—such as subjects, predicates, or parts of predicates—you can avoid repetition and simplistic prose by compounding the common elements with simple coordinators like *and, but,* and *or;* with correlative coordinators like *not only . . . but also, either . . . or, both . . . and;* and with expressions like *in addition to, as well as, but not.*

SEPARATED:	Garlic contains natural antibiotics. Onions also contain these substances.
COMBINED SUBJECTS:	Garlic and onions contain natural antibiotics.
SEPARATED:	The players didn't seem to understand what had happened. And the referees didn't either.

COMBINED SUBJECTS: Neither the players nor the referees seemed to understand what had happened.

SEPARATED: The Great Wall of China was built entirely by hand. It took hundreds of years to complete.

COMBINED PREDICATES: The Great Wall of China was built entirely by hand and took hundreds of years to complete.

sent style 33a

SEPARATED: Leafy trees add beauty to your landscape. They also help lower your energy bill in the summertime.

COMBINED PREDICATES: Leafy trees not only add beauty to your landscape but also help lower your energy bill in the summertime.

SEPARATED: Your body requires the macronutrients (fats, carbohydrates, and proteins). It also requires the micronutrients (vitamins and minerals).

COMBINED DIRECT OBJECTS: Your body requires the macronutrients (fats, carbohydrates, and proteins) as well as the micronutrients (vitamins and minerals).

SEPARATED: He was willing to assume the privileges of the office. He was not, however, willing to assume the responsibilities.

COMBINED OBJECTS OF INFINITIVES: He was willing to assume the privileges of the office but not the responsibilities.

SEPARATED: She was a well-known jazz singer. She was also a well-respected portrait artist.

COMBINED COMPLEMENTS: She was both a well-known jazz singer and a well-respected portrait artist.

(3)   Subordinate with adverb clauses.

One structure very useful for combining ideas is the adverb clause, which expresses time, place, cause, purpose, condition, manner, and contrast. The nature of the information in the adverb clause is clearly signaled through the use of an introductory subordinating conjunction such as *when, until, where, because, so that, if, as though, although,* and the like. (See 6b.3 and 7c.1.) Thus, adverb clauses can improve clarity in prose by flatly stating, through the subordinating conjunction, how one idea relates to another. In addition, since most adverb clauses can introduce sentences, they provide a way to vary sentence beginnings.

SEPARATED: Billie Jean King won nineteen tournaments in 1971. She became the first woman tennis player ever to earn $100,000 a year.

COMBINED: When Billie Jean King won nineteen tournaments in 1971, she became the first woman tennis player ever to earn $100,000 a year.

SEPARATED: Our school system offers almost no instruction in financial planning. Few of us learn to handle our finances in an intelligent manner.

COMBINED: Since our school system offers almost no instruction in financial planning, few of us learn to handle our finances in an intelligent manner.

SEPARATED: Mid-afternoon drowsiness is often called the "post-lunch dip." It occurs regardless of when, or if, we eat.

COMBINED: Although mid-afternoon drowsiness is often called the "post-lunch dip," it occurs regardless of when, or if, we eat.

(4) Subordinate with adjective clauses.

The adjective clause can help eliminate the choppy prose that results from too much repetition of nouns and personal pronouns. In this structure, ideas are joined with relative words like *which, who/whom/whose, when,* and *where.* (See 2c and 7c.2.)

SEPARATED: The last stop on the tour was King's Tavern. This tavern was originally a hostel at the end of the Natchez Trace.

COMBINED: The last stop on the tour was King's Tavern, which was originally a hostel at the end of the Natchez Trace.

SEPARATED: Hamlin Garland spent his youth on farms in Wisconsin, Iowa, and South Dakota. He learned firsthand about grim pioneer life on these farms.

COMBINED: Hamlin Garland spent his youth on farms in Wisconsin, Iowa, and South Dakota, where he learned firsthand about grim pioneer life.

SEPARATED: I was forced to go to my first dance with Father's nephew, Talbot. His hair was longer than mine. And he danced like a trained bear.

COMBINED: I was forced to go to my first dance with Father's nephew, Talbot, whose hair was longer than mine and who danced like a trained bear.

(5) Subordinate with verbal phrases.

The essential element in a verbal phrase is a verbal—a verb form (*to see, seeing, seen*) functioning as a noun, an adjective, or an adverb. In addition, a verbal phrase contains one or more of the following: a subject, object, complement, or modifiers. (See Chapter 5.) Subordinating with verbal phrases can eliminate repetition of nouns and personal pronouns and provide a source for varying sentence beginnings.

SEPARATED: The wedding date was already set. She felt compelled to go through with the marriage.

COMBINED: Having already set the wedding date, she felt compelled to go through with the marriage.

SEPARATED: You can dust the face lightly with a white, frosted powder. This procedure will produce a faint glow.

COMBINED: To produce a faint glow, you can dust the face lightly with a white, frosted powder.

SEPARATED: Vines covered the entire house. They almost concealed it from the casual observer.

SEPARATED: Vines covered the entire house, almost concealing it from the casual observer.

(6) Subordinate with appositives.

The appositive, one of the most versatile structures in prose, re-states or renames a word or phrase. When immediately following the word or phrase it renames, the appositive adds information. When introducing a sentence, it serves as a descriptive lead-in to the subject and an unusual beginning for a sentence. And if postponed until the end of a sentence, it lends a bit of drama and suspense. The following examples demonstrate how the appositive works to make prose more efficient and structure more interesting.

SEPARATED: This automobile is an up-to-date mechanical achievement. It has a permanently engaged, all-wheel drive system.

APPOSITIVE INSIDE: This automobile, an up-to-date mechanical achievement, has a permanently engaged, all-wheel drive system.

SEPARATED: The Anchor Pub is the last survivor of the many Southwark taverns. It was built on the site of the Globe Theatre.

APPOSITIVE AT BEGINNING: The last survivor of the many Southwark tav-
~~erns, the Anchor Pub was built on the site of~~
the Globe Theatre.

SEPARATED: For the ten years of her imprisonment, Marie
concentrated on revenge. It was the only
thing that kept her alive.

APPOSITIVE AT END: Only one thing kept Marie alive for the ten
years of her imprisonment: <u>the thought of
revenge.</u>

sent
style
33a

Writers frequently use appositives to add ideas after an independent clause. Appositives like these can prevent short, repetitious
sentences and vague pronoun references. One way to employ the
technique is to repeat a word or words in the preceding structure.

SEPARATED: Chaucer tells us of a pilgrimage to the shrine of a saint. The
pilgrimage is more social than religious.

COMBINED: Chaucer tells us of a pilgrimage to the shrine of a saint, <u>a
pilgrimage more social than religious.</u>

SEPARATED: Our climate is precariously balanced. This means that a tiny
variation in the earth's orbit could cause another ice age.

COMBINED: Our climate is precariously balanced—<u>so precariously that
a tiny variation in the earth's orbit could cause another ice
age.</u>

Another way to use the technique is to begin the appositive
with a word or phrase that summarizes the preceding idea or ideas.

VAGUE PRONOUN: Health experts recommend that we decrease fat and
increase fiber in our diets. This may lower our risk of
cancer.

COMBINED: Health experts recommend that we decrease fat and
increase fiber in our diets, <u>two steps that may lower
our risk of cancer.</u>

VAGUE PRONOUN: Because so much of the business world now provides
information rather than goods, many adults must

return to school for retraining. This will change the recruiting tactics of universities.

COMBINED: Because so much of the business world now provides information rather than goods, many adults must return to school for retraining—a trend that will change the recruiting tactics of universities.

33b EMPHASIS

Most of the sentences in a composition should be direct and unadorned with stylistic flourish. They should not have parts that are unusually long or artfully balanced. They should not call out to a reader for special notice. Sometimes, however, an idea warrants such notice. You can then create a dramatic structure by rearranging the parts of an ordinary sentence, by expanding a part beyond the reader's expectations, by building to a climactic conclusion, or by noticeably balancing the parts. These kinds of dramatic structures should appear sparingly because too many will make prose seem artificial and contrived. Used occasionally, however, and in the right situations, dramatic sentences will strengthen prose.

(1) Periodic sentences

The most common kind of sentence is the "loose" construction, which begins with the main idea in an independent clause, followed by less-important details. This order is considered normal because English speakers seem naturally to progress from subject to verb to complement, with additions and modifiers tacked on. In the periodic sentence, the normal order is reversed, and the main idea is postponed until the end. A periodic order seems to hang the reader in suspension—anticipating the outcome.

LOOSE: This house was the last of the century-old buildings we had tried in vain to protect.

PERIODIC: Of the century-old buildings we had tried in vain to protect, this house was the last.

LOOSE:	Don't order spaghetti when you go to an important business lunch, where you must present a neat, efficient, controlled image.
PERIODIC:	When you go to an important business lunch, where you must present a neat, efficient, controlled image, don't order spaghetti.

When exaggerated, a periodic sentence calls attention not only to the idea at the end but also to the structure itself. In the following example, the writer begins with a long, detailed modifier, postponing the main idea until a final short clause, *the realities emerged.* The result is a fairly dramatic sentence that a reader will notice and enjoy.

sent
style
33b

> Through the motes of cracker dust, corn meal dust, the Gold Dust of the Gold Dust Twins that the floor had been swept out with, the realities emerged. (Eudora Welty)

In the next example, an introductory adverb clause and the parenthetical *you may ask* delay the point and thus add to the humor of the question—when it finally comes.

> If Man has benefited immeasurably by his association with the dog, what, you may ask, has the dog got out of it? (James Thurber)

In the following passage, two consecutive periodic sentences heighten the intensity of the writer's main idea: *the only difference between music and Musak is the spelling* and *it's all the same to me.*

> First off, I want to say that as far as I am concerned, in instances where I have not personally and deliberately sought it out, the only difference between music and Muzak is the spelling. Pablo Casals practicing across the hall with the door open—being trapped in an elevator, the ceiling of which is broadcasting "Parsley, Sage, Rosemary, and Thyme"—it's all the same to me. (Fran Lebowitz)

(2)   Cumulative sentences

The cumulative sentence is an exaggerated loose structure that piles up—or accumulates—structures at the end. One type of exaggeration is a long series of modifiers, like the *who* clauses in the following sentence.

> Grant was one of a body of men who owed reverence and obeisance to no one, who were self-reliant to a fault, who cared hardly anything for the past but who had a sharp eye for the future. (Bruce Catton)

A series of phrases at the end of a sentence can also produce a cumulative effect.

> This time the sorrel mare was in the lot before he heard it at all, the rider collarless and even bareheaded, trembling, speaking in a shaking voice as the woman in the house had done, his father merely looking up once before stooping again to the horse he was buckling, so that the man on the mare spoke to his stooping back. (William Faulkner)

**sent
style
33b**

In the next sentence, the writer begins with two main clauses and then tacks on a series of examples after the word *say*. The length of the structure and the number of details creates an attention-getting sentence.

> Summer will be admitted to our breakfast table as usual, and in the space of a half a cup of coffee I will be able to discover, say, that Ferguson Jenkins went eight innings in Montreal and won his fourth game of the season while giving up five hits, that Al Kaline was horse-collared by Fritz Peterson at the stadium, that Tony Oliva hit a single off Mickey Lolich in Detroit, that Juan Marichal was bombed by the Reds in the top of the sixth at Candlestick Park, and that similar disasters and triumphs befell a couple of dozen-odd of the other ballplayers—favorites and knaves—whose fortunes I follow from April to October. (Roger Angell)

(3)   Climactic sentences

Another strategy for achieving emphasis is the climactic sentence, in which multiple ideas move up a scale—from less important to more important, from simple to complex, from the ordinary to the extraordinary. The climactic sentence can also build to a point, then shift suddenly from the literal to the ironic or from the normal to the unexpected. The effect is that the last idea expressed receives the most emphasis.

> The letter, written in pencil, expressed intense admiration, confessed regrets about the past, revealed deep sorrows—and was never mailed.

Like us, stars have a cycle of life from birth, through youth and maturity, to decline and death.

He fidgeted, took practice swings, spit, adjusted his clothes, kissed his bat, stepped into the batter's box, and struck out.

When the content lends itself to drama, the climactic sentence can be particularly effective, as the following sentence illustrates.

Thus it is that the mouse seems always to dangle so languidly from the jaws, lies there so quietly when dropped, dies of his injuries without a struggle. (Lewis Thomas)

(4) Balanced sentences

A balanced sentence creates a symmetry—a noticeable and deliberate symmetry—achieved with parallel structure and often with repetition of key vocabulary. The "echo" of structure and words emphasizes the comparison or contrast of ideas.

You cannot get a job without experience, and you cannot get experience without a job.

From afar, the island looked like a tropical paradise of white sand and sparkling blue sea; up close, the island looked like a garbage dump of trash and polluted water.

When the structure and vocabulary of a sentence are perfectly balanced, the result can be quite dramatic. For example, the second sentence in the following passage has perfectly balanced independent clauses, with the subject and complement of the first clause (*seamen, gentlemen*) reversed in the second clause (*gentlemen, seamen.*)

There were gentlemen and there were seamen in the Navy of Charles II. But the seamen were not gentlemen, and the gentlemen were not seamen. (Lord Macaulay)

Consecutive sentences can also be balanced; that is, a structure can be repeated and vocabulary carried over for two or more sentences in a row. In the next passage, the echo effect is created by the repetition of *when* clauses with *power* as the subject, followed by independent clauses with *poetry* as the subject.

When power leads man toward arrogance, poetry reminds him of his limitations. When power narrows the areas of man's concern, poetry reminds him of the richness and diversity of his existence. When power corrupts, poetry cleanses, for art establishes the basic human truths which must serve as the touchstone of our judgment. (John Kennedy)

A balanced structure can highlight an idea or keep prose from sounding monotonous. Remember, however, that if overused, this kind of structure, especially when exaggerated, will seem pretentious and will rapidly wear on a reader's nerves.

33c STREAMLINING

Effective writing is easy to read. It allows a reader to move smoothly through sentences without laboring to discover structure and meaning. If your pose seems cumbersome and hard to read, you may be obscuring the meaning by packing too much into single sentences, by including too many empty or passive verbs, or by clouding the connection between subjects and verbs. Practicing the following techniques can help you streamline your writing and produce crisp, clear sentences that throw no obstacles in a reader's path.

(1) Empty verbs and nominalizations

Empty verbs, such as *be, have,* and *make,* have little or no meaning themselves and must absorb meaning from their contexts. Since these verbs do not express action, they are frequently accompanied by a nominalization, that is, an expression of action in noun form. Using unnecessary nominalizations can result in cumbersome structures, as the following sentence illustrates.

> Rescue teams are making attempts to uncover the mine shaft, but authorities have no expectations of success.

Expressing the action in verbs rather than nouns tightens and streamlines the structure.

> Rescue teams are attempting to uncover the mine shaft, but authorities do not expect success.

In revising, you should keep an eye out for nominalizations that weaken structure and pad your prose. The following pairs of sentences demonstrate how easily you can eliminate unnecessary nominalizations. Often the solution is simply to express the action in a strong verb or verbal. Notice that the revised versions are shorter and crisper.

ORIGINAL: We <u>had hopes</u> that the students would vote <u>for the abolition</u> of the curfews.

REVISED: We <u>hoped</u> that the students would vote <u>to abolish</u> the curfews.

ORIGINAL: <u>The basis of the achievement of</u> your goal is <u>the develop-ment of</u> a positive attitude.

REVISED: <u>To achieve</u> your goal, you <u>must develop</u> a positive attitude.

ORIGINAL: <u>To make a discovery about</u> how many people <u>felt a necessity</u> for longer lab hours, I <u>made use of</u> a simple questionnaire.

REVISED: <u>To discover</u> how many people <u>needed</u> longer lab hours, I <u>used</u> a simple questionnaire.

(2)   Weak passives

In an active sentence, the agent of the action appears in the subject position, and the receiver of the action appears as the direct object. In a passive sentence, this order is reversed. The receiver of the action appears in the subject position but still receives the action. The agent of the action can appear as an object of the preposition *by*.

ACTIVE: Locusts ruined their crops.

PASSIVE: Their crops were ruined by the locusts.

A passive sentence can be useful in certain situations. For example, a writer can choose the passive to emphasize the receiver of the action. The following pair of sentences illustrates the different emphasis found in active and passive constructions.

ACTIVE: The Etruscans and the Greeks influenced the earliest Roman sculpture.

PASSIVE: The earliest Roman sculpture was influenced by the Etruscans and the Greeks.

The active sentence focuses attention on the agents (*the Etruscans and the Greeks*), whereas the passive sentence focuses attention on the receiver of the action (*earliest Roman sculpture*).

Also, a writer can choose the passive because the agent is unknown or unimportant in the context. In such cases, the phrase containing *by* or *with* and the agent is usually left out.

PASSIVE: The telephone lines were cut.

PASSIVE: Equity courts in the United States are called Courts of Chancery.

**sent
style
33c**

The passive may be preferable in some situations, but in others, it may be unnecessarily weak and wordy, especially when a *by* phrase supplies the agent. Active versions tend to be more concise, emphatic, and lively than their passive counterparts because the subject acts and the verb does not require the *be* auxiliary. Also, when the agent of the action figures significantly in the content, the active focuses a reader's attention on the right words.

WEAK PASSIVE: Booster cables should never be connected to a frozen battery <u>by you</u>.

ACTIVE: You should never connect booster cables to a frozen battery.

WEAK PASSIVE: The investors were swindled out of 10 million dollars <u>by Arnold and Slack</u>.

ACTIVE: Arnold and Slack swindled the investors out of 10 million dollars.

Compare the following two passages. The passive version obscures the important role of the host, calling attention instead of the result of his actions.

WEAK PASSIVE

Before a Japanese tea ceremony, the tea room and surrounding gardens were cleaned by the host. Then a fire is made in the hearth and the water is put on to boil. When the guests arrive, the tea bowl, tea caddy, utensils for tending the fire, incense burner, and other necessary tools are carried in by the host. After the tea is prepared in a historical ritual, each guest is served. Finally, all utensils having been removed, the guests are bowed to, the signal that the ceremony has been completed.

In contrast, the active version is livelier and emphasizes the importance of the agent (the host) in the action (the ceremony).

ACTIVE

Before a Japanese tea ceremony, the host cleans the tea room and surrounding gardens. Then he makes a fire in the hearth and puts the water on to boil. When the guests arrive, he carries in the tea bowl, tea caddy, utensils for tending the fire, incense burner, and other necessary tools. After preparing the tea in a historical ritual, the host serves each guest. Finally, he removes all utensils and bows to guests, the signal that the ceremony is over.

**sent
style
33c**

(3)   Unnecessary *that, who,* and *which* clauses

When revising prose, look for adjective clauses that begin with *that, who,* or *which* followed by a form of the verb *be* (*that is, who are, which were,* etc.). Frequently, these are empty words that can be deleted. The deletion converts this kind of clause to a word or phrase—a more efficient structure.

UNNECESSARY CLAUSE: The teacher had a smile that was skeptical.

REVISED: The teacher had a skeptical smile.

UNNECESSARY CLAUSE: W. C. Fields often played swindlers who were dedicated to the rule "never give a sucker an even break."

REVISED: W. C. Fields often played swindlers dedicated to the rule "never give a sucker an even break."

UNNECESSARY CLAUSE: Radon, which is a radioactive gas that forms naturally underground, can seep into buildings.

REVISED: Radon, a radioactive gas that forms naturally underground, can seep into buildings.

(4) Excessive verb forms

If a sentence seems congested and difficult to follow, check it to see whether it contains too many verb forms. Any verb form—main verb, infinitive, or participle—is the potential basis for a sentence. As a result, the addition of each verb form to a sentence complicates the structure. Consider, for instance, the following sentence with four verb forms.

> Residents who reveal in the city's tradition of eccentricity expect 25,000 visitors to join in the dancing under the palm trees.

Embedded are four potential sentences.

> Residents reveal in the city's tradition of eccentricity.

> Residents expect 25,000 visitors.

> The visitors will join in.

> The visitors will dance under the palm trees.

Because there are only four verbs, the sentence is not unduly complicated. But when too many verb forms are packed into a sentence, the structure will groan and collapse under its own weight, as in this sentence from a government document.

> EXCESSIVE VERB FORMS
>
> After conducting surveys concerning public opinion toward automated highway systems, the department decided to abandon plans to allocate funds for studying such systems and is investigating mass transit systems that might help to alleviate congestion on highways leading into metropolitan areas.

Asking a reader to plow through eleven ideas in one sentence is simply asking too much. The solution is to split the sentence into smaller units and to eliminate some of the empty verbs that contribute nothing to the meaning. For example, *conducting surveys* can be expressed as *surveying; to allocate funds for studying* can be expressed as *to fund studies.* And because *decide to* and *help to* do not contribute information or clarity, they can be eliminated.

> REVISED
>
> After surveying public opinion toward automated highway systems, the department abandoned plans to fund studies of such

systems. Instead, the department is investigating mass transit systems that might alleviate congestion on highways leading into metropolitan areas.

Now the first sentence has four verb forms, and the second has three. The result is a more streamlined passage that is easier to read.

(5) A clear connection between subject and verb

To understand a sentence readily, a reader must make a swift connection between the subject and its verb. If too many words intervene between the two, the vital connection is obscured, and the reader must grope for the sense. In the following example, 14 words intervene between the subject (*Second City*) and the verb (*has launched*).

OBSCURE CONNECTION: Second City, originally a group of University of Chicago students who formed an improvisational repertory company, has launched an astonishing number of our best comic actors.

Since most sentences can be revised in several ways, the revision you choose depends on the meaning you want to convey. For instance, to emphasize *Second City,* the subject of the preceding example, you should probably leave it at the beginning—a place of emphasis. In this case, a possibility is to split the sentence. The original subject plus the intervening words could be made into a complete sentence. Adding a little transition between the two sentences would make their relationship clear.

CLEAR CONNECTION: Second City was originally a group of University of Chicago students who formed an improvisational repertory company. Since its origin, the group has launched an astonishing number of our best comic actors.

To emphasize *comic actors* instead of *Second City,* you could shift to a passive sentence. In this version, the original subject and intervening words move to the end, and the new subject *an astonishing number of our best comic actors* is now closer to its verb.

CLEAR CONNECTION:	An astonishing number of our best comic actors have been launched by Second City, originally a group of University of Chicago students who formed an improvisational repertory company.

In the next example, 29 words separate the subject (*police officers*) from its verb (*are*).

OBSCURE CONNECTION:	Police officers, who are apparently the only members of our society with legitimate excuses to use an assortment of deadly weapons and to drive fast with lights flashing and sirens blaring, are the favorite subjects of television writers.

Because the subject and the subject complement (*favorite subjects*) are interchangeable, switching the two elements can clarify the sentence.

CLEAR CONNECTION:	The favorite subjects of television writers are police officers, who are apparently the only members of our society with legitimate excuses to use an assortment of deadly weapons and to drive fast with lights flashing and sirens blaring.

If this solution seems unappealing, an alternative is to rewrite the original intervening words as an adverb clause and move it to the beginning of the sentence. Thus, you bring together the subject and verb.

CLEAR CONNECTION:	Because they are apparently the only members of society with legitimate excuses to drive fast, blare sirens, flash lights, and knock heads, police officers are the favorite subjects of television writers.

A compound subject, especially one containing modifiers, can be so cumbersome that the subject-verb connection is obscured.

OBSCURE CONNECTION:	Osteoclasts, dismantling cells that destroy old bone, and osteoblasts, construction cells that

help form new bone, combine to create a continuous remodeling process.

The complete subject contains the simple subjects (*osteoclasts, osteoblasts*) as well as the appositives (*dismantling cells, construction cells*) and adjective clauses (*that destroy . . . , that help . . .*).
This lengthy construction overwhelms the verb (*combine*). One
way to solve the problem is to move the shorter noun phrase from
the end to the subject position.

CLEAR CONNECTION: A continuous remodeling process results from a
combination of osteoclasts, dismantling cells that
destroy old bone, and osteoblasts, construction
cells that help form new bone.

Another way to clarify the connection between subject and verb is vi-
sual: parentheses can help the reader isolate the subjects and "read
around" the appositives. Also, this solution eliminates four commas.

CLEAR CONNECTION: Osteoclasts (dismantling cells that destroy old
bone) and osteoblasts (construction cells that help
form new bone) combine to create a continuous
remodeling process.

If the sentence still sounds cumbersome, it can be split, expanding
the original subject to one sentence and the original predicate to
another. Again, enclosing the appositives in parentheses reduces
commas.

CLEAR CONNECTION: Dismantling cells (osteoclasts) destroy old bone,
whereas construction cells (osteoblasts) help form
new bone. This combination creates a continuous
remodeling process.

As the examples demonstrate, the problem with long sentences is frequently not the length itself but rather the distance between the subject and the verb. Thus, when you revise your
writing, pay attention to the subject-verb connection; make sure it
is immediately clear. In the process, you will also streamline your
prose, making it easier to read.

33d FIGURES OF SPEECH

Figures of speech communicate through comparison or association rather than through literal meaning. For example, the familiar expression *shed light on the matter* is not literal, but figurative. No reader would think of light in its actual sense of electromagnetic radiation. Instead readers make this association: *light* makes things clearer, more visible; therefore *shed light* means *make clear.* The concreteness and vividness of effective figures of speech can often communicate more directly and more intensely than abstractions and generalizations.

Probably the most common figures of speech are metaphor, simile, personification, and hyperbole. In a metaphor, two dissimilar things are said or implied to be the same. Thus, one thing (usually unfamiliar or abstract) becomes clearer because of its similarity with the other thing (usually familiar or concrete). For example, Churchill uses the concrete *tossing sea* and *firm ground* to contrast two abstract ideas.

> I pass with relief from the tossing sea of Cause and Theory to the firm ground of Result and Fact. (Winston Churchill, *The Malakand Field Force*)

In some metaphors the abstract ideas are not expressed but suggested. For example, Canby uses the concrete *fabric* to suggest the abstract idea of structure—something holding writing together. He uses *jelly* to suggest the idea of a formless mass—something without shape or structure.

> Without the support of reasoned thought the fabric of writing may collapse into a jelly of words. (Henry Seidel Canby, *Better Writing*)

Like the metaphor, the simile compares two dissimilar actions or things. Unlike the metaphor, the simile must include the comparative word *like* or *as.*

SIMILE WITH *LIKE:*   Like a monster of the sea, the nuclear-powered research submarine NR-1 prowls the twilit depth of the Bahamas during a practice dive. (Emory Kristof, "NR-1, The Navy's Inner-Space Shuttle," *National Geographic*)

SIMILE WITH *AS:*   Humor can be dissected, as a frog can, but the thing dies in the process and the innards are discouraging to any but the pure scientist. (E. B. White, "Some Remarks on Humor," *The Second Tree from the Corner*)

A personification is a special type of metaphor in which something not human (animal, object, place, idea) is given some human characteristic: *patient forest, marriage of flavors, eloquence of the museum, heart of the atom, sister continent.* In the following quotation, the writer personifies the winds:

> I'm alone here for much of the summer, these hot winds my only dancing partner. (Gretel Ehrlich, "A Season of Portraits")

A hyperbole is an exaggeration. For example, instead of being literal (*they spend too much money*), a writer can intensify the reader's awareness of size by writing a hyperbole (*the national defense budget couldn't pay their bills for one month*).

Although figures of speech are common in poetry and fiction, they should be used only sparingly in nonfiction. If you do use occasional figures of speech, try to avoid those that seem inappropriately exaggerated ("the fraternity system is a cancer, malignant and festering, which must be excised") or trite ("he is a stubborn as a mule"). Instead, try to choose those that help to clarify and enliven your writing.

33e SOUND AND RHYTHM

All human beings respond to the sounds of words and phrases. Children in the process of learning language constantly engage in sound play. They chant in games: *Red Rover, Red Rover, send Rachel right over; Cinderella, dressed in yellow, went upstairs to kiss her fellow.* They experiment with tongue twisters: *Peter Piper picked a peck of pickled peppers.* They show off with Pig Latin: *An-cay ou-yay eak-spay is-thay?* They delight in spoonerisms: *Mardon me padam; this pie is occupewed. Allow me to sew you to another sheet.*

Most adults rarely indulge in sound play just for fun, but they do respond to the music of the language. Television advertising, for instance, relies heavily on sound gimmicks to sell products and ensure that consumers remember brand names and slogans. Politicians use sounds and rhythmic patterns to capture the emotions of audiences. And of course, sound and rhythm help separate poetry from prose.

English speakers seem to respond to certain sounds in rather predictable ways. For example, /j/ and /ch/ often suggest noise (*jabber, jingle, chime, chirp*). Short words that end in /p/, /t/, and /k/ have a crisp, staccato effect (*pop, tap, pat, whack*). Repetition of /l/ can produce a liquid effect (*lily, lullaby, lyrical*). The sequence of /uh/ or /ih/ plus an /f/ and a /y/ can make a word seem as light as air (*fluffy, puffy, whiffy*).

In addition to individual sounds, the language also has phrasal rhythms that can wed sound to ideas. For example, phrases with lots of unstressed syllables seem to move fast: *It's funny how rapidly phrases go running along on the page.* Phrases made up mostly of stressed syllables seem to move much slower: *Like gunmen at high noon, some words walk slow.*

In the following excerpt from *An Essay on Criticism,* Alexander Pope admirably demonstrates how sound can reinforce sense. The first two lines state Pope's thesis—that a writer must deliberately make use of sound symbolism.

(1) 'Tis not enough no harshness gives offense,

(2) The sound must seem an echo to the sense:

(3) Soft is the strain when Zephyr gently blows,

(4) And the smooth stream in smoother numbers flows;

(5) But when loud surges lash the sounding shore,

(6) The hoarse, rough verse should like a torrent roar:

(7) When Ajax strives some rock's vast weight to throw,

(8) The line too labors, and the words move slow;

(9) Not so when swift Camilla scours the plain,

(10) Flies o'er the unbending corn, and skims along the main.

In the third line of the excerpt, the repetition of /s/ suggests the sighing of the wind. In the fourth, the /sm/ and /st/ make silk-like sounds, and the long vowels in *smooth, stream, smoother,* and *flows* make the line flow slowly. The /g/, /sh/, and /r/ sounds in lines (5) and (6) echo the noise of the surf pounding the shore. Lines (7) and (8) have many more stressed than unstressed syllables and so seem to have *vast weight* and to *move slow.* In lines (9) and (10), the predominance of unstressed syllables makes words *skim along.* Thus Pope makes the sound *an echo to the sense.*

Another technique writers use for rhythmic effect is repetition of words and phrases. Consider Winston Churchill's famous "Dunkirk" speech before the House of Commons during World War II. The repetition of *we shall* and *we shall fight* sets up a cadence, culminating in the bold line *we shall never surrender.*

> We shall not flag or fail. We shall go on to the end. We shall fight in France, we shall fight on the seas and oceans, we shall fight with growing confidence and growing strength in the air, we shall defend our island, whatever the cost may be, we shall fight on the beaches, we shall fight on the landing grounds, we shall fight in the fields and in the streets, we shall fight in the hills; we shall never surrender.

sent style 33e

In the next example, Adlai Stevenson not only repeats the words *rule* and *law* but also repeats a structure: compound nouns joined by *and.*

> As citizens of this democracy, you are the rulers and the ruled, the law givers and the law-abiding, the beginning and the end.

To achieve this moving passage about the carrying of the Olympic flame across the country in 1984, Lance Morrow uses sound to complement sense.

> The flame came fluttering out of the darkness into an early morning light. Americans in bathrobes would sometimes stand by the sides of two-lane roads, and as a runner carried the Olympic torch toward them, they would signal thumbs up and break the country silence with a soft, startling cheer. Their faces would glow with a complex light—a patriotism both palpable and chastened, a kind of reawakened warmth, something fetched from a long way back.

The passage begins with the repetition of /f/ sounds, suggesting softness, the way the flame must have looked in the *early morning light.* In the second sentence, Morrow uses a number of /s/ sounds, again suggesting softness. He ends the sentence with *a soft, startling cheer,* startling the reader with an unusual idea—that something soft can also be startling. The rhythm of the last sentence is made interesting by the three appositives after the dash, which have a chantlike quality. Also the choice of the verb *fetched* is perfect. It is a crisp word, a no-nonsense word; and it is an old-fashioned word, appropriate for something from a long way back. The passage ends with three, single-syllable words to slow the movement, *long way back.* And the final word ends with the crack of a /k/.

As the examples indicate, effective writing is not merely clear and correct. It also sounds good. You may not be able to manipulate the sounds of the language with the expertise of the writers quoted here. You should, nevertheless, practice listening to what you write. Read it aloud. Try several versions. Pick the one that sounds the best, the one that is "an echo to the sense."

sent
style
33e

A

SPELLING

SP

The English spelling system is often criticized for its "inconsistencies," that is, for its failure to reflect pronunciation accurately. For example, the pronunciation of the word *answer* does not include a /w/ sound, and the pronunciation of the word *night* does not include either a /g/ or an /h/ sound. The sound "ah" can be spelled with an *a* (as in *father*) or an *o* (as in *not*). A *d* sometimes represents the sound /d/ (as in *bagged*) and sometimes the sound /t/ (as in *jumped*). In other words, many English words are not pronounced as their spellings might indicate.

One reason for the inconsistencies is the tendency of English to borrow words from other languages. These words, such as the French *naive* or the Dutch *yacht,* reflect the spelling systems of those languages rather than of our own. But receptiveness to foreign words is one of the strengths of English, making it flexible, adaptable, able to survive. Spelling peculiarities seem a small price to pay for that strength.

Another reason for inconsistencies in the English spelling system is the large number of regional dialects, which frequently have differing pronunciations of the same words. Thus, English spelling often seems to contradict phonetics. But it must. If our spelling were phonetic, English speakers from different regions would have to spell words differently. Consequently, a New Yorker would have to struggle to read an Atlanta newspaper, and written communication between an American and an Australian would require translation.

In addition, the pronunciation of English has changed throughout history. To reflect pronunciation accurately, spelling would have to change over the years, and these changes would create a very inefficient writing system. The written records of the past would too quickly become obscure: knowledge of law, history, and literature, for instance, would be available only to those who knew the old tongues.

Obviously, the primary requirement of a spelling system is not that it be logical but that it be as stable as possible from dialect to dialect and from era to era. Furthermore, it is imperative that you observe the system, no matter how illogical it seems. To most readers in the worlds of business, commerce, and scholarship, spelling is a mark of a person's education, sense of responsibility, and even intelligence. Therefore, you cannot afford to take a casual attitude toward spelling; it is to your professional advantage to take spelling seriously.

SPa   TIPS FOR IMPROVING SPELLING

SPa

Some people seem to have a natural talent for spelling, an ability that allows them to visualize words correctly. These people can simply look at commonly used words and know immediately if the spelling is correct. Thus, natural spellers rely on dictionaries to spell only unusual or technical words. But many people do not have this talent and instead must always be alert to the possibility of misspelled words in everything they write. If you fall into this second category of spellers, you may want to adopt some or all of the following five techniques for improving spelling.

(1)   Use the dictionary.

The best way to solve spelling problems is to use a dictionary. Poor spellers often counter this suggestion with "If I don't know how to spell a word, I can't find it in the dictionary." This assumption usually is not true. With a few exceptions (such as *kn, ph, sc*), an initial consonant is almost always predictable. And initial vowels are almost as easy to predict as consonants—a word like *envision* may begin with either an *i* or an *e,* but it certainly is not likely to begin with an *a,* an *o,* or a *u.* Thus, finding the right section of the dictionary requires little effort. At that point, the word can be located rather quickly.

Suppose, for example, you want to look up the correct spelling of a common word like *concept*. From its sound, you can guess that the first letter is going to be *c* or *k*. The first vowel, if not *a,* is likely to be *o*. It is certain that an *n* will follow that vowel. Next comes an /s/ sound, rarely spelled any way except *s* or *c*. After that comes a sound usually represented by an *e*. Finally, the *p* and *t* are almost completely predictable. In summary, if *concept* is not in the *k*'s, it will certainly be in the *c*'s. And from that point, it should take only a few minutes to track the word down.

(2)   Practice pronunciation.

Once you have found a word in the dictionary, be sure you know exactly how to pronounce it. To fix the pronunciation in your mind, say the word aloud several times, pausing between syllables. Then say the word aloud a number of times without pausing. If you have difficulty understanding the pronunciation symbols of dictionaries, you might try the *Oxford American,* which uses an Americanized pronunciation key much simpler than those of most other dictionaries.

SPa

(3)   Practice writing the word.

After you are sure of the pronunciation, write the word a dozen times or so. This practice not only will help fix the word in your motor memory but also will let you see how it looks in your own handwriting. If possible, also type the word a number of times to help you recognize it in print. When you know a word in sound, script, and type, you are not likely to forget how to spell it.

(4)   Keep a word list.

You might find it helpful to keep a list of words that you tend to misspell. You can include those words that instructors have marked on your papers as well as words you must frequently look up in the dictionary. Studying your list and using it when you edit papers will help you master the words you find particularly troublesome.

You can also consult lists of commonly misspelled words, such as those at the end of this chapter. You can single out the words you do not spell with confidence and add them to your individual list.

(5)   Study spelling patterns.

Get familiar with spelling patterns, also called "spelling rules." Remember, however, that a rule in spelling is an observation—a description of a pattern that recurs in the language, not an iron-clad law never violated.

SPb   SPELLING PATTERNS

Inconsistencies do exist between the spelling system and the sound system. And bizarre spellings do occur, although usually with scientific terms, esoteric words, and proper names. But on the whole, patterns predominate.

SPb

(1)   Silent *e* with long vowels

Many words end with an unpronounced letter *e*—commonly called "silent *e*." Actually, the silent *e* is a key to pronunciation, as the following pairs of words illustrate.

van/vane	lop/elope
gap/gape	dot/dote
spit/spite	occur/cure
forbid/abide	sum/consume

The word pairs show that silent *e* follows a stressed (accented) syllable with a long vowel, a vowel that requires the muscles in the mouth to tense during pronunciation.

ee in *theme*	*ay* in *mate*
oo in *rude*	*iy* in *bite*
oh in *hope*	

The *e* may attach to a single-syllable word or to a word stressed on the last syllable.

The absence of the *e* on a stressed (accented) syllable indicates a short vowel. Short vowels like the following allow the muscles in the mouth to remain lax during pronunciation.

ih in *fit*	*aw* in *bought*
eh in *bet*	*ah* in *spa*
uh in *cup*	*aeh* in *mat*

The pattern is as follows:

- stressed syllable with long vowel: silent *e* (*tape, ride*)

- stressed syllable with short vowel: no *e* (*tap, rid*)

The rule does not apply when the stressed final syllable has

- more than one vowel in a row (*boom, appear*)

- more than one consonant in a row (*comb, dodge*)

(2)   Silent *e* with suffixes

SPb

When a suffix is added to a word that ends in silent *e*, the *e* drops if the suffix begins with a vowel and remains if the suffix begins with a consonant.

BASE	SUFFIX WITH VOWEL, DROP THE *E*	SUFFIX WITH CONSONANT, RETAIN THE *E*
arrange	arranging	arrangement
like	likable	likely
sincere	sincerity	sincerely
name	naming	nameless
intense	intensify	intensely
tone	tonal	toneless
waste	wasting	wasteful
excite	exciting	excitement
love	lovable	lovely

EXCEPTION: Three common exceptions to this pattern are *truly, argument,* and *judgment.*

EXCEPTION: The letter *c* may represent the hard sound /kuh/ as in *cup* or the soft sound /s/ as in *circle*. The letter *g* may represent the hard sound /guh/ as in *gum* or the soft sound /juh/ as in *gentle*. With the suffixes *-able* and *-ous*, silent *e* is retained in two situations:

- After soft *c:*   service/serviceable
                     notice/noticeable

- After soft *g:*   outrage/outrageous
                     advantage/advantageous

(3)   Doubled consonants with verbs

With regular verbs, the past tense and past participle are made by adding *-d* or *-ed* to the base form. (See 4a.) The spelling pattern is as follows.

- When the verb ends in a stressed syllable and a single consonant, the consonant is doubled and *-ed* is added (*pin/pinned, uncap/uncapped*).

- When the verb ends in a stressed syllable and a silent *e,* a *-d* is added to the base (*dine/dined, escape/escaped*).

BASE FORM	PAST FORM AND PAST PARTICIPLE
bar	barred
bare	bared
refer	referred
interfere	interfered
grip	gripped
gripe	griped
occur	occurred
cure	cured
mat	matted
mate	mated

The present participle is made by adding *-ing* to the base form of the verb. The spelling pattern is as follows.

SPb

- When the verb ends in a stressed syllable and a single consonant, the consonant is doubled and *-ing* is added (*pin/pinning, uncap/uncapping*).

- When the verb ends in a stressed syllable and a silent *e,* the *e* is dropped and *-ing* is added (*dine/dining, escape/escaping*).

BASE FORM	PRESENT PARTICIPLE
bar	barring
bare	baring
refer	referring
interfere	interfering
grip	gripping
gripe	griping
occur	occurring
cure	curing
mat	matting
mate	mating

(4) Doubled consonants with prefixes, suffixes, and compounds

SPb

When a prefix ends with the same consonant that the base begins with, both consonants are retained.

dis + satisfied	dissatisfied
over + rate	overrate
un + necessary	unnecessary

When a suffix begins with the same consonant that the base ends with, both consonants are retained.

mental + ly	mentally
stubborn + ness	stubbornness
heel + less	heelless

When the first part of a compound word ends with the same consonant that the second part begins with, both consonants are retained.

book + keeper   bookkeeper
beach + head   beachhead
room + mate   roommate

(5) *I* before *e*

Almost everyone knows the "i before e" school rhyme:

"I before *e* except after *c*
or when sounding like *a* as in *neighbor* and *weigh."*

The rule in this rhyme works with many *ie* words.

achieve   relief
believe   thief
friend   view

It also works with many *c* plus *ei* words.

ceiling   deceive
conceit   perceive
conceive   receive

And *ei* does appear in words that sound like *weigh.*

eight   neighbor
feign   sleigh
freight   veil

But many words without the *c* or the *weigh* sound are spelled with *ei.*

either   neither
foreign   seize
height   weird

The rhyme does cover words like *believe* and *receive,* but it is not completely reliable. The best solution to the *ie/ei* problem is the dictionary.

(6)   *-Cede, -ceed,* and *-sede*

Since *-sede, -ceed,* and *-cede* are pronounced identically, writers sometimes confuse them, spelling *proceed,* for example, as *procede.* Mastering the "cede" words, however, is a simple matter of memorizing the spelling of four words: *supersede, exceed, proceed,* and *succeed.*

> *Supersede* ends in *-sede.*
> *Exceed, proceed,* and *succeed* end in *-ceed.*
> All the rest end in *-cede: recede, secede, concede,* and so on.

SPc   LISTS OF FREQUENTLY MISSPELLED WORDS

Several lists of frequently misspelled words are grouped according to the characteristics that cause problems.

Easily Confused Words

accept/except	dairy/diary
advice/advise	descent/dissent
affect/effect	device/devise
all ready/already	die/dye
all together/altogether	ensure/insure
allusion/illusion	envelop/envelope
ally/alley	formally/formerly
aloud/allowed	forth/fourth
altar/alter	foul/fowl
analysis/analyze	hear/here
ascent/assent	heard/herd
assistance/assistants	idol/idle
board/bored	incidence/incidents
breath/breathe	its/it's
bridal/bridle	know/no
capital/capitol	later/latter
censor/censure	lead/led
choose/chose	lessen/lesson
cite/site/sight	lightning/lightening
cloths/clothes	loan/lone
coarse/course	loose/lose

complement/compliment
conscience/conscious
council/counsel
currant/current
passed/past
peace/piece
personal/personnel
presence/presents
principal/principle
prophecy/prophesy
quiet/quit/quite
right/write
road/rode
sail/sale
shone/shown
stationary/stationery
statue/stature

maybe/may be
moral/morale
muscle/mussel
naval/navel
straight/strait
than/then
their/there/they're
through/threw
to/too/two
vain/vein
waist/waste
wait/weight
weather/whether
were/we're/where
which/witch
who's/whose
your/you're

Words with *s, ss, c,* and *sc*

SPc

absence
accessible
adolescent
ascend
assassinate
assistance
associate
conscience
conscious
decision
necessary
nuisance
occasion
permissible
persistence
physical
possession
reminisce
resistance

descend
discussion
ecstasy
embarrass
expense
fascinate
insistent
license
mischievous
muscle
scarcity
sincerely
source
succeed
succession
suspicious
unconscious
unnecessary
vicious

Words with *-able* or *-ible*

acceptable
admissible

incredible
irresistible

advisable   irritable
~~believable~~   ~~likeable~~
changeable   movable
collapsible   noticeable
comfortable   peaceable
compatible   permissible
credible   possible
dependable   probable
edible   profitable
eligible   resistible
flammable   responsible
flexible   separable
gullible   visible
impossible

Words with *-ence* or *-ance*

abhorrence   dependence
abundance   difference
acquaintance   endurance
appearance   existence
appliance   guidance
assistance   independence
attendance   inference
conference   insistence
deference   intelligence
defiance   interference
magnificence   prominence
maintenance   providence
nuisance   reference
occurrence   resemblance
patience   significance
permanence   surveillance
persistence   temperance
preference   tolerance
prevalence   vengeance

SPc

B

ENGLISH AS A SECOND LANGUAGE

ESL

Children acquire language very easily. Any languages children hear often, they learn to speak; and any languages children read often, they learn to write. Furthermore, children can learn language without any formal study because they internalize the grammatical rules as they hear and see individual sentences.

But for most adults, language is not so simply acquired. Although hearing and seeing a language is essential, most adults also need at least some formal study of grammar. In other words, they need information about the underlying system of a language.

This appendix is designed to help non-native speakers understand the most basic elements underlying English grammar: the components of the noun phrase and the verb phrase. In addition, the appendix includes methods for recognizing complete sentences and for forming questions and negatives. The appendix is best used along with Parts I and II of this textbook, which explain and illustrate grammatical principles. Therefore, you should pay attention to the cross references that point to other sections of the book, and you should review material from Parts I and II whenever you need additional information.

ESLa   THE NOUN PHRASE

The term **noun phrase** refers to a single word or a group of words that can function in a noun position—such as subject of a verb, object of a verb, object of a preposition, and so forth. A noun phrase may contain a single noun or a series of modifiers plus a noun. (See Chapter 1.)

information
much information
not much useable information

houses
the houses
the first three red brick houses on Baker Street

announcer
the radio announcer
the same tiresome radio announcer

milk
twice the milk
twice the milk in the recipe

memories
Jane's memories
some of Jane's most pleasant childhood memories

As the examples show, the noun phrase can be expanded from a single word to a rather long string of words. The order of the words, however, is not random but fairly fixed. If you think of a noun phrase as a series of positions, you can more easily discover the proper order. Sections ESLb through ESLf explain the positions and the kinds of items that may appear in those positions.

ESLb

ESLb   HEAD NOUNS

A **head noun** is the obligatory position in a noun phrase (ESLa). All other words in the noun phrase depend upon it grammatically; that is, they "modify" the head noun. Furthermore, the modifiers depend to some extent on whether the head noun is a count noun or a non-count noun.

(1)   Count Nouns

A **count noun** names something that can be counted: *one desk, two desks, three desks,* and so forth. Therefore, a count noun usually has a singular and a plural form. In the singular form, a count noun requires a determiner: *a desk, my desk* (ESLc). In the plural form, however, a count noun can appear with or without a determiner: *desks, the desks.* Remember that count nouns can be preceded by *many* but not by *much.*

> POSSIBLE: her <u>many accomplishments</u>
>
> IMPOSSIBLE: her <u>much accomplishments</u>

(2)   Non-count nouns

A **non-count noun** names something that cannot be counted: *news, information, furniture, butter, milk, homework.* Non-count nouns have no plurals, but you can refer to their parts or amounts by using a phrase that indicates measurement: *half of the butter, some of the information, two pieces of furniture.* Remember that non-count nouns can be preceded by *much* but not by *many.*

> POSSIBLE: <u>much good luck</u>
>
> IMPOSSIBLE: <u>many good luck</u>

ESLc

ESLc DETERMINERS

A **determiner** indicates that a noun will appear. The noun may not immediately follow the determiner, but it will appear at some point. Determiners can be classified as articles, demonstrative pronouns, and possessives.

(1)   The indefinite article

The **indefinite article** is *a/an.* The *a* form precedes words that begin with a consonant sound (not necessarily a written consonant): *a* *tree, a book, a unicorn* [pronounced *yew-nuh-corn*]. The *an* form precedes words that begin with a vowel sound (not necessarily a written vowel): *an apple, an uncle, an herb* [pronounced *erb*].

Since *a/an* means roughly "one," it accompanies singular count nouns (ESLb.1); it is not appropriate with non-count nouns. Use *a/an* when you introduce a singular count noun into the discourse. Do not use *a/an* with a noun you have already mentioned or with a synonym of that noun. Otherwise, you mislead the reader to think that the noun is new and has not been previously mentioned.

> POSSIBLE: Senator Perez is sponsoring a bill [first mention] for reforming the income tax system. If passed, the bill [the same bill] would establish a "flat tax," with everyone paying the same rate regardless of income. Because the proposal [synonym for the same bill] is quite sensible, it is sure to be defeated.

> IMPOSSIBLE AND   Senator Perez is sponsoring a bill for reforming the
> MISLEADING: income tax system. If passed, a bill would establish a "flat tax," with everyone paying the same rate regardless of income. Because a proposal is quite sensible, it is sure to be defeated.

(2)   The definite article

The **definite article** is *the*. This article can precede both count and non-count nouns and both singular and plural nouns. Most of its numerous uses are explained below.

ESLc

- Use *the* with a common noun (see 1a) that has been previously mentioned in the discourse. You use *the* regardless of whether the noun appears in the same form or as a synonym.

  > Low-maintenance landscaping is easy if you stick to ground cover and shrubs. The ground cover provides a neat appearance and discourages weeds, while the shrubs provide design and create interest.

  > Gold is one of the oldest marks of wealth. From the earliest times, possession of the bright yellow metal [synonym] indicated prestige.

- Use *the* with a common noun when a modifier after the noun makes it specific.

The car in the garage belongs to Andrew.

The people downstairs moved into the apartment yesterday.

The package that we received on Thursday was left in the rain.

- Use *the* with a common noun that names something universally known or familiar in everyday life.

    At most parties, everyone gravitates toward the kitchen.

    The siesta is my favorite Mexican custom.

- Use *the* with an ordinal number (*first, second,* etc.).

    I took the first empty seat on the plane.

    He was the third applicant on the list.

- Use *the* with the superlative degree of an adjective (*best, biggest,* etc.).

    She got an award for the best science project.

    Geography is the most interesting of all my courses.

- Use *the* with a plural proper name.

    The first guests to arrive were the Powells.

    The Gleesons opened a bed-and-breakfast inn.

ESLc

- Use *the* with a public institution.

    My group toured the Library of Congress.

    The Smithsonian Institute issues a sale catalogue.

- Use *the* with a unique phenomenon or unique individual—in other words, when there can be only one.

    Some early astronomers thought the sun revolved around the earth.

    While in Rome, he sought an audience with the Pope.

    How is the Israeli prime minister chosen?

    Some cultures trace ancestry through the mother.

(3) Demonstrative pronouns

The **demonstrative pronouns** are *this, these, that,* and *those.* (See 2b.) They are used primarily to refer to nouns previously mentioned in the discourse or as a kind of summary substitute for material that has preceded. In general, use *this* and *these* with present and future time and *that* and *those* with past time.

> Leaf-cutter ants cultivate a fungus in large underground gardens. When a queen ant moves on to start a new colony, she takes a pellet of this fungus with her.

> When hiking, do not neglect to pack food, water, matches, and a first-aid kit. These items can save your life.

> As Napoleon approached Moscow, the Russians retreated and destroyed everything in their path—leaving the French without food or shelter from the freezing winds. That disaster was the beginning of the end for Napoleon.

> A car key and a house key were found at the crime scene, but police did not know whether those keys belonged to the victim or to the murderer.

(4) Possessives

As determiners, **possessives** may be pronouns or proper nouns.

ESLc

PERSONAL PRONOUNS:	*my, your, his, her, its, our, their*
INDEFINITE PRONOUNS:	*one's, anyone's, nobody's, somebody's,* etc.
PROPER NAMES:	*Tan's, George's, Asia's, Panama's,* etc.

> All players must turn in their score cards.

> Medical records should not be open to everyone's scrutiny.

> Thailand's Buddhist temples are brilliantly colored.

Possessive common nouns do not ordinarily appear first in a noun phrase but instead are preceded by a determiner.

> The university's funding was cut back.

My church's congregation is very young.

The weather controls a farmer's life.

A few possessive common nouns, however, can appear first in a noun phrase. These possessives usually indicate time.

Have you heard today's news?

They always left the mountains at summer's end.

ESLd   PRE-DETERMINERS

When a **pre-determiner** appears in the noun phrase, it comes first—regardless of whether the phrase includes a determiner. Usually, pre-determiners indicate a quantity, and most of them are phrases. Some pre-determiners precede count nouns only, some precede non-count nouns only, and some can precede either. The lists below include the most common pre-determiners.

Preceding count nouns only: *both, both of, either of, neither of, few of, a few of, each, each of, several of, many of, not many of,* etc.

Either of the books will be acceptable.

Both the proposals were excellent.

Each table was set for four guests.

Not many of his ideas were usable.

Preceding non-count nouns only: *a great deal of, much of, not much of, a little of,* etc.

The project will take only a little of your time.

Much of the wood was cherry.

A great deal of the jewelry was stolen.

Preceding both count and non-count nouns: *all, all of, any of, some of, a lot of, half of, a quart of, a bowl of, twice, two (three, four) times,* etc.

They expect twice the number [count] of runners as participated last year.

The agency received <u>twice</u> the money [non-count] requested.

<u>Some of</u> his answers [count] were hilarious.

<u>Some of</u> the information [non-count] was misleading.

We ate <u>a quart of</u> strawberries [count].

We drank <u>a quart of</u> milk [non-count].

NOTE: Pre-determiners that include the phrase *part of* can precede either count or non-count nouns, as long as the nouns are singular.

<u>One part of</u> the paper [count] was missing.

<u>Part of</u> the fabric [non-count] was faded.

<u>A part of</u> the problem is morale [non-count].

ESLe   PRE-NOUN MODIFIERS

In between the determiner and the head noun, various other positions are possible in a noun phrase. The items in these positions are usually called **pre-noun** (or **pre-nominal**) **modifiers** because they come before the noun and modify or describe it. Occasionally, the order of the positions might vary slightly. But by and large, variation is rare, and the order is fixed.

Of course, you are not likely to find a noun phrase with all positions filled. It would be too long, too cumbersome, and probably too silly. Nevertheless, all the positions described below are grammatically possible as long as they are filled in the order listed.

ESLe

1. **Specifiers:** *same, other, chief, main, principal, primary,* etc.

   the <u>other</u> subjects

   both of the <u>principal</u> contributors

2. **Ordinal numbers:** *first, second, third,* etc.
   (Note: *Next* may substitute for an item in the middle of the series and *final* or *last* may substitute for the item at the end.)

   our <u>second</u> meeting

   the <u>last</u> game

3. **Cardinal numbers:** *one, two, three,* etc.

    <u>four</u> bracelets

    the first <u>ten</u> applicants

4. **Superlative adjectives:** *best, worst, least, most, tallest, most valuable,* etc.

    the <u>worst</u> ideas

    the five <u>best</u> performances

5. **Adjectives of size:** *big, huge, enormous, little, medium-sized,* etc.

    an <u>enormous</u> mansion

    several of the <u>small</u> boats

6. **Adjectives of shape:** *square, round, circular, rectangular,* etc.

    the <u>rectangular</u> table

    both of the huge <u>circular</u> driveways

7. **Descriptive adjectives:** *friendly, cruel, obnoxious, extraordinary, thoughtful, kind, beautiful, peculiar, reckless, cautious, peaceful, serene, lazy, clever, stupid, happy, outrageous,* etc.

    a <u>peaceful</u> setting

    their three tiny <u>playful</u> dogs

8. **Adjectives of age:** *old, young, middle-aged, ancient,* etc.

    Luis's reckless <u>young</u> brother

    a lot of lazy <u>old</u> cows

9. **Colors:** *red, green, black, yellow, fuchsia,* etc.

    either of the <u>pink</u> sheets

    all four oblong <u>yellow</u> lanterns

10. **Nationalities:** *German, Honduran, Japanese, Australian,* etc.

    a <u>Portuguese</u> family

    twice the <u>German</u> immigrants

ESLe

11. **Religions:** *Jewish, Protestant, Hindu, Buddhist,* etc.

this large Protestant community

the first Jewish school

12. **Materials:** *gold, silver, wooden, brick, slate,* etc.

an old silver tray

several large concrete barriers

13. **Nouns as modifiers:** *kitchen, fence, heart, tennis, radio,* etc.

my kitchen cabinets

a crooked wooden fence post

ESLf POST-NOUN MODIFIERS

Post-noun modifiers in the noun phrase follow the head noun (ESLb). These modifiers can be single words, prepositional phrases, or adjective clauses.

• Single-word modifiers

Generally, the single-word modifiers locate the noun in time or space—for example, *upstairs, outside, inside, yesterday, tomorrow,* etc.

our first meeting tomorrow

the black limousine outside

a reading room upstairs

• Prepositional phrases

Very often, prepositional phrases also locate the noun in time or space.

a luncheon around noon

the carnival before Lent

a wedding in May

several layers below the surface

their lodge in the Rocky Mountains

the land across the river

ESLf

Of course, prepositional phrases can also express other relationships besides those of time and space. (See 6a.)

> a room with a balcony

> all students except three

> the fall of Rome

> a doll for his daughter

- Adjective clauses

  Adjective clauses are introduced by a relative pronoun (such as *who, which, that*) or a relative adverb (such as *when, why, where*). The relative introducer follows and renames the head noun being modified. (See 7c.2, 21c, and 33a.4.)

  > We need evergreen plants that grow in rocky soil.

  > Spring is the time when study is the hardest.

  > I recommend Yan He, who was my laboratory assistant last fall.

ESLg   THE ACTIVE-VOICE VERB PHRASE

An **active-voice verb** expresses the action of the subject or links the subject to what follows (4e).

> A city employee checks the meters. [*Employee* acts.]

> Firefighters rushed to the blaze. [*Firefighters* act.]

> Juan is an honor student. [*Juan* linked to *student.*]

> The room seems stuffy. [*The room* linked to *stuffy.*]

The **active-voice verb phrase** in English includes four possible verb forms. This section and ESLh–j explain those forms and their proper order. Before reading further, however, you may want to look over Chapter 4, Verbs and Verb Phrases. There you will find information about basic forms, auxiliaries, tense forms, progressive forms, voice, and mood.

Mastering the verb phrase is not difficult if you think of the active-voice verb phrase as four possible positions, in the order shown. Position 4 must be filled; the other three are optional.

1	2	3	4
~~MODAL AUXILIARY~~	*HAVE* ~~AUXILIARY~~	*BE* AUXILIARY	MAIN VERB

Six rules, with no exceptions, govern the phrase.

1. The modal auxiliary must be followed by a base form (*call, bring, go,* etc.)
2. The auxiliary *have* must be followed by a past participle (*called, brought, gone,* etc.).
3. The auxiliary *be* must be followed by a present participle (*calling, bringing, going,* etc.).
4. The main verb, which carries the meaning, must be present.
5. If the modal auxiliary is present, the verb phrase does not show tense.
6. If the modal auxiliary is not present, the first verb in the phrase shows tense.

The following examples show verb phrases in the proper order and form.

- main verb with tense

    Helmuth told the truth.

- modal auxiliary + base form of main verb

    Helmuth should tell the truth.

- *have* with tense + past participle of main verb

    Helmuth has told the truth.

- *be* with tense + present participle of main verb

    Helmuth is telling the truth.

ESLg

- *have* with tense + past participle of *be* + present participle of main verb

    Helmuth had been telling the truth.

- modal auxiliary + base form of *have* + past participle of *be* + present participle of main verb

    Helmuth may have been telling the truth.

Sections ESLi through ESLj discuss in turn the components of the active-voice verb phrase.

ESLh TENSE

English has special verb forms only for the present and past tenses. (See 4c for a complete discussion of verb tense.)

- A **present tense** verb is marked by an *-s* ending when its subject is any singular noun or any singular pronoun except *I* and *you*.

  Abdul writes his family every Monday.

  She wants to photograph the lions.

  It sits in the corner of my grandmother's living room.

  Everyone likes the new student union.

- A **present tense** verb requires the base form when its subject is *I, you,* any plural noun, or any plural pronoun.

  The sisters make all their own clothes.

  I hope you will visit soon.

  You pay at the end of each month.

  We eat at the cafeteria on weekdays.

  Both of them play the piano.

- A regular verb in the **past tense** is marked by *-d* or *-ed* ending regardless of the subject.

  We moved to a new apartment during semester break.

  Antonia helped organize the conference.

  I hiked through Tibet one summer.

- The **past tense** of an irregular verb is not predictable and must be learned. (See *Irregular Verb* in the Glossary of Terms.)

  Thomas forgot to turn off the oven.

  The sun shone so brightly that we could not see.

  The bell in the steeple fell during the hurricane.

ESLh

ESLi   MODAL AUXILIARIES

Modal auxiliaries express concepts such as ability, advisability, and probability. When modals appear in the verb phrase, they come first and do not permit tense. The examples below suggest the uses of modals. Notice that the verb immediately following the modal is always in the base form.

* Ability: *can, could*

    Maria can help you with your algebra.

    The maintenance department could have replaced the carpet.

* Advisability: *should, would, ought to*

    We should leave for the airport an hour before boarding time.

    If I were you, I would stop smoking.

    The school ought to adopt a dress code.

* Necessity: *must*

    The dean must sign your withdrawal slip.

    All data must be analyzed by next week.

* Possibility: *may, might*

    It may snow before nightfall.

    Our professor said that he might drop our lowest grade.

* Prediction: *will*

    The party will be over before we get there.

    You will learn the accounting program in a few days.

* Fact: *will*

    Oil will float on water.

    The recipe will serve eight people.

* Invitation: *shall*

    Shall we go to dinner?

ESLi

ESLj   AUXILIARIES *HAVE* AND *BE*

The **auxiliaries *have*** and ***be*** may appear alone, in combination, or after a modal.

- *have* auxiliary

  Any form of the *have* auxiliary is always followed by a past participle (*seen, hoped, given,* etc.).

  > Her family has lived in Tokyo since 1980.

  > The crowd had dwindled since late afternoon.

- *be* auxiliary

  In the active voice, any form of the *be* auxiliary is always followed by a present participle (*seeing, hoping, giving,* etc.).

  > Susan is taking German this semester.

  > The street vendors were selling handmade pottery.

- *have* and *be* auxiliaries in combination

  When *have* and *be* auxiliaries appear together, *have* comes first, followed by *been.*

  > Susan has been taking German this semester.

  > The street vendors had been selling handmade pottery.

- *have* and *be* auxiliaries after a modal

  After a modal, *have* and *be* appear in the base form.

  > Her family may be living in Tokyo.

  > The crowd must have dwindled.

ESLk   PASSIVE-VOICE VERB PHRASE

The **passive voice** is used to indicate that the subject does not act but instead receives action. (See 4e, 17d, and ESLg.)

> Kyle was given a scholarship. [*Kyle* receives action.]

> The car was badly damaged. [*Car* receives action.]

There are four possible positions in the **passive-voice verb phrase** in the order shown. Positions 3 and 4 must be filled; the other two are optional.

1 MODAL AUXILIARY	2 *HAVE* AUXILIARY	3 *BE* AUXILIARY	4 MAIN VERB

Six rules, with no exceptions, govern the phrase. Compare these rules with those governing the active-voice verb phrase (ESLg).

1. The modal auxiliary must be followed by the base form *have* or the base form *be*.
2. The auxiliary *have* must be followed by the past participle *been*.
3. The auxiliary *be* must appear and must be followed by a past participle (*seen, planned, made, bought,* etc.).
4. The main verb, which carries the meaning, must be present.
5. If the modal auxiliary is present, the verb phrase does not show tense.
6. If the modal auxiliary is not present, the first verb in the phrase shows tense.

The following examples show verb phrases in the proper order and form.

- *be* with tense + past participle of main verb

  The art work was displayed in the park.

- modal auxiliary + *be* + past participle of main verb

  The art work will be displayed in the park.

- *have* with tense + *been* + past participle of main verb

  The art work had been displayed in the park.

- modal auxiliary + base form of *have* + *been* + past participle of main verb

  The art work should have been displayed in the park.

ESL1 *DO* AUXILIARY

Do auxiliary is unique. Its three forms (*do, does, did*) appear only with the base form of the main verb, and they cannot com-

ESL1

bine with other auxiliaries or with modals. Most commonly, the *do* auxiliary is used to form questions and negative sentences (ELSn–p).

> STATEMENT: The committee <u>approved</u> the proposal.
>
> QUESTION: <u>Did</u> the committee <u>approve</u> the proposal?
>
> NEGATIVE: The committee <u>did</u> not <u>approve</u> the proposal.

In addition, *do* can convey emphatic contrast when no other auxiliary or modal is present in the sentence. In conversation, this emphatic contrast often expresses a protest, and the major stress of the sentence is always on the form of *do*.

> FIRST SPEAKER: He doesn't play soccer.
>
> SECOND SPEAKER: Yes, he <u>does</u> play.

The emphatic contrast also appears in written sentences. If read aloud, these sentences would place major stress on the *do* auxiliary.

> The Aztecs had no alphabet; they <u>did</u>, however, develop rebus writing.

> We do not prepare budgets, but we <u>do</u> provide financial consultants.

ESLm   CHAINS OF VERBS

Some main verbs in English are often followed either by an infinitive (the *to* form of the verb) or by a present participle (the *-ing* form of the verb). Thus are formed **chains of verbs.**

> Alicia <u>intended to study</u> medicine.

> We <u>regret losing</u> your order of last week.

> My counselor <u>encouraged</u> me <u>to stay</u> in school.

> She <u>promised to stop pretending</u>.

Verb chains can be divided into categories according to the patterns they produce. The lists below are not complete, but they do indicate the large number of verbs that chain. Note that some verbs appear in more than one category.

- verb + infinitive

agree
decide
fail
forget
hesitate
hope
intend
neglect
offer   } to go
plan
prefer
pretend
promise
refuse
remember
try

- verb + actor + infinitive

allow
ask
convince
encourage
force
hire
instruct
invite   } me to write
permit
persuade
remind
teach
tell
want

ESLm

- verb + actor + infinitive without *to* (base form)

have
let   } him apply
make

Verbs that express perception or observation often follow this pattern.

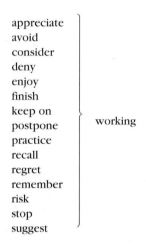

feel
hear
notice
observe
see
watch
} it fall

- verb + participle

appreciate
avoid
consider
deny
enjoy
finish
keep on
postpone
practice
recall
regret
remember
risk
stop
suggest
} working

ESLm

- verb + actor + participle

feel
hear
notice
observe
see
watch
} it burning

The patterns frequently combine to form longer chains. In such cases, the strings of verbs can include infinitives as well as participles.

The labor union refused even to begin to negotiate.

Should we consider trying to replace old equipment?

A doctor convinced my father to start eating properly.

The judges decided to let her finish skating.

If the chains get too long, however, the sentences become awkward.

AWKWARD: Do you remember promising to remind me to finish practicing?

AWKWARD: I wanted to offer to hire someone to teach her to ski.

ESLn   QUESTIONS

Any of the following verb forms can produce a **question** by shifting to the front of the sentence: the main verb *be,* a modal, the *have* auxiliary, or the *be* auxiliary.

She is bilingual. → Is she bilingual?

The sign will blink. → Will the sign blink?

Our pizza has arrived. → Has our pizza arrived?

Kites were invented in China. → Were kites invented in China?

If the verb phrase does not contain a form of *be,* a modal, or *have* auxiliary, you make the question with the *do* auxiliary: do/does/did + subject of sentence + base form of main verb. The appropriate form of *do* depends on the subject of the sentence and the tense of the verb.

ESLn

- For a present tense verb that ends in *-s,* use *does.*

   Mint grows well in sandy soil. → Does mint grow well in sandy soil?

- For a present tense verb that does not end in *-s,* use *do.*

   Wild tigers live in Asia. → Do wild tigers live in Asia?

- For any past tense verb, use *did.*

   Mr. Sato owned the factory. → Did Mr. Sato own the factory?

   Mr. Sato's daughters bought the factory. → Did Mr. Sato's daughters buy the factory?

ESLo NEGATIVE SENTENCES

To make a sentence **negative,** you must alter the positive version of the verb phrase. Basically, there are three possibilities.

1. If verb phrase contains more than one word, insert *not* after the first word or use a negative contraction of the first word.

   My cat <u>will</u> <u>eat</u> lettuce. →

   My cat <u>will</u> <u>not</u> <u>eat</u> lettuce.

   My cat <u>won't</u> <u>eat</u> lettuce.

   The church <u>has</u> <u>been</u> <u>remodeled</u> since its construction. →

   The church <u>has</u> <u>not</u> <u>been</u> <u>remodeled</u> since its construction.

   The church <u>hasn't</u> <u>been</u> <u>remodeled</u> since its construction.

2. If the only verb is a form of *be,* insert *not* after the verb or use a negative contraction of the verb.

   My music professor <u>is</u> a good pianist. →

   My music professor <u>is</u> <u>not</u> a good pianist.

   My music professor <u>isn't</u> a good pianist.

   The beaches <u>are</u> public. →

   The beaches <u>are</u> <u>not</u> public.

   The beaches <u>aren't</u> public.

3. If the only verb is anything except *be,* insert the *do* auxiliary. Use *do/does/did* + *not* + base form of verb, or use a negative contraction of *do/does/did* + base form of verb.

   She <u>makes</u> her pottery on a wheel. →

   She <u>does</u> <u>not</u> <u>make</u> her pottery on a wheel.

   She <u>doesn't</u> <u>make</u> her pottery on a wheel.

   The robins <u>eat</u> the holly berries. →

   The robins <u>do</u> <u>not</u> <u>eat</u> the holly berries.

   The robins <u>don't</u> <u>eat</u> the holly berries.

The movie got good reviews. →

The movie did not get good reviews.

The movie didn't get good reviews.

ESLp   TAG QUESTIONS TO IDENTIFY SENTENCES

One way you can identify a complete sentence is to add a **tag question** at the end. This "tagged on" question asks for a *yes/no* answer.

This class is dull, isn't it?

The lawn hasn't been mowed, has it?

You used my racquet, didn't you?

A tag question begins with one of the following:

* a past or present tense form of the main verb *be* or auxiliary *be: am, is, are, was, were*

* a present or past tense form of the auxiliary *have: have, has, had*

* a present or past tense form of the auxiliary *do: do, does, did*

* a modal auxiliary: *can, will, shall, may, must, might, should, could, would*

The tag-question test is easy to apply. Consider, for example, these six word groups.

ESLp

She is clever.

The car has been repaired.

Non-voters should not complain.

Meeting the deadline will not be possible.

Some oak trees lose their leaves.

You returned the book.

1. Begin the tag question with the main-verb form of *be* or the first auxiliary in the main-verb phrase. If neither exists, supply *do/does* for present time and *did* for past time.

She is clever, is. . . .

The car has been repaired, has. . . .

Non-voters should not complain, should. . . .

Meeting the deadline will not be possible, will. . . .

Some oak trees lose [present time] their leaves, do. . . .

You returned [past time] the book, did. . . .

2. **If the sentence is positive, make the tag question negative. If the sentence is negative, make the tag question positive.**

She is [positive] clever, isn't [negative]. . . .

The car [positive] been repaired, hasn't [negative]. . . .

Non-voters should not [negative] complain, should [positive]. . . .

Meeting the deadline will not [negative] be possible, will [positive]. . . .

Some oak trees lose [positive] their leaves, don't [negative]. . . .

You returned [positive] the book, didn't [negative]. . . .

3. **Supply a pronoun to match the subject of the sentence.**

She is clever, isn't she?

The car has been repaired, hasn't it?

Non-voters should not complain, should they?

Meeting the deadline will not be possible, will it?

Some oak trees lose their leaves, don't they?

You returned the book, didn't you?

ESLp

All six word groups pass the tag-question test; therefore, all are complete sentences. In contrast, sentence fragments (see Chapter 8) cannot pass the test. Some, like the next two examples, do not have a subject and main verb phrase to make the question.

FRAGMENT: Standing on the corner under his leaky umbrella.

IMPOSSIBLE: Standing on the corner under his leaky umbrella, isn't he?

FRAGMENT: The coffee overflowing into the saucer.

IMPOSSIBLE: The coffee overflowing into the saucer, isn't it?

Although dependent clause fragments (8a) do have a subject and verb, they still do not allow tag questions. The introductory subordinate conjunction (7c) prevents the clause from making a statement. Therefore, the tag question cannot ask for confirmation in the form of a *yes/no* answer.

FRAGMENT: When Maria goes out in the rain.

IMPOSSIBLE: When Maria goes out in the rain, doesn't she?

FRAGMENT: Because he thought he didn't deserve it.

IMPOSSIBLE: Because he thought he didn't deserve it, did he?

ESLp

GLOSSARY OF USAGE

This glossary provides a brief guide for commonly confused words and phrases, such as *illusion, delusion; ensure, insure; differ from, differ with.* In addition, the glossary serves as a guide for usage, that is, the acceptable use of words and phrases. Usage is sometimes determined by clarity and logic but other times merely by the preferences of influential writers and language experts. Thus, usage is subject to controversy and to change. The advice here is based on information found in current dictionaries and usage guides. However, you should bear in mind that some readers—your instructor, for example—may occasionally have other preferences.

A, An

Use *a* before words with an initial consonant sound; use *an* before words with an initial vowel sound. Remember that the sound, not the letter, controls your choice: *a thought, an idea; a heel, an honor; a unicorn, an uncle; a "k," an "s."*

Accept, Except

Accept is a verb that generally means "to receive something or someone willingly" or "to believe": *We accept your terms. Jefferson accepted the ideas of deism. Except* is usually a preposition meaning "with the exclusion of" or a conjunction (often coupled with *that*) meaning "if it were not for the fact that": *The walls of every room except the kitchen were decorated with silk screens. He is fairly well qualified for the position except that he has no experience in public relations.*

usage

294

Adverse, Averse

Adverse usually describes some position or thing that is hostile or antagonistic: *adverse criticism, adverse reaction, adverse publicity, adverse report. Adverse* can also refer to something unfavorable or harmful: *The pioneers struggled against the adverse conditions of the Rocky Mountain winter. Antibiotics kill infection but can have an adverse effect on the digestive system.*

Averse is part of the idiom *averse to,* which describes someone who dislikes or opposes something: *The Mormons are averse to any kind of artificial stimulant. The editorial board, averse to all Democratic candidates, used the magazine as a Republican forum.*

Advice, Advise

Advice is a noun, with the *c* pronounced as an /s/ sound: *Your advice is welcome. Advise* is a verb, with the *s* pronounced as a /z/ sound: *We advise beginning students to take BASIC.*

Affect, Effect

Affect is usually a verb that means "to influence" or "to bring about a change": *The weather often affects our emotions.* Sometimes *affect* is a verb meaning "to pretend": *Although he was actually from Wisconsin, Gibbs affected a British accent.* The use of *affect* as a noun is confined to psychology, where it refers to a feeling or an emotion as opposed to a thought or action: *He denied feeling guilty, but his affect was revealed in his blushing and stammering.*

Effect is usually a noun that means "a result": *The prolonged cold spell had a devastating effect on the citrus crop.* As a noun, *effect* is also used in idioms like *take effect* and *come into effect: The drug should take effect within two hours. When will the new regulations come into effect?* But *effect* occasionally is used as a verb meaning "to bring about": *Her efforts effected a change.*

Aggravate, Irritate

In formal English, the verb *aggravate* means "to make worse," "to make more troublesome or more serious": *Unusually heavy traffic aggravated the deterioration of the bridge pilings. The star's frequent lateness aggravated the tension among the cast members. Irritate* means "to annoy," "to exasperate," "to provoke": *Khrushchev's behavior at the UN irritated the Western delegates.*

Informally, some people use *aggravate* for *irritate: The dog's constant barking aggravated the neighbors.* This usage, however, is not acceptable to many readers and should be avoided in formal writing.

usage

Agree to, Agree with, Agree on *or* about

Used with *to, agree* means "to give consent": *The board agreed to hear the evidence on Friday.*

Agree with usually indicates accord: *He agreed with the philosophy of the transcendentalists. Agree with* can also refer to health or constitution: *Mexican food doesn't agree with many people. The desert air agrees with me.*

With *on* or *about, agree* indicates a coming to terms: *We agreed on a meeting in May. The judges could not agree about the criteria for evaluating the contestants.*

All, All of

Before noun phrases, especially in written English, *all* is appropriate: *All the circuits were busy. In all the excitement, I forgot where I parked the car.* However, *all of* is also acceptable: *All of the circuits . . . In all of the excitement . . .*

Before pronouns or proper nouns, *all of* is required: *All of us were embarrassed. In all of Europe, the plague raged.*

In the subject position, *all* takes a singular verb when the meaning is "everything": *All is forgiven. All* takes a plural verb when referring to individuals in a group: *All were refunded their money.*

All Ready, Already

All ready is pronounced with a distinct pause between the two words and means "everything or everyone in a state of readiness": *The floral arrangements were all ready for delivery. The swimmers were all ready to begin the competition.*

The single word *already* means "previously," "by this or that time," "before this or that time": *By the time dinner was served, some of the guests had already left. By January, local hotels are already booked for the summer.*

usage

All Right

All right should always be written as two words, not run together as *alright.*

All That

Do not use *all that* in formal writing to imply comparison: *The movie was not all that bad.* Instead, write something like *The movie was better than we had expected.*

All Together, Altogether

The two-word phrase *all together* means "all at one time," "all in one place," "collectively": *They were standing all together against the menace. The students were housed all together in one run-down barrack.*

The adverb *altogether* means "completely," "in all," or "on the whole": *These statistics are not altogether accurate. The meal cost fifty dollars altogether. Altogether, I wish I had never met the man.*

Allusion, Delusion, Illusion

The noun *allusion* comes from the verb *allude,* which means "to make an indirect reference to something or someone." Thus, *allusion* means "an indirect reference" or "a hint": *Although she was never specific, she made a vague allusion to something sinister in his past.*

Deriving from the verb *delude,* which means "to mislead deliberately and harmfully," *delusion* means "a deception": *Her innocence was a delusion she cultivated cunningly.*

The noun *illusion* has no corresponding verb form. It means "a false perception of reality": *The actor's stature was an illusion; he usually stood on a box to kiss his leading lady.*

Almost, Most

In very informal prose, some people use *most* as an adverb to mean "almost." In formal prose, *almost* is required: *We go to San Francisco almost* [not *most*] *every year. Almost* [not *most*] *all the cement has dried.*

A Lot (of), Lots (of)

These expressions are informal substitutes for such words as *much, many, frequently: You're in a lot of trouble. We went to the movies a lot that summer. He uses lots of Tabasco in his chili. I miss you lots.*

Do not write *a lot* as one word (*alot*).

Among, Between

Many guides dictate the use of *between* only with two items or persons and *among* with more than two: *Rivalry between the two teams was intense. Rivalry among the three teams was intense.*

usage

Nevertheless, the *Oxford English Dictionary,* the most scholarly of word collections in English, states, "In all senses *between* has been, from its earliest appearance, extended to more than two. . . . It is still the only word available to express the relation of a thing to many surrounding things severally and individually; *among* expresses a relation to them collectively and vaguely: we should not say 'the space lying *among* three points,' or 'a treaty *among* three powers,' or 'the choice lies *among* the three candidates in the select list,' or 'to insert a needle among the closed petals of a flower.'"

Between is also used with more than two when it refers to intervals occurring regularly: *Between dances, the boys stood around sweating and the girls combed their hair. I cannot stop eating between meals.* Certainly *among dances* and *among meals* would make very little sense.

Among is more properly used to suggest a relationship of someone or something to a surrounding group: *She lived among the natives for almost ten years. There is honor among thieves.*

Amount, Number

Amount should be used with nouns that name something that cannot be counted (or made plural), such as *noise, information, linen, mud: Judging from the amount of noise inside, we expected the movie to be outrageous.*

Number should be used with nouns that name things that can be counted (or made plural), such as *shrieks, statistics, handkerchiefs, rocks: Judging from the number of shrieks inside, we expected the movie to be outrageous.*

And Etc.

Etc. is an abbreviation for the Latin phrase *et cetera,* which means "and other (things)." Therefore, the expression *and etc.* is redundant. See also **Et Al., Etc.**

And/Or

Writers sometimes use *and/or* to indicate three options: *Merit is rewarded by promotion and/or salary increase* means that merit is rewarded (1) by promotion or (2) by salary increase or (3) by both. Some readers, however, object to the *and/or* device outside of legal, business, or technical writing. To be on the safe side, you can write out the options.

Ante-, Anti-/Ant-

Ante is Latin for "before" or "in front of." It serves as a prefix in English in such forms as *antebellum* ("before the Civil War") and *antechamber* ("a small room in front of, or entry to, a larger room"). *Anti/ant* comes from Greek, meaning "against" or "opposite," and serves as a prefix in such forms as *antibiotic* ("against bacteria") and antacid ("opposing acid"). A hyphen after *anti-* can clarify reading when the root word begins with a capital letter (*anti-Truman*) or an *i* (*anti-intellectualism*).

Anxious, Eager

In conversation, *anxious* and *eager* are often used interchangeably: *I am eager to move into my new apartment. I am anxious to move into my new apartment.* Nevertheless, in formal situations, most usage experts recommend *anxious* to convey apprehension and *eager* to convey impatient desire: *The pilot was anxious about the high winds. The Senator was anxious to avoid scandal. An eager understudy waited in the wings. The fans were eager for victory.*

Any More, Anymore

The two-word adjective *any more* means "some more" or "additional": *Are any more tests necessary to confirm the presence of radiation? The department has not hired any more clerks since 1994.*

The single-word adverb *anymore* means "presently" or "from now on": *The deer aren't seen in the marshes anymore. Will the shop carry imported cheeses anymore?*

Any One, Anyone

The two-word phrase *any one* refers to any person, place, thing, idea, and so on. It is followed by *of* when it precedes a noun or pronoun: *Any one of the desks will serve our purposes. Any one of you is qualified to serve. Any one* may occur without *of* if its referent has been previously stated: *Four options are available. Choose any one.*

The single word *anyone* means "anybody"; it is never followed by *of* and does not precede nouns and pronouns: *Anyone with drive and a high-energy level can succeed.*

Anyplace, Anywhere

Anyplace is usually restricted to informal situations; *anywhere* is acceptable in both formal and informal English.

Any Way, Anyway, Anyways

The two-word phrase *any way* refers to any course or any direction: *They were trapped any way they turned. Anyway* means "nevertheless" or "regardless of circumstances": *The plot is weak, but the film succeeds anyway. Anyways* is a nonstandard variant of *anyway* and should be avoided.

As, Like

In informal situations, speakers often substitute *like* for the subordinate conjunctions *as, as if, as though* to introduce dependent clauses: *Unfortunately, he dances like he sings. It looks like it's going to rain.* But most usage experts agree that in formal situations *like* should not introduce dependent clauses; the *as* conjunctions are more appropriate: *In a democracy, the government acts as the people dictate. The speaker clutched her throat as if she were gasping for air.*

usage

As To

As to occurs frequently in published prose, particularly in journalism: *The weather service kept residents posted as to the position of the hurricane. The mayor and city council members refused to make any comment as to whether the project would require higher taxes. We consulted an efficiency expert as to how to proceed.* In all cases, *about* may be substituted and probably sounds better.

Averse, Adverse (See Adverse, Averse.)

Awful, Awfully

Awful is an adjective meaning "fearsome," "awesome," or "great"; *awfully* is the adverb form of *awful: The dragon's awful roar shook the knight's confidence. The dragon roared awfully, shaking the knight's confidence.*

Informally, some speakers use *awful* and *awfully* as intensifiers equivalent to *very: The children were awful [awfully] tired.* Such use, however, should be avoided in formal writing or speaking.

A While, Awhile

The two-word phrase *a while,* consisting of an article and a noun, functions as the object of a preposition: *After a while in the city, I began to long for the quiet nights of the country. They stopped for a while in a roadside park.* The single word *awhile,* an adverb, does not occur after a preposition: *The fire will smoke only awhile.*

Bad, Badly

Bad is properly an adjective and thus should modify nouns and pronouns: *We always have bad weather this time of year. This headache is a particularly bad one. Badly* is properly an adverb of manner and should modify verbs and verbals: *She performed the piece badly. The editor soon tired of reading badly written poems.*

Confusion between the two words often occurs after a linking verb in a subject complement position, typically after the verb *feel,* in a sentence such as *I feel badly about not calling my parents.* In this sentence, the position after *feel* is a subject complement position and should be filled with an adjective modifying *I,* not an adverb modifying *feel.* Thus, the correct usage is *I feel bad about not writing my parents often enough.*

Sports announcers frequently use *bad* for *badly* in such expressions as *He's playing bad today* and *He just threw the ball bad.* Standard usage is *playing badly* and *threw the ball badly.*

usage

Beside, Besides

The preposition *beside* means "at the side of" (*she was seated beside the guest speaker*) or "compared with" (*my game looked shabby beside his expertise*) or "having nothing to do with" (*in this case, your opinion is beside the point*).

Besides can function as a preposition meaning "other than" (*Jamison had no ambition besides doing a good job*) or as a transitional expression meaning "moreover" (*the restaurant was too expensive; besides, the food was only mediocre*).

Be careful not to substitute *beside* for *besides: Besides* [not *beside*] *being lazy, the new secretary could not type.*

Between, Among (See Among, Between.)

Between You and I, Between You and Me
Because *between* is a preposition, it requires an objective case pronoun. Thus *between you and I* (or *he, she, they*) is incorrect. Use *between you and me* (or *him, her, them*).

Bring, Take
In standard English, both *bring* and *take* mean "to convey." However, *bring* suggests movement toward the speaker or focal point, whereas *take* suggests movement away from the speaker or focal point: *The teacher asked the students to bring a newspaper article to class. The governor took three antique chairs from the mansion when he left office.*
   In some dialects, speakers use *bring* to mean "convey away from," as when one speaker says to another in the same location, *I'll bring you to work this morning.* This substitution, however, is not acceptable in formal English.

Bunch
Conversationally, *bunch* is frequently used to mean a group: *A bunch of guys went to the ball game.* In formal English *bunch* should refer only to things growing together in a cluster—like *a bunch of grapes.*

Burst, Bust
The standard verb *burst, burst, burst* usually means "to explode" or "to fly apart suddenly." In formal English, the verb *bust, busted, busted* is inappropriate for these meanings: *The tank burst* [not *busted*] *suddenly.*

But However, But Yet
In informal situations, speakers sometimes combine *but* with contrastive adverbs—possibly for emphasis: *He was practicing medicine, but yet he had never been to medical school.* Such combinations are not acceptable in formal English. Write, *By 1800, the French were satisfied with wounding an opponent, but* [not *but however*] *American dueling practice still demanded death.*

But That, But What
Informally, writers sometimes introduce dependent clauses with *but that* and *but what* (particularly after a negative and the word *doubt*): *No one*

usage

doubted but that [or *what*] *Miss Marple would persevere.* In formal English, the proper connector is *that: No one doubted that Miss Marple would persevere.*

Can, May

Can indicates ability (*we can meet the deadline if we work the whole weekend*) or power (*a dean can overrule a department head*). *May* indicates permission (*you may invite three guests*). Generally, in formal writing, *can* should not replace *may.* In negative contractions, however, most usage experts accept *can't* for permission, since *mayn't* seems stilted and archaic: *You can't* [not *mayn't*] *be excused from the graduation exercises except in dire emergencies.* Also, many experts accept *cannot* for permission in negatives: *May I have this dance? No, you cannot.*

Can't Help But

Can't help but, a rather common idiom, is appropriate only in informal situations: *I can't help but wish I had kept my old Volkswagen bug.* The idiom can be deleted with no change of meaning.

Capital, Capitol

Capital usually means "head," "very serious," "principal": *capital city, capital error.* It also refers to crimes involving the death sentence: *capital offense, capital punishment.* And in finance, *capital* refers to money or property, particularly that used for investment: *capital for the venture, capital gain, capital goods. Capitol* refers to the building in which a legislature meets.

Censor, Censure

The verb *censor* means "to examine material for immoral or harmful content" or "to ban material" for those reasons: *Some state school boards appoint committees to censor textbooks.* The verb *censure* means "to criticize, blame, or rebuke": *Admiral Stanley was censured for unnecessarily endangering the lives of his men.*

usage

Center Around

Most usage experts prefer *revolve around* to *center around: The controversy revolves* [not *centers*] *around misappropriation of funds.* This notion rests on the argument that one thing cannot logically "center around" something else; thus *centers* is more properly followed by *on* or *in: The controversy centers on* [or *in*] *misappropriation of funds.* Nevertheless, language does not follow the logic of mathematics, and *center around* is widely used by many respectable writers.

Climatic, Climactic

Confusion of *climatic* and *climactic* is not a matter of usage but rather a matter of meaning. The adjective *climatic* refers to climate, to weather: *Fluctuations in the earth's orbit probably affect climatic conditions.* The adjective *climactic* refers to climax, to a turning point or high point: *My childhood was so uneventful that the climactic moment occurred when I was chosen a bus-patrol boy.*

Complected, Complexioned

Complected is a regional variation of *complexioned.* In formal situations, use *complexioned: She was so fair complexioned* [not *complected*] *that she used a number forty-four sunscreen.*

Complement, Compliment

Complement derives from *complete;* thus the verb *complement* usually means "something that completes or perfects": *The oriental garden complemented the architecture of the house.* The verb *compliment* means "to praise or congratulate": *She complimented the photographer on his ability to capture mood.*

Comprise, Compose

Strictly, the whole comprises the parts; the parts compose the whole: *The bureau comprises five departments. Five departments compose the bureau.* The passive expression *is comprised of* is often used to mean "is composed of": *The bureau is comprised of five departments.* Even though *Webster's Collegiate* points out that this usage has been in existence since the eighteenth century, some readers still find it objectionable. To be safe, you should probably avoid *is comprised of* altogether and use instead *is composed of* or *is made up of.*

Conscience, Conscious

The noun *conscience* means "moral sensibility," "recognition of right and wrong": *How could you in good conscience use my money to pay your debts?* The adjective *conscious* means "aware" or "deliberate": *She was suddenly conscious of a shadowy figure ahead. I am certainly not guilty of a conscious insult.*

usage

Consensus

Consensus comes from Latin *con* ("together") and *sentire* ("to think" or "to feel"). Thus, *consensus of opinion* is considered by many to be redundant. In any case, the phrase has become a cliché and should be avoided. *Consensus* is sufficient.

Continual, Continuous

Careful writers distinguish between the two adjectives *continual* and *continuous*. Strictly speaking, *continual* indicates recurring actions, repeated regularly and frequently; *continuous* indicates something unceasing, occurring without interruption: *Continual irrigation of crops is dangerously lowering the water table. The continuous motion of the sea lulled me to sleep.*

Theodore Bernstein offers a mnemonic device for remembering the difference: "*Continuous* ends in *o u s,* which stands for *o*ne *u*ninterrupted *s*equence."

Convince, Persuade

Most people do not distinguish between *convince* and *persuade;* however, careful writers associate *convince* with belief, and *persuade* with action: *He convinced me of his sincerity. The recruiting officer persuaded her to enlist.* One difference between the two words is that *persuade,* but not *convince,* is best followed with an infinitive: *They persuaded me* [not *convinced me*] *to get back on the horse.*

Could have, Could of

Could of is a misrepresentation of the way *could have* sounds in running speech. Write *I could have* [not *could of*] *left.*

Credible, Creditable, Credulous

Credible means "believable," "plausible": *Her account of the day's events was too amusing to be credible. Creditable* usually means "deserving commendation": *Only one of the divers gave a creditable performance. Credulous* means "believing too readily," "gullible": *Lisa was too credulous to be a probation officer.* (See also **Incredible, Incredulous.**)

usage

Data

Data is the plural of the Latin noun *datum,* which means "fact." Rarely do writers use the singular *datum;* instead they use a more familiar word, such as *fact, result, statistic.* But *data* is very commonly used, traditionally with a plural verb: *The data show that most voters in this area vote for the candidate rather than the party. The data are in question; therefore, we cannot accept the conclusions of the study.*

Increasingly, however, in technical writing, *data* is considered a noncountable noun like *information* and is used with a singular verb: *Our data proves that the oyster beds beyond 2 miles should not be harvested. The data is inconclusive.* Outside of technical writing, the safe route is to use a plural verb with *data.*

Device, Devise

~~Confusion between these two words is usually a matter of spelling.~~ *Device,* the noun, is pronounced /dih viyce/ and means "something constructed for a specific purpose": *We need a device for holding the jack in place. Devise,* the verb, is pronounced /dih viyze/ and means "to construct something for a specific purpose": *She devised a scheme for undermining her partner's credibility.*

Differ From, Differ With

The phrases are closely related, but *differ from* usually means "to be dissimilar," and *differ with* means "to disagree": *The two dialects differ from each other mainly in the pronunciation of vowels. Most experts differed with Jones's hypothesis.*

Different From, Different Than

Although some usage experts insist that *different* be followed by *from,* not by *than,* the rule is oversimplified. Because *from* is a preposition, *different from* should always have a noun or pronoun object—either stated or implied: *Moseley's batting stance is different from Griffin's [batting stance]. Different than* is preferable when a clause (usually an elliptical clause) follows: *James worked on a different assignment than we did.* To use *different from* in this example, you would have to insert an object for *from: James worked on a different assignment from the one we did.*

Discreet, Discrete

Discreet means "cautious," "unobtrusive," "tactful": *The Secret Service made discreet inquiries into Mark's background. Discrete* means "separate," "distinct": *The language institute and the university were two discrete entities.* To help avoid confusion, you can remember that the noun forms of the two adjectives are different: *discreet, discretion; discrete, discreteness.*

usage

Disinterested, Uninterested

Correct usage of *disinterested* and *uninterested* has long been disputed. Apparently, the word *disinterested* originally meant "not interested" but later took on the additional meanings of "free from self-interest" and "altruistic." *Uninterested* originally meant "impartial" but later came to mean "not interested." The best solution to the current problem of usage is to follow conservative guides. Use *disinterested* to mean "impartial," "uninfluenced by thoughts of personal gain" and *uninterested* to mean "not interested": *Some couples have a disinterested party to negotiate prenuptial financial agreements. Acting uninterested in class is likely to irritate the instructor.*

Due To
Due to introduces adjective phrases and either immediately follows a noun or appears as a subject complement: *Many cases of depression due to chemical deficiencies go undetected. Many cases of depression are due to chemical deficiencies.* Because many people object to the substitution of *due to* for *because of* in adverbials, you are probably wise to avoid a construction such as *Due to advanced technology, contemporary ball players cannot realistically be compared to those of the past.* Write instead, *Because of advanced technology.* . . .

Due to the Fact That
Due to the fact that is an unnecessarily wordy bureaucratic phrase; *because* is the better choice.

Each and Every
Each and every is one of the favorite clichés of politicians and hucksters. Use simply *each* or *every* but not both.

Eager, Anxious (See Anxious, Eager.)

Effect (See Affect, Effect.)

Emigrate, Immigrate
Emigrate means "to leave a country"; *immigrate* means "to enter." One *emigrates* from a place, but *immigrates* to it.

Ensure, Insure
Ensure means "to guarantee" or "to make safe": *Organic gardening will ensure that produce is safe to eat. Safety goggles will ensure the worker against eye injury. Insure* means "to provide insurance against loss, damage, injury, etc.": *Our company will insure your home against loss due to flood, fire, and nuclear attacks.*

Enthused
Enthused has not been fully accepted, although it is often substituted for *enthusiastic.* Avoid *enthused* in formal prose: *Everyone on the staff was enthusiastic* [not *enthused*] *about the new personal shopper service.*

Et Al., Etc.
Et al. is the abbreviation for the Latin *et alii* or *et aliae,* meaning "and other people." This abbreviation is used in some documentation systems for citing books with more than two authors: *Yanella, D., et al.*

usage

Etc. is the abbreviation for *et cetera,* meaning "and other things." *Etc.* ~~is common in business memos and some technical documents but not in~~ formal or literary writing. To punctuate *etc.,* put a comma before it when more than one item precedes but not when only one item precedes: *Use only the title and the last name—Ms. Jones, Mr. Jones, Dr. Jones, etc. Dress out completely with pads etc.* (See also **And Etc.**)

Every Day, Everyday
The two-word phrase *every day* means "each day": *Mrs. Sommes went to the gym every day.* The single word *everyday* means "common" or "used on ordinary days." *He came to the dinner party in everyday work clothes.*

Every One, Everyone
The two-word phrase *every one* refers to every person, place, thing, idea, and so on. It is followed by *of* when it precedes a noun or pronoun: *Every one of the candidates has an image problem. Every one of these ancient civilizations had vanished by 500 B.C. Every one* can occur without *of* if its referent has been previously stated: *Four proposals were submitted, and every one called for a budget of over $500,000.*

The single word *everyone* means "everybody"; it is never followed by *of* and does not precede nouns and pronouns: *Everyone in the audience stood and cheered Ms. Gordon for over fifteen minutes.*

Except, Accept (See Accept, Except.)

Except for the Fact That
Shorten this long, bureaucratic phrase to *except that.*

Explicit, Implicit
Explicit means "not implied or suggested but stated outright": *The job description was so explicit that it even prescribed height and weight requirements. Implicit* means just the opposite, "implied or suggested, not stated outright": *Implicit in the advertisement was the notion that waxing floors is a joyful experience.*

usage

Farther, Further
Farther usually refers to distance; *further* usually means "in addition" or "additionally": *The mountains are farther away than they appear. Regular exercise promotes weight loss, and further, increases the energy level.* Also, as a verb, *further* means "to help to progress": *Derrick would use any means available to further his career in Hollywood.*

Fewer, Less

Fewer is used with nouns that can be counted and made plural: *fewer files, fewer paintings, fewer letters. Less* is used with nouns that cannot be counted or made plural: *less software, less art, less mail.*

Further, Farther (See Farther, Further.)

Good, Well

In formal English, *good* is always an adjective, appearing either before a noun or after a linking verb like *be, seem, look, feel, sound, smell, taste: The good food lifted our flagging spirits. The newly mowed grass smelled good. That hat looks good on you.*

Well functions as an adverb when it refers to the manner in which an action is performed: *She spoke German well. He hits the ball well but his concentration is not good. Well* functions as an adjective only when it refers to health. *Don't you feel well? Get well soon.*

Had Better

Had better means "ought to." In running speech, the *had* sometimes disappears but should never be omitted in writing, except in dialogue. Write *The cabinet had better* [not *better*] *be more responsive to foreign affairs and less to partisan politics.*

Had Ought To

Had ought to is nonstandard; instead, use *ought to: We ought to* [not *had ought to*] *send a housewarming gift.*

Half

You may write *a half* or *half a,* but most usage guides do not approve *a half a: The distance of the cabin from the lake was only a half mile* [or *only half a mile; not only a half a mile*].

Hanged, Hung

In every sense but one, the correct forms of the verb *hang* are *hang, hung, hung.* However, in the sense of execution, the verb is *hang, hanged, hanged: The picture was hung. The traitor was hanged.*

Hardly

Because *hardly* has a negative meaning ("insufficiency"), it should not be used with another negative—particularly, with *can't* or *couldn't.* Instead of *can't hardly* or *couldn't hardly,* write *can hardly* or *could hardly.* Also, when *hardly* means "barely," a completing clause begins with *when,* not *than: Hardly had the class started when* [not *than*] *the alarm sounded.*

usage

Healthy, Healthful

Healthy describes people, animals, plants, and economies in a state of good health. *Healthful* describes such things as climate and food that contribute to good health. Increasingly, writers use *healthy* for both senses, but a distinction between the terms often adds clarity.

Hisself

Never use *hisself,* a nonstandard variation of *himself.*

Historic, Historical

Historic narrowly means "making history"; *historical* means "relating to history." *Uncle Tom's Cabin* is a "historic" novel, which affected history. *Gone with the Wind* is a "historical" novel, which uses history as the setting.

Hopefully

Hopefully is a generally accepted adverb meaning "full of hope": *We watched hopefully for a change in the weather.* Many people, however, object to its use as a sentence modifier meaning "it is hoped": *Hopefully, the weather will change.* Logically this second use of *hopefully* makes as much sense as *fortunately, happily, regrettably,* or *certainly,* and according to *Webster's Collegiate Dictionary,* has been in well-established use since 1932. But as the *American Heritage Dictionary* wisely points out, "This usage is by now such a bugbear to traditionalists that it is best avoided on grounds of civility, if not logic."

If, Whether

In some sentences, *if* and *whether* are equally acceptable and clear: *I do not know if* [or *whether*] *the plan is feasible.* But in some sentences *if* is ambiguous, expressing either an alternative or a condition: *Tell me if they are late.* An alternative is more clearly expressed with *whether: Tell me whether they are late.* A condition is more clearly expressed when the *if* clause is moved to the front of the sentence: *If they are late, tell me.*

usage

Illusion, Allusion, Delusion (See Allusion, Delusion, Illusion.)

Immigrate, Emigrate (See Emigrate, Immigrate.)

Implicit, Explicit (See Explicit, Implicit.)

Imply, Infer

Imply means "to suggest"; *infer* means "to arrive at a conclusion." Words and actions can imply meaning. From them, readers, listeners, and observers can infer meaning. *The toss of her head implied a defensive attitude. From the toss of her head, he inferred a defensive attitude.*

In, Into
Into rather than *in* more clearly shows movement from outside to inside: *The fumes seeped into the room.*

Incredible, Incredulous
Incredible describes something that is hard to believe: *The circus act was incredible. Incredulous* describes someone who is skeptical: *She was incredulous despite their assurances.*

Infer, Imply (See Imply, Infer.)

In Regards to
To mean "in reference to," write *in regard to, with regard to, regarding,* or *as regards*—never *in regards to.*

Insure, Ensure (See Ensure, Insure.)

Into, In to
Into, written as one word, is a preposition: *into the water, into the room, into the matter.* Sometimes *in* is a part of a phrasal verb and is followed by the word *to.* Then, *in* and *to* are not joined: *She went in to check the temperature. Turn your papers in to me.*

Irregardless, Regardless
Never write *irregardless* to mean *regardless: I am going regardless* [not *irregardless*] *of the weather.*

usage

Irritate, Aggravate (See Aggravate, Irritate.)

Is When, Is Where
When refers to time, and *where* refers to place. The words are misleading in contexts that do not have these meanings. For example, do not write *A hologram is when people use a laser to create a three-dimensional photograph.* Instead write *A hologram is a three-dimensional photograph produced by a laser.* Also, do not write *A quarterback sneak is where the quarterback, with the ball, plunges into the line.* Instead write *A quarterback sneak is a play in which the quarterback, with the ball, plunges into the line.*

It's, Its

The apostrophe in *it's* shows that the word is a contraction meaning "it is" or "it has." *Its,* like the other possessive personal pronouns that end in *s* (*hers, his, yours, ours, theirs*), contains no apostrophe. The form *its'* does not exist.

Kind of, Sort of

The expressions *kind of* and *sort of* to mean "somewhat" or "rather" are informal. Avoid them in formal writing: *The work was somewhat* [not *kind of*] *tedious.*

Kind of (a), Type of (a), Sort of (a)

The *a* should not appear in expressions such as *this kind of a book, this sort of a plan, this type of a day.*

Later, Latter

Later (pronounced /layt r/) refers to time; *latter* (pronounced /lat r/) means "the second of two."

Lay, Lie

The forms of these two verbs are

	To Lay (To Put or Place)	*To Lie (To Rest or Recline)*
Present	lay	lie
Past	laid	lay
Participles	laid, lying	lain, lying

When *lay* (present tense of *lay*) means "put" or "place," it has an object: *Lay the cards on the table.* When *lay* (past tense of *lie*) means 'reclined," it has no object and either has or could have the word *down* after it: *The dog lay [down] in the mud.* Write *The valuable diamond lies* [not *lays*] *in a case unprotected. He lay* [not *laid*] *in bed all day. I was lying* [not *laying*] *on the beach.* When there is no object and when the meaning is "recline," the proper verb is *lie* (*lay, lain, lying*).

usage

Lend, Loan

Some people prefer the verb *lend* (*lent, lent*) and scorn the verb *loan* (*loaned, loaned*) even though *loan* has a long history, especially in America. The verb *loan* is common in financial contexts: *The bank loaned the money.*

Less, Fewer (See Fewer, Less.)

Lie, Lay (See Lay, Lie.)

Like, As (See As, Like.)

Lose, Loose
Lose is pronounced /looz/ and means "misplace" or "get rid of." *Loose* is pronounced /loos/ and means "not tight." *If you lose your receipts, you can't be reimbursed. To hide his weight gain, he wore only loose-fitting clothes.*

May, Can (See Can, May.)

May Be, Maybe
The verb *may be* is two words. The adverb *maybe* (meaning "perhaps") is one word. *We may be late. Maybe we are late.*

Might Have, Might of
Might of is a misinterpretation of the way *might have* sounds in running speech. *I might have [not might of] picked the winning numbers.*

Moral, Morale
Moral (meaning "ethical" or "ethical lesson") is pronounced with the stress on the first syllable /mor′ al/: *The moral of the fable is "haste makes waste." Morale* (meaning "spirit") is pronounced with the stress on the second syllable /mo ral′/: *The defeat destroyed the team's morale.*

Most, Almost (See Almost, Most.)

Must Have, Must of
Must of is a misinterpretation of the way *must have* sounds in running speech. *They must have [not must of] left the play during the third act.*

usage

Myself, Me or I
Confusion about whether to use *me* or *I* in compound constructions probably leads to the incorrect use of *myself: The staff and myself thank you. Myself* must refer to a previous *I* or *me* in the same sentence: *I saw the incident myself. I wrote myself a note. They told me to answer the letter myself.*

Noplace, Nowhere
Use *nowhere,* not *noplace,* in formal prose.

Number, Amount (See Amount, Number.)

Of
In formal writing

- Do not use *of* after words such as *large* and *good: That is too large* [not *too large of*] *a meal.*

- Do not use *of* after *off: The cat jumped off* [not *off of*] *the ledge.*

- Do not omit *of* after *type: What type of* [not *type*] *car did you buy?*

O.K.
O.K., also spelled *OK* and *okay,* is informal. In formal writing use instead an expression such as *acceptable, satisfactory,* or *correct.*

Oral, Verbal
The distinction between *oral* and *verbal* can be useful, even though the two meanings are very close. Whereas *verbal* refers to either spoken or written words, *oral* refers specifically to spoken words.

Orient, Orientate
As verbs, both *orient* and *orientate* can mean "to get properly adjusted or aligned." In American English, *orient* is more common: *Orient yourself to the map before you start through the unfamiliar area.*

People, Persons
Persons implies a small and specific group: *The elevator will hold only six persons. People* is more versatile and can refer to any group.

Percent, Per Cent, Percentage
When you do not specify an amount, *percentage* is preferred in formal writing: *A large percentage* [not *percent*] *of the text was destroyed.* When you do specify an amount, use *percent* or *per cent: Employees get a 20 percent discount.*

usage

Persuade, Convince (See Convince, Persuade.)

Playwrite, Playwright
Even though a playwright writes plays, he or she is not called a "playwrite." The correct term is *playwright. Wright* (as in *wheelwright* and *shipwright*) means "one who makes or constructs something" and has no relation to *write.*

Plenty

In writing, avoid *plenty* as an intensifier. Instead, use words such as *very* and *quite: Legal action was quite* [not *plenty*] *appropriate.*

Plus

In formal writing, do not use *plus* to mean *and: They couldn't find summer jobs, and* [not *plus*] *they owed the school tuition.*

Practicable, Practical

Practicable means that something is possible; *practical* means that something is sensible: *A new bridge is practicable but not practical because of the cost.*

Precede, Proceed

The root *cede/ceed* means "go." The prefix *pre-* means "before," and the prefix *pro-* means "forward"; therefore, *precede* means "go before," and *proceed* means "go forward."

Principal, Principle

Because *principal* and *principle* sound alike, they are frequently confused. *Principle* is an abstract noun meaning a "truth," "law," "rule," "code": *He advocates the principle of separation of church and state. Principal* can be both a noun and an adjective. As a noun it generally means "chief official," "main participant"; and as an adjective it means "most important," "chief": *The principal of the school insisted on a dress code. The principal role in the drama is that of the son.*

Proceed, Precede (See Precede, Proceed.)

Prosecute, Persecute

Prosecute usually means "to start legal action." *Persecute* means "to treat oppressively." *The Allies prosecuted those who had persecuted the Jews.*

Quote, Quotation

The use of the verb *quote* for the noun *quotation* is informal. In formal prose, use *The speaker began with a quotation* [not *quote*] *from Emerson.*

Raise, Rise

Raise (raised, raised) usually means "to lift" and always has an object: *They raised the Confederate ship from the muddy bottom of the Mississippi. Rise (rose, risen)* usually means "to go up" and has no object: *The sun rose before we could get good photographs of the eclipse.*

usage

Real, Really

The use of *real* as an adverb to mean "very" is informal. Instead of *real angry,* write *really angry* or *very angry.*

Rear, Raise

One of the meanings of *rear* is "to nurture a child," although many people now use *raise* in this same sense. According to Theodore Bernstein, this meaning of *raise* is established. He comments: "At one time . . . the battle cry was, 'You raise pigs, but you rear children.' However, in this country at least . . . we raise both pigs and children, and some parents will testify that you can't always tell the difference."

Reason Is Because, Reason Is That

Instead of *reason is because,* write *reason is that: The reason for the lack of job openings is that* [not *because*] *people are retiring at the age of seventy, not sixty-five.*

Regardless, Irregardless (See Irregardless, Regardless.)

Respectfully, Respectively

Respectfully means "showing respect": *She respectfully responded to the request. Respectively* means "in a specific order": *The record and the tape cost $8.99 and $9.99, respectively.*

Right

Right as a modifier is vague; it can mean "somewhat" or "to a large degree": *right confusing, right ridiculous, right dumb.* Consequently, it should be avoided in writing.

Same

Same is a substitute for *it* or *them* in legal documents but in no other writings: *After you have written the letter, submit it* [not *same*] *for approval.*

usage

Scarcely

In a negative construction, *scarcely* is nonstandard. Do not write *Without scarcely a notice, they moved.* Instead write *With scarcely a notice, they moved.* Do not write *I couldn't scarcely breathe.* Instead write *I could scarcely breathe.*

Scarcely When, Scarcely Than

Scarcely when is preferred over *scarcely than: Scarcely had the announcement been written, when* [not *than*] *the reporters arrived.*

Seldom, Seldom Ever

Ever is unnecessary in the phrase *seldom ever.* Do not write *We seldom ever attend movies.* Instead, write *We seldom attend movies. Ever* is acceptable in the phrase *seldom if ever: We seldom if ever attend movies.*

Set, Sit

The verb *sit, sat, sat* does not have an object: *Sit in row H.* The verb *set, set, set,* meaning "to position or place," must have an object: *Set your glass on the coaster.* A few special meanings of *set,* however, require no object: *The sun sets. The hen sets on her nest.*

Shall, Will

In the past, grammars dictated that *shall* be used with the subjects *I* and *we, will* with other subjects. These grammars also prescribed that for emphasis, promise, determination, or command, the pattern be reversed: *will* with *I* and *we, shall* with other subjects.

Attention to actual usage shows that even in formal prose, people have never used *shall* and *will* consistently in this fashion. Instead, *will* appears commonly with *I* and *we* and also with other subjects in emphatic statements: *I will visit China. They repeated that they will strike if their demands are not met. Shall* seldom appears except in a question with *I* or *we* as the subject: *Shall we reject the offer? Where shall I look?* Frequently, the question is an invitation: *Shall we have lunch? Shall we dance?* In other contexts, *shall* seems extremely formal—almost stuffy.

Should, Would

Following the pattern of *shall* and *will,* many early grammars prescribed the use of *should* with the subjects *I* and *we, would* with all other subjects. (See **Shall, Will.**) The prescription, however, is seldom followed. *Should* is used with all subjects to indicate obligation or expectation: *The public should support the bill. He should be here shortly.* With all subjects *would* can indicate promise: *I swore that I would work out two hours every day.* Furthermore, with all subjects *would* can express a hypothetical situation: *If the schedule were more realistic, more people would fly the shuttle.* Finally, either *should* or *would* is acceptable in certain idioms expressing desire or preference: *I would [should] like to direct your attention to paragraph 3. We would [should] prefer to delay discussion until the next meeting. Would* is more common than *should* in American English.

Should Have, Should of

Should of is a misinterpretation of the way *should have* sounds in running speech: *I should have written* [not *should of written*].

usage

Sit, Set (See Set, Sit.)

Situation

Do not unnecessarily add the word *situation* to a sentence: *If you are in an accident* [not *accident situation*], *you may need legal advice. The questions were too vague to be used on tests* [not *in a testing situation*].

Slow, Slowly

Both *slow* and *slowly* have long been used as adverbs but in special ways. *Slow* occurs only after the verb and usually in short commands: *Drive slow. Slow* also occurs frequently with the verb *run: The clock runs slow. The trains were running slow.* If the rhythm and sense are satisfied, *slowly* can occur either before or after the verb: *The cat slowly stalked the robin across the yard* or *The cat stalked the robin slowly across the yard.*

When the adverb follows a verb describing a process, either *slow* or *slowly* is acceptable, particularly with a compound adverb: *The boat drifted slow [slowly] and steady [steadily] toward the reef.*

Only *slowly* can occur as a sentence adverb. In such cases, it usually appears at the beginning of the structure: *Slowly, Earp rose to his feet, laid four aces on the table, and drew his gun.*

So, So That

So that makes the sentence structure clearer and the tone more formal than *so: Keep a record of your blood pressure so that* [not *so*] *your doctor can make an accurate interpretation.*

So, Very

In writing, do not use *so* to mean "very": *The film was very* [not *so*] *maudlin.*

Some

In formal writing, do not use *some* to mean "somewhat": *The way we speak may differ somewhat* [not *some*] *in the locker room and at a cocktail party.*

usage

Someplace, Somewhere

Someplace is more informal than *somewhere*. In formal prose, write *Supposedly, there is a symbol somewhere* [not *someplace*] *in the poem.*

Sometime, Sometimes

Sometime means "at some unspecified time": *I plan to read the complete works of Shakespeare sometime. Sometimes* means "now and then": *Stray radio signals sometimes open garage doors.*

Sort of

Sort of is more informal than *somewhat* or *to some extent.* In formal prose, write *They are somewhat* [not *sort of*] *confused by the instructions.*

Stationary, Stationery

Stationary means "fixed"; *stationery* means "writing paper." Remember that stationERy is made of papER.

Such a

In formal writing, do not use *such a* to mean "very": *It was a very* [not *such a*] *witty play. Such a* should be used only when it is followed with a *that* clause stating a result: *It was such a witty play that I would like to see it again.*

Suppose to, Supposed to

Do not write *suppose to* for *supposed to.* Although the d sound often is not pronounced in running speech, it should always be written: *We were supposed to* [not *suppose to*] *attend the conference.*

Sure

Sure as an adverb is more informal than *surely* or *certainly* and should be written only in friendly correspondence and dialogue. In formal prose, write *The book surely* [not *sure*] *is radical.*

Sure to, Sure and

Use *sure to,* not *sure and,* in a construction like *Be sure to* [not *sure and*] *go.*

Take, Bring (See Bring, Take.)

Than, Then

Than, a conjunction, completes a comparison; *then* indicates time: *We then learned that the matter was more serious than we had thought.*

That, Which

Although the distinction is not always observed, to be unquestionably correct, you should use *that* to introduce restrictive clauses (no commas) and *which* to introduce nonrestrictive clauses (commas): *Flashman is a book that makes a shameless cad entertaining. Flashman, which makes a shameless cad entertaining, is worth reading.*

Their, There, They're

Their, which shows possession, appears only before a noun: *their work, their music, their beliefs. There* indicates location (*go there*) or introduces an inverted sentence (*there are three possible answers*). *They're* means *they are* (*they're late*).

Theirselves, Themselves
Never write *theirselves* instead of *themselves*: *They declared themselves* [not *theirselves*] *bankrupt.*

Them, Those
A phrase such as *them people* or *them pencils* is considered illiterate. Instead, always write *those people* or *those pencils.*

Then, Than (See Than, Then.)

This Here, That There
This here and *that there* are not standard English. Omit the *here* and *there*: *This* [not *this here*] *attempt was unsuccessful. He did not hear that* [not *that there*] *warning.*

This Kind of, These Kinds of
Use the singular *this* with *kind of* and the plural *these* with *kinds of*: *this kind of food, these kinds of food.*

Thusly
An -*ly* added to *thus* is unnecessary; *thus* is already an adverb. *We will thus* [not *thusly*] *cancel plans.*

Till, Until
Till and *until* are both correct and interchangeable. The spelling *'til* is incorrect.

To, Too
To can be a preposition (*to them, to school*) or an infinitive marker (*to go, to win*). *Too* is an adverb meaning "excessively" (*too tired, too much*) or "also" (*we too left*).

usage

Toward, Towards
Toward and *towards* have the same meaning; however, the sound of *toward* is usually preferable: *The camera faced toward* [or *towards*] *the crowd.*

Try to, Try and
Write *try to,* not *try and: You should try to* [not *try and*] *understand.*

-type

The suffix *-type* can be used to create adjectives: *A-type personality, European-type clothes, a* Playboy-*type publication*. If you use an adjective with a *-type* suffix, be sure that the suffix creates the right meaning. *A Bogart hero* refers to one of the characters Humphrey Bogart made famous. *A Bogart-type hero* only resembles those characters. In some constructions the addition of *-type* is unnecessary: *compact car* (not *compact-type car*), *spy novel* (not *spy-type novel*), *suspension bridge* (not *suspension-type bridge*).

Type, Type of

Do not omit the *of* after the noun *type: It is the type of* [not *type*] *computer they recommend.*

Uninterested, Disinterested (See Disinterested, Uninterested.)

Unique

Some people object to phrases like *more unique, somewhat unique, almost unique,* or *very unique.* They argue that *unique* is absolute and thus cannot be compared, modified, or intensified. According to *Webster's Collegiate Dictionary, unique* is absolute when meaning "without like or equal"; but when meaning "distinctively characteristic" or "unusual," *unique* can properly appear in phrases such as *a very unique region* and *a somewhat unique school.*

Until, Till (See Till, Until.)

Up

Omit *up* in verb phrases where it adds no meaning, as in *join up, check up, end up, fold up, call up, divide up, lift up.*

Use, Utilize

The verb *use* means "to put to use." *Utilize* means "to find a special purpose for something." Although these verbs are sometimes thought of as synonyms, *utilize* actually has a narrower meaning than *use: They used the detergent for washing clothes. They utilized the detergent as an insecticide.*

Use to, Used to

Do not leave the *d* out of *used to: The family used to* [not *use to*] *believe in flying saucers.*

Verbal, Oral (See Oral, Verbal.)

Wait for, Wait on

Some people say *wait on* to mean "await." But the expression is not standard English; write instead *wait for*: *He waited for me* [not *on me*] *under the clock at Holmes'.*

Way, Ways

Write *They have a long way* [not *ways*] *to drive.*

Well, Good (See Good, Well.)

Whether, If (See If, Whether.)

Which, That (See That, Which.)

Which, Who

Do not use *which* to introduce a relative clause modifying a person or people: *They reprimanded the doctor who* [not *which*] *prescribed the drug.* Do not use *who* with animals and things: *The plate pictured an eagle, which* [not *who*] *clutched an olive branch.*

Who's, Whose

Do not confuse *who's* and *whose*. *Who's,* which is somewhat informal, means *who is: Who's going? Whose* is the possessive form of *who: Whose responsibility is the statistical analysis?*

Will, Shall (See Shall, Will.)

Would, Should (See Should, Would.)

Would Have

In *if* clauses, use *had,* not *would have: If they had* [not *would have*] *checked the engine, the accident would not have occurred.*

usage

Would Have, Would of

Would of is a misinterpretation of the way *would have* sounds in running speech: *Except for the Vietnam War, in 1968 Lyndon Johnson would have* [not *would of*] *run for President.*

Your, You're

Your is the possessive form of *you: your idea, your order, your assignment. You're,* which is somewhat informal, is a contraction of *you are: You're indecisive. You're trapped.*

GLOSSARY
OF TERMS

This glossary provides a quick reference to terms—some useful and some essential for writers to know. Many definitions provide all the necessary information. Other definitions may require supplementary information from the text.

Absolute Phrase

An absolute phrase—usually a participial or infinitive phrase—modifies the whole sentence to which it is connected: *Speaking of problems, have you seen our new assignment? To be blunt, Jones has no sense of rhythm.* An absolute phrase that begins with a subject is sometimes called a nominative absolute: *The reservation confirmed, we called a cab. The climbers struggled up the mountain, their lungs aching.* (Section 5d)

terms

Abstract Noun

An abstract noun names something with no physical existence: *beauty, fury, dishonesty.*

Acronym

An acronym is a word formed from the initial letters or syllables of the words in a phrase: *awol* (absent without leave), *COBOL* (common business-oriented language), *CINCPAC* (Commander in Chief, Pacific), *Fiat* (Fabrica Italiana Automobili, Torino).

Active Voice

A verb is in the active voice when its subject acts or controls the action: *Harry bet on the winner. The jury convicted him.* (See also **Passive Voice.**) (Section 4e)

Adjective

An adjective is a word that describes, limits, or qualifies a noun or a noun equivalent: *a tart apple, a foolish remark, a successful opening.* (Section 3a)

Adjective Clause

An adjective clause modifies a noun or pronoun. These clauses are introduced by relative pronouns (*who/whom/whose, which, that*) or relative adverbs (*when, where, why*): *The game, which will be televised, is a sellout. I returned to Pocatello, where I had spent my first ten years.* (Section 7c.2)

Adverb

An adverb modifies an adjective (*fairly complex*), adverb (*very carefully*), verb (*moved backward*), or whole sentence (*Certainly, we want to go*). (Section 3b)

Adverb Clause

An adverb clause modifies a verb, adjective, adverb, or whole sentence. Adverb clauses are introduced by subordinate conjunctions (*when, until, because, since, if, unless, although*, etc.): *After they left Vermont, they moved to Quebec. He thought he was a woodsman because he bought clothes at L.L. Bean.* (Section 7c.1)

Adverbial Conjunction (See Conjunctive Adverb.)

terms

Agreement

The term *agreement* refers to the correspondence of both verbs with subjects and pronouns with antecedents. A verb must agree in number with its subject, and a pronoun must agree in number with its antecedent (singular verb with singular subject, singular pronoun with singular antecedent; plural verb with plural subject, plural pronoun with plural antecedent): *The raccoon washes its food.* [*Raccoon, washes,* and *its* are all singular.] *Raccoons wash their food.* [*Raccoons, wash,* and *their* are all plural.] (Chapters 10 and 13)

Alliteration

Alliteration is the repetition of the initial sounds of words to create a musical effect: "sunless sea," "the weary, way-worn wanderer," "the hunter home from the hill," "dusty death."

Antecedent

An antecedent is the noun or noun phrase that a pronoun refers to: *In the 1960s Bob Dylan was at the height of his success.* [*Bob Dylan* is the antecedent of *his.*] *Mosquitoes filled the air; they ruined the entire picnic.* [*Mosquitoes* is the antecedent of *they.*]

Appositive

An appositive renames, restates, or explains the word or words it refers to: *She bought an expensive car, a BMW luxury model.* (Section 33a.6)

Article

An article is a word (*a, an, the*) that signals the presence of a noun. (Section ESLc.1–2)

Auxiliary Verb

An auxiliary verb combines with a main verb to form a verb phrase: *is burning, did stand, has been grown, could have watched.* (See also **Helping Verb.**) (Sections 4b and ESLi-j, l)

Balanced Sentence

A balanced sentence has a noticeable symmetry of structure and often vocabulary. This kind of sentence heightens comparison or contrast: *What is true about losing weight is not magic, and what is magic about losing weight is not true.* (Section 33b.4)

terms

Case

Case refers to the special forms of nouns and pronouns that indicate their function. Some pronouns have three cases.

> Subjective (or nominative) case—used for subjects and subject complements: *I, we, he, she, they, who*
> Objective case—used for objects: *me, us, him, her, them, whom*
> Possessive (or genitive) case—used to show ownership, authorship, source, and description: *my/mine, our/ours, his, her/hers, their/theirs, whose*

Nouns and all other pronouns have two cases.

Common case—used for all functions except possession: *Linda, every-one, friends, actors*

Possessive (or genitive) case—used for the same functions as the possessive pronouns and formed by adding *'s* to singular forms and *'* to most plural forms: *Linda's, everyone's, friends', actors'.* (Chapter 14)

Clause

A clause is a grammatical construction with both a subject and predicate. Independent (main) clauses may stand by themselves as sentences: *My car had a flat.* Dependent (subordinate) clauses must be attached to independent clauses: *I was late because my car had a flat.* (Chapter 7)

Cleft Sentence

A cleft sentence is a construction that emphasizes an element that follows a form of *be.* The construction occurs when an ordinary sentence with a subject-verb-object pattern is changed to one with this pattern: *it* plus a form of *be* plus the element to be emphasized plus a *who, which,* or *that* clause. The term *cleft* refers to the fact that the ordinary sentence is cleft, or cut, into parts. The ordinary sentence *The pitcher hit the home run* can be changed to these cleft sentences: *It was the pitcher who hit the home run. It was a home run that the pitcher hit.*

Cliché

A cliché is an expression made stale and boring by overuse: *quick as a wink, last but not least, hour of need.* (Section 32c.1)

Climactic Sentence

The ideas in a climactic sentence move up a scale from less important to more important, from less intense to more intense, or from ordinary to extraordinary: *Once, in the early days before the buffalo herds had dwindled, Grinnel saw a Cheyenne Indian noiselessly ride his horse close to the side of a huge bull, and springing gracefully on his back, ride the beast for some distance, and then, with his knife, give it its death stroke.* (Section 33b.3)

Collective Noun

A collective noun refers to a group that forms a unit: *family, team, army, audience.* (Sections 10h and 13e)

Comma Splice

A comma splice, a punctuation error, occurs when two independent clauses are connected, or spliced together, with only a comma: *Alcohol en-*

terms

hances confidence, at the same time, it impairs judgment. Two independent clauses must be joined with a comma and a coordinating conjunction or with a semicolon: *Alcohol enhances confidence, but at the same time, it impairs judgment. Alcohol enhances confidence; at the same time, it impairs judgment.* (Chapter 9)

Comparative Conjunction

A comparative conjunction is a subordinate conjunction with two parts: *as . . . as, so . . . that, such . . . that*, a comparative modifier *. . . than*, a superlative modifier *. . . that.* These conjunctions express comparisons: *He laughed so loud that we got embarrassed. The train was more comfortable than we had expected. She was the hardest teacher that I ever had.* (Section 6b.4)

Comparative Degree

The form of an adjective and adverb used to compare two items is called the "comparative degree." An *-er* ending and the words *more* or *less* usually indicate the comparative degree: *May was wetter than June. Cod is more plentiful than flounder. This paper is less expensive.* (See also **Superlative Degree.**) (Section 3c)

Complement

In a clause, a complement "completes" the meaning of the predicate. A complement may be

- The object of a transitive verb: *They ate pizza.*

- The indirect object of a transitive verb: *He told me a lie.*

- The object complement of a transitive verb: *They called the storm Frederic.*

- The subject complement following *be* or a linking verb: *The book is a challenge. The water felt hot.*

Complex Sentence

A complex sentence contains one independent clause (ind.) and at least one dependent clause (dep.): *The bus filled* [ind.] *until even the aisle was jammed with people* [dep.]. *When the bell rang* [dep.], *the students raced from the room* [ind.]. (Section 7e.3)

Compound-Complex Sentence

A compound-complex sentence contains two or more independent clauses (ind.) and at least one dependent clause (dep.): *In New England earthworms are called nightwalkers* [ind.]; *in the Midwest, where they are best known as bait* [dep.], *they are called fishing worms* [ind.]. (Section 7e.4)

Compound Sentence

A compound sentence contains two or more independent clauses (ind.): *English has a phonetic alphabet* [ind.]; *Chinese has a pictographic system* [ind.]. (Section 7e.2)

Concrete Noun

A concrete noun names a material object that can be seen, touched, heard, tasted, or smelled: *rock, hamburger, wallet.*

Conjugation

A conjugation is a list of all the forms of a particular verb—its tenses (present, past, future, present perfect, past perfect, and future perfect), its voices (active and passive), its moods (indicative, imperative, and subjunctive), its persons (first, second, and third), and its numbers (singular and plural).

Conjugation of *Choose, Chose, Chosen*
INDICATIVE MOOD

PRESENT TENSE

ACTIVE VOICE:	I/You/We/They choose.
	He/She/It chooses.
PASSIVE VOICE:	I am chosen.
	He/She/It is chosen.
	You/We/They are chosen.

PAST TENSE

ACTIVE VOICE:	I/You/He/She/It/We/They chose.
PASSIVE VOICE:	I/He/She/It was chosen.
	You/We/They are chosen.

FUTURE TENSE

ACTIVE VOICE:	I/You/He/She/It/We/They will choose.
PASSIVE VOICE:	I/You/He/She/It/We/They will be chosen.

terms

PRESENT PERFECT TENSE

ACTIVE VOICE: I/You/We/They have chosen.
He/She/It has chosen.

PASSIVE VOICE: I/You/We/They have been chosen.
He/She/It has been chosen.

PAST PERFECT TENSE

ACTIVE VOICE: I/You/He/She/It/We/They had chosen.

PASSIVE VOICE: I/You/He/She/It/We/They had been chosen.

FUTURE PERFECT TENSE

ACTIVE VOICE: I/You/He/She/It/We/They will have chosen.

PASSIVE VOICE: I/You/He/She/It/We/They will have been chosen.

SUBJUNCTIVE MOOD

PRESENT TENSE

ACTIVE VOICE: I/You/He/She/It/We/They choose.

PASSIVE VOICE: I/You/He/She/It/We/They be chosen.

PAST TENSE

ACTIVE VOICE: (same as indicative mood)

PASSIVE VOICE: I/You/He/She/It/We/They were chosen.

PRESENT PERFECT TENSE

ACTIVE VOICE: I/You/He/She/It/We/They have chosen.

PASSIVE VOICE: I/You/He/She/It/We/They have been chosen.

PAST PERFECT TENSE

ACTIVE AND PASSIVE VOICE: (same as indicative mood)

IMPERATIVE MOOD

PRESENT TENSE

ACTIVE VOICE: Choose.
PASSIVE VOICE: Be chosen.

(See also **Progressive Forms.**)

terms

Conjunction

A conjunction is a grammatical connector that links sentence elements—words, phrases, or clauses. (See also **Coordinating Conjunction, Correlative Conjunction,** and **Subordinating Conjunction.**) (Section 6b)

Conjunctive Adverb (Adverbial Conjunction)

A conjunctive adverb serves as a transitional expression to link ideas: *however, therefore, thus, in addition, on the other hand,* and so on. (See also **Transitional Expression.**)

Connotation

Connotation refers to the feelings and memories evoked by a word. (See also **Denotation.**) (Section 32b.1)

Coordinating Conjunction

Coordinating conjunctions (*and, but, or, nor, for, so, yet*) connect grammatically equal structures—words, phrases, clauses. (Section 6b.1)

Coordination

Coordination is the process of combining two or more grammatically equal structures—for example, two or more nouns, verbs, predicates, prepositional phrases, dependent clauses, or independent clauses. For techniques that use coordination, see Sections 33a.1–33a.2.

Correlative Conjunction

A correlative conjunction is a coordinating conjunction that consists of a pair of words or phrases: *both . . . and, not . . . but, not only . . . but also, either . . . or, neither . . . nor.* (Section 6b.2)

Count Noun

A count noun names something that can be counted. Thus, count nouns have plural forms. *Desk* and *bracelet* are count nouns with the plural forms *desks* and *bracelets. Furniture* and *jewelry* with no plural forms are not count nouns. (See also **Mass Noun** and **Non-Count Noun.**)

Cumulative Sentence

A cumulative sentence begins with an independent clause and then piles up—or accumulates—structures at the end in order to create a dramatic effect: *Last night I had very discomforting dreams—full of evil creatures, plunges down precipices, and prolonged re-creations of embarrassing moments from my past.* (Section 33b.2)

terms

Dangling Modifier

A modifier with nothing nearby to modify is called "dangling." A dangling modifier is usually a verbal or an elliptical clause that appears at the beginning of a sentence: *Despising the habit, a resolution was made to quit smoking tomorrow.* The word modified should appear close to the modifier and should be the agent of the action expressed by the verb or verbal in the modifier: *Despising the habit, she resolved to quit smoking tomorrow.* (Section 16a)

Demonstrative Pronoun

The demonstrative pronouns are *this* and *that,* along with their corresponding plurals, *these* and *those.* These demonstratives fill a noun position or precede a noun and function as a determiner: *this pen, that tape, these marks, those noises.* (Sections 2b and ESLe.3)

Denotation

The denotation of a word is its literal and explicit meaning independent of any emotional association. (See also **Connotation.**) (Section 32b.1)

Dependent Clause

A dependent clause (also called a *subordinate clause*) has a subject and predicate but must be tied to an independent clause as a modifier or noun element: *When I noticed the menu's eight-dollar hamburger, I quickly left. They insisted that I say for the weekend.* (Section 7c)

Determiner

A determiner is a word like *a, the, our, this,* or *Susan's* that signals the presence of a noun. (Section 6c)

Direct Address

terms

Words in direct address (set off from the rest of the sentence with commas) name whoever or whatever is being spoken to: *This time, Ed, I'll pay. Get in the car, old dog.* (Section 21g)

Direct Object

A direct object is a word, phrase, or clause that receives or is affected by the verb's action: *Jessica likes historical romances. He said that he felt dizzy.*

Direct Quotation

A direct quotation, enclosed in quotation marks, duplicates the exact words of a speaker or writer: *"The first rule for taxi drivers," Mr. Geno* said, "is to be sure the passenger is in the car." The Times *called it "the latest American humbug." (See also* **Indirect Quotation.***) (Section 27a)*

Double Negative
No, not, nothing, hardly, scarcely, and barely are considered negatives in English. Use only one of these words to create a negative statement: *I have no cash. They have hardly begun.* A double negative is redundant and incorrect: *I don't have no cash. They haven't hardly begun.*

Elliptical Construction
In an elliptical construction, a word or several words are omitted, but their sense is clearly understood: *The bus takes an hour; a taxi, only thirty minutes.* [*Takes* is omitted in the second clause.] (Section 7d)

Emphatic Pronoun
An emphatic pronoun (also called an intensive pronoun) ends with *-self* or *-selves* and emphasizes a noun or another pronoun: *The Constitution itself says so. We were reprimanded by the conductor himself.* (See also **Reflexive Pronoun.**) (Section 2a)

Euphemism
A euphemism, an expression such as *revenue enhancers* for *taxes* or *passed away* for *died,* is used for evading or glorifying reality. (Section 32c.2)

Expletive
An expletive is a meaningless word (*there* or *it*) that fills out a sentence's structure and allows its subject to be delayed: *There is a fly in the room. It is hard to translate the story.* (Section 6d)

terms

Figures of Speech
Figures of speech communicate through comparisons and associations. Common figures of speech are the metaphor, simile, personification, and hyperbole. (Section 33d)

Finite Verb
A finite verb serves as the main verb of a clause or sentence. Unlike nonfinite verbs (infinitives, participles, and gerunds), finite verbs do not serve as modifiers and nominals.

Fragment

A fragment is an incomplete sentence punctuated as if it were a complete sentence: *When the team lost eighty-two games.* A fragment can be corrected by incorporation into another sentence: *When the team lost eighty-two games, no one was playing well.* A fragment can also be rewritten as a complete sentence: *The team lost eighty-two games.* (Chapter 8)

Function Word

Function words (prepositions, conjunctions, determiners, or expletives) create structure. (Chapter 6)

Fused Sentence

A fused sentence (sometimes called a *run-on sentence*) contains two independent clauses not separated by a conjunction or proper punctuation: *The students take regular classes however, all the subjects are taught in French.* The clauses must be separated: *The students take regular classes; however, all the subjects are taught in French.* For other ways of correcting fused sentences, see Chapter 9.

Gender

In English, *gender* refers to the sex represented by third-person singular pronouns: masculine (*he, him, his*), feminine (*she, her, hers*), and neuter (*it, its*). A few nouns reflect gender: masculine (*actor*) and feminine (*actress*).

General/Specific Words

General words refer broadly to categories: *food, book, person.* Specific words refer more narrowly to a member or members of a category: *burrito, telephone directories, Joe.* (Section 32b.2)

terms

Genitive Case

Genitive case is a term for possessive case or for an *of* phrase showing possession: *the coach's rule, the rule of the coach.* (See also **Possessive Case.**)

Gerund

A gerund is a verb form (the present participle, or *-ing* form) functioning in a sentence as a noun. A gerund phrase is a gerund plus another element—an object, subject, or modifier: *Writing well can be important in getting a good job.* [*Writing* is a gerund subject; *getting* is a gerund object of preposition. *Writing well* and *getting a good job* are both gerund phrases.] (Section 5c)

Gobbledygook

Gobbledygook (also called bureaucratic language, double-talk, officialese, and doublespeak) is the abstract and confusing language used by officials who think simple, direct prose will not impress readers. (Section 32d.1)

Helping Verb

Helping verb is a name sometimes given to an auxiliary verb. (See also **Auxiliary Verb.**)

Hyperbole

A hyperbole is a figure of speech that uses exaggeration rather than a literal statement to make a point: *We must have walked a thousand miles on this shopping trip.* (Section 33d)

Idiom

An idiom is an expression peculiar to a language or dialect. The meaning of idiomatic speech is not always clear from the meaning of each word: *put up with his foolishness, carry on about the problem, makes off with the loot.*

Imperative Mood

Verbs in the imperative mood are those used to give commands. *You* is always the understood subject: *Look out! Answer the roll. Delete the conjunction.* (Section 4f.2)

Indefinite Pronoun

An indefinite pronoun (*anyone, everybody, each, either, both,* etc.) does not require an antecedent and need not refer to a specific person or thing. (Section 2e)

terms

Independent Clause

An independent clause, sometimes called a *main clause,* is a structure with a subject and predicate. It need not be connected to any other structure: *We drove to Atlantic City.* (Section 7b)

Indicative Mood

Verbs in the indicative mood make statements and questions: *I saw the movie. Was the movie good?* (Section 4f.1)

Indirect Object

An indirect object, usually a noun or pronoun, appears between a transitive verb and a direct object. The indirect object may be converted to a prepositional phrase with *to, for,* or *of* and moved after the direct object: *They gave the school an award. [They gave an award to the school.]*

Indirect Quotation

In an indirect quotation, the exact words of a source are paraphrased. No quotation marks surround an indirect quotation: *Soren explained that he was curious about their everyday life.* (See also **Direct Quotation.**) (Section 27a)

Infinitive

An infinitive is a verbal made of *to* plus a verb: *to live, to listen, to appear.* An infinitive may function as a noun or as a modifier; it may appear alone or as part of an infinitive phrase: *To finish was his dream. [To finish* is an infinitive noun subject.] *She had the determination to finish the assignment. [To finish the assignment* is an infinitive phrase used as a modifier.] Though *to* is called the "sign" of the infinitive, it may be omitted after a few verbs like *let, make,* and *hear.* (Section 5a)

Inflection

An inflection is a change in the form of a word that signals a change in meaning or in grammatical relation to another word. The parts of speech, or word classes, that have inflection are nouns (*bird, birds, bird's, birds'*), verbs (*go goes, went, gone, going*), pronouns (*it, its*), adjectives (*tall taller, tallest*), and adverbs (*badly, worse, worst*).

terms

Intensifier

An intensifier is a modifier that adds emphasis: *very ill, extremely successful, really hopeful.* (See also **Qualifier.**)

Intensive Pronoun (See Emphatic Pronoun.)

Interjection

An interjection is an expression of emotion or exclamation (such as *oh, well,* or *wow*) structurally unconnected to a sentence: *Well! it's about time. Oh, I forgot the key.* (Sections 21g and 25g)

Interrogative Pronoun

An interrogative pronoun (*who, whom, whose, which,* or *what*) introduces a question that asks for information. *Whose, which,* and *what* can
function as a pronoun or as a determiner: *Whose is this? Which job is available?* (Section 2d)

Intransitive Verb

An intransitive verb expresses action but has no object: *The substance vanished. The package arrived quickly.*

Irregular Verb

The past tense and past participial forms of irregular verbs do not follow the
predictable pattern of adding *-d* or *-ed*. Following is a list of most of the irregular verbs in English and their principal parts.

Base	*Past*	*Past Participle*
arise	arose	arisen
awake	awoke, awaked	awakened
be	was	been
bear	bore	borne
beat	beat	beaten
become	became	become
befall	befell	befallen
begin	began	begun
behold	beheld	beheld
bend	bent	bent
bet	bet, betted	bet, betted
bid*	bade, bid	bidden, bid
bind	bound	bound
bite	bit	bitten, bit
bleed	bled	bled
blow	blew	blown
break	broke	broken
breed	bred	bred
bring	brought	brought
build	built	built
burn	burnt, burned	burnt, burned
burst	burst	burst
buy	bought	bought
cast	cast	cast
catch	caught	caught
choose	chose	chosen

*When the verb refers to offering a price, *bid* is appropriate for both the past and past participle. Otherwise, either *bade* or *bid* is appropriate for the past; either *bidden* or *bid* is
appropriate for the past participle.

Base	Past	Past Participle
cling	clung	clung
clothe	clothed, clad	clothed, clad
come	came	come
cost	cost	cost
creep	crept	crept
cut	cut	cut
deal	dealt	dealt
dig	dug	dug
dive	dived, dove	dived
do	did	done
draw	drew	drawn
drink	drank	drunk
drive	drove	driven
eat	ate	eaten
fall	fell	fallen
feed	fed	fed
feel	felt	felt
fight	fought	fought
find	found	found
flee	fled	fled
fling	flung	flung
fly	flew	flown
forbid	forbade, forbad	forbidden
forecast	forecast, forecasted	forecast, forecasted
forget	forgot	forgotten
forgive	forgave	forgiven
freeze	froze	frozen
get	got	got, gotten
give	gave	given
go	went	gone
grind	ground	ground
grow	grew	grown
hang	hung, hanged*	hung, hanged*
have	had	had
hear	heard	heard
hide	hid	hidden
hit	hit	hit
hold	held	held
hurt	hurt	hurt
inlay	inlaid	inlaid
keep	kept	kept
kneel	knelt	knelt
knit	knitted, knit	knitted, knit
know	knew	known

*When the verb refers to execution, *hanged* is preferred for both past and past participle. Otherwise, *hung* is preferred.

terms

Base	Past	Past Participle
lay	laid	laid
lead	led	led
leap	leaped, leapt	leaped, leapt
learn	learned, learnt	learned, learnt
leave	left	left
lend	lent	lent
let	let	let
lie	lay	lain
light	lit, lighted	lit, lighted
lose	lost	lost
make	made	made
mean	meant	meant
meet	met	met
melt	melted	melted, molten
mistake	mistook	mistaken
mow	mowed	mowed, mown
pay	paid	paid
prove	proved	proved, proven
put	put	put
quit	quit	quit
read	read	read
rid	rid, ridded	rid, ridded
ride	rode	ridden
ring	rang	rung
rise	rose	risen
run	ran	run
saw	sawed	sawed, sawn
say	said	said
see	saw	seen
seek	sought	sought
sell	sold	sold
send	sent	sent
set	set	set
sew	sewed	sewn, sewed
shake	shook	shaken
shave	shaved	shaved, shaven
shear	sheared	sheared, shorn
shed	shed	shed
shine	shone	shone
shoe	shod	shod
shoot	shot	shot
show	showed	shown, showed
shrink	shrank, shrunk	shrunk, shrunken
shut	shut	shut
sing	sang	sung
sink	sank	sunk, sunken

terms

terms

Base	Past	Past Participle
sit	sat	sat
slay	slew	slain
sleep	slept	slept
slide	slid	slid
sling	slung	slung
slink	slunk	slunk
slit	slit	slit
sow	sowed	sown, sowed
speak	spoke	spoken
speed	sped, speeded	sped, speeded
spell	spelled, spelt	spelled, spelt
spend	spent	spent
spill	spilled, spilt	spilled, spilt
spin	spun	spun
spit	spat	spat
split	split	split
spread	spread	spread
spring	sprang	sprung
stand	stood	stood
steal	stole	stolen
stick	stuck	stuck
sting	stung	stung
stink	stank, stunk	stunk
stride	strode	stridden
strike	struck	struck, stricken*
string	strung	strung
strive	strove	striven
swear	swore	sworn
sweep	swept	swept
swell	swelled	swollen, swelled
swim	swam	swum
swing	swung	swung
take	took	taken
teach	taught	taught
tear	tore	torn
tell	told	told
think	thought	thought
throw	threw	thrown
thrust	thrust	thrust
understand	understood	understood
upset	upset	upset
wake	woke, waked	woken, waked
wear	wore	worn
weave	wove	woven

Stricken is normally used to mean "afflicted," as with disease: *"She was stricken with polio."*

Base	Past	Past Participle
weep	wept	wept
win	won	won
wind	wound	wound
withdraw	withdrew	withdrawn
withhold	withheld	withheld
withstand	withstood	withstood
wring	wrung	wrung
write	wrote	written

Jargon

Jargon is the specialized vocabulary of a group such as lawyers, sociologists, and linguists. Jargon should be avoided when it obscures meaning or over-burdens style. (Section 32d.1)

Linking Verb

A linking verb requires a subject complement to complete its meaning. An adjective complement modifies and a noun complement renames the subject of the clause. Common linking verbs are *be, become, seem, look, feel: The discussion was painful. The supplies grew scarce.*

Loose Sentence

A loose sentence begins with the main idea and then adds modifiers: *Computer chess programs allow stronger play because new methods of searching have improved the evaluation of positions and moves.* (See also **Periodic Sentence.**) (Section 33b.1)

Main Clause (See Independent Clause.)

Mass Noun

A mass noun, also called a *non-count noun,* names something that cannot be counted. Thus, mass nouns have no plural form. In their normal senses, *clothing, money, water, garbage,* and *equipment* are examples of mass nouns. (See also **Count Noun.**)

Metaphor

A metaphor is a figure of speech that conveys information in a nonliteral way by stating or implying that two things are similar: *The book is a passport into exotic, untrodden lands.* (Section 33d)

terms

Misplaced Modifier

A misplaced modifier seems to relate to the wrong element in a sentence: *The delivery service brought the package to the house in a van.* [seems to modify *house*] Modifiers should be positioned so that they clearly modify the intended word: *In a van, the delivery service brought the package to the house.* [clearly modifies *brought*] (Section 16b)

Mixed Metaphor

Sometimes several metaphors are strung together to form a mixed metaphor, an expression that begins with one overused metaphor and shifts into another or several: *We were out on a limb; but since we knew we were playing with fire and had all our eggs in one basket, we continued the struggle.*

Modal Auxiliary

A verb auxiliary that cannot undergo conjugation is called a modal auxiliary: *can, could, shall, should, will, would, may, might,* and *must.* Modals express such ideas as ability, advisability, necessity, and possibility. (Section ESLi)

Modifier

A modifier is a word, phrase, or clause that describes, limits, or qualifies some other word, phrase, or clause. Adjectives and adverbs (and words functioning as such) are modifiers: *The tribe had no written language. Without warning, the horse stumbled. I got a unicycle, which I could never learn to ride.*

Mood

The mood of a verb is shown by form and meaning. The indicative mood expresses a fact or a question: *I attended. Was the problem solved?* The imperative mood expresses a command: *Buy bonds. Get help.* The subjunctive mood expresses desire or possibility: *I wish I were there.* (See also **Indicative Mood, Imperative Mood,** and **Subjunctive Mood.**) (Section 4f)

Nominalization

A nominalization is an expression of action in noun form: *contribution, development, failure, inclusion.* Unnecessary nominalizations can sometimes be changed to more forceful verb equivalents: *contribute, develop, fail, include.* (Section 33c.1)

Nominative Absolute (See Absolute Phrase.)

Nominative Case (See Case.)

Non-count Noun

A non-count noun, also called a *mass noun,* names something that cannot be counted. Thus, non-count nouns have no plural form. In their normal senses, *water, sand, furniture,* and *wealth* are examples of non-count nouns. (See also **Count Noun.**) (Section ESLb.2)

Nonfinite Verb (See Finite Verb.)

Nonrestrictive Element

A nonrestrictive element does not restrict or limit the word or phrase it modifies. Commas should surround a nonrestrictive element to indicate its loose connection with a sentence: *I heard someone called a "dork," which can't refer to anything complimentary. The research has led to the CD GUIDE, a successful software product.* (Section 21c)

Noun

A noun names things in the physical and nonphysical worlds: *Jim, sister, novel, field, generosity, grief,* and so on. (Chapter 1 and Section ESLa–b)

Noun Clause

A noun clause is a dependent clause that functions in the same ways that all nouns do—as subjects, objects, and complements: *What you should do is quit. I know that cheval means "horse." The winner will be whoever spends the most money.* (Section 7c.3)

Number

Number refers to the form of a noun, pronoun, or verb that shows singularity (one) or plurality (more than one): singular—*car, it, sings;* plural—*cars, they, sing.* (Section 1b)

Object (See Direct Object, Indirect Object, and Object of Preposition.)

Object Complement

An object complement, either an adjective or a noun, completes a clause's structure by modifying or renaming the direct object: *The drought made water scarce. She named her dog Josh.*

Objective Case (See Case.)

terms

Object of Preposition

An object of a preposition, usually a noun, noun phrase, or pronoun, combines with a preposition to form a prepositional phrase: *at school, after washing the car, in front of them.* (Section 6a)

Parallelism

In grammar, *parallelism* refers to the use of the same grammatical structure for items in a compound structure, a series, a list, or an outline. (Chapter 20)

Parenthetical Element

A parenthetical element in a sentence is set off with commas, dashes, or parentheses to show its loose, interruptive, or nonessential nature: *A robot, at least to most people, is a manlike creature. The production—how can I put it politely?—lacks interest. In the story, Zeus had a child by Pluto (not to be confused with the god of the underworld).* (Sections 21f.1, 24d, 24e)

Participle

A participle is a verb form used as an adjective. Participles have two basic forms—the present participle (*-ing* verb form) and past participle (the form that follows *have* in a verb phrase). A participial phrase is a participle plus another element—an object, subject, or modifier: *Remembering, Eugene started over. Meat cut very thin is called scallopini.* [*Remembering* and *cut* are both participles modifying the subjects of both sentences. *Cut very thin* is a participial phrase.] (See also **Absolute Phrase.**) (Section 5b and 5d)

Part of Speech

Part of speech refers to the grammatical classification of a word based on its form, function, or meaning. Traditionally, a word is classified as a noun verb, adjective, adverb, pronoun, preposition, conjunction, or interjection.

Passive Voice

A verb is in the passive voice when its subject receives the action. The verb consists of a form of *be* plus a past participle: *The purse was stolen. Your account has been credited.* (See also **Active Voice.**) (Sections 4e and ESLk)

Past Participle

The past participle is the form of a verb that normally follows *have.* The past participle of regular verbs adds *-d* or *-ed* to the base form:

called, increased, pitched, assumed. Irregular verbs do not have predictable past participles. The forms for the past participles of irregular verbs can be found in dictionaries and in appropriate lists. (See also **Irregular Verb.**)

Perfect Tenses

The perfect tenses are formed by combining *has/have/had* or a modal and *have* with the past participle: *has escaped, had rebuilt, will have withdrawn, could have read.* (Sections 4c and 4d)

Periodic Sentence

In a periodic sentence the main idea is postponed until the end: *Just at the height of his power when he could have become an American monarch, Washington went home to farm.* (See also **Loose Sentence.**) (Section 33b.1)

Person

For pronouns, the term *person* refers to the form that indicates whether a reference is to the speaker or spokesperson (first person: *I, we*), to the person(s) spoken to (second person: *you*), or to the person(s) or thing(s) spoken about (third person: *he, she, it, they*). All other pronouns and nouns are in the third person. For verbs, the term refers to the form that goes with each of the three persons.

Personal Pronoun

A personal pronoun refers to a specific person or people (*I, you, she, they,* etc.) or to a specific thing or things (*it, them,* etc.). (For a complete list of the personal pronouns, see Section 2a.)

terms

Personification

Personification is a figure of speech in which something nonhuman is given a human characteristic: *The printer ate the paper. The unplugged TV stared blankly.* (Section 33d)

Phrase

A phrase is a group of related words that together have a single function (as a noun, verb, or modifier). Unlike a clause, a phrase has no subject and finite verb: *a heavy eater, has been applied, in a rural town, tending to be jealous, to close the letter, the meal over.*

Positive Degree

Positive degree refers to the simple, uncompared form of adjectives and adverbs: *crazy, evenly, complex, quick, angrily*. (See also **Comparative Degree** and **Superlative Degree.**) (Section 3c)

Possessive Case

The possessive case is the form of a noun or pronoun that indicates ownership (*Sue's job, their vacation*), authorship (*Poe's story, her essay*), source (*paper's headline, teacher's assignment*), measurement (*a mile's distance*), and description (*a child's bike*). (See also **Case.**) (Chapter 14)

Predicate

The predicate joins with the subject to form a clause. A predicate consists of at least one finite verb and may also include modifiers and completing words: *The dress was cut low in the front and lower in the back. He sent his grandmother a poinsettia for Christmas.*

Predicate Adjective

A predicate adjective, also called a subject complement, follows *be, seem, appear, become, grow, remain, taste, look, smell, sound,* or *feel* and modifies the subject: *The topic was boring. He remained angry.*

Predicate Noun

A predicate noun or nominative, also called a subject complement, follows *be, become, remain, seem,* and *appear* and names or refers to the subject: *The topic was euthanasia. He remained an enemy.*

terms

Prefix

A prefix is a syllable that attaches to the beginning of a root to add or alter meaning: *pre-* in *preview* means "before"; *de-* in *devalue* means "reduce"; *mal-* in *malfunction* means "badly."

Preposition

A preposition is a function word like *in, to, from, by,* and *through* that connects its object to the rest of the sentence. The preposition plus its object is called a prepositional phrase: *Over the past year, the school in our neighborhood has deteriorated to the point of needing extensive repairs.* (Section 6a)

Present Participle

The present participle is the form of a verb that ends in *-ing: surviving, making, breathing, lying.* (See also **Participle, Gerund,** and **Progressive Forms.**)

Principal Parts

The principal parts of verbs are the base form (*see, step*), the past form (*saw, stepped*), and the past participle form (*seen, stepped*). (Section 4a)

Progressive Forms

The progressive forms of a verb indicate actions in progress. These forms appear in all six tenses and are made with a form of *be* plus the present participle (*-ing* form): *is looking, was looking, will be looking, has been looking, had been looking, will have been looking.* (Section 4d)

Pronoun

Pronouns are words that appear in the same positions as nouns. A pronoun usually substitutes for a previously stated noun or noun phrase, called its *antecedent: The language was easy to learn because it had many words similar to Latin. Pigs were used in the research; they were fed large amounts of sugar.* (See also **Personal Pronoun, Interrogative Pronoun, Relative Pronoun, Demonstrative Pronoun, Indefinite Pronoun, Reciprocal Pronoun, Reflexive Pronoun,** and **Emphatic Pronoun.**) (Chapter 2)

Proper Noun and Adjective

Proper nouns and adjectives are specific names that begin with a capital letter: *Churchill, Xerox, Crimean War, Natchez Trace, Florida vacation, Easter service, October weather.* (Section 31b)

Qualifier

A qualifier is an adverb that serves to intensify or restrict an adjective or adverb: *very tired, highly motivated, somewhat bitter, rather large.*

Quotation (See Direct Quotation and Indirect Quotation.)

Reciprocal Pronoun

The reciprocal pronouns, *each other* and *one another,* are only used as objects: *The two always give each other help. The noise was so loud we could not hear one another.* (Section 2e)

terms

Reflexive Pronoun

A reflexive pronoun, ending in *-self* or *-selves,* is always an object that refers to or "reflects" the subject of the clause: *I wrote myself a note. They couldn't imagine themselves as losers.* (See also **Emphatic Pronoun.**) (Section 2a)

Regular Verb

A regular verb adds *-d* or *-ed* to the base to form the past tense and the past participle: *use, used, used; warn, warned, warned.*

Relative Pronoun

A relative pronoun (*who, whom, whose, whoever, which, whichever, what, whatever,* and *that*) introduces a dependent clause: *No one was injured by the tank that exploded. You can't trust whoever looks honest.* (Section 2c)

Restrictive Element

A restrictive element restricts, limits, or identifies the word or phrase it modifies. A restrictive element is not set off by commas: *The coach created an offense that used a variety of sets.* (See also **Nonrestrictive Element.**) (Section 21c)

Root

The root of a word provides its base, or primary, meaning. For example, the root of *telegraphy* is *graph,* which means "write"; the root of *amorphous* is *morph,* which means "shape."

Run-on Sentence (See Fused Sentence.)

Sentence

A sentence is an independent statement, question, or command beginning with a capital letter and ending with some terminal punctuation. Except for exclamations like "Oh!" and idioms like "The more, the merrier," sentences contain a subject and predicate, usually with modifiers and complements: *A man wearing sweaty, seedy clothes pushed his way in. Why did he enter a race that he was sure to lose?*

Sentence Fragment (See Fragment.)

Sentence Modifier

A sentence modifier is an adverbial element that has an independent or parenthetical meaning. Sentence modifiers, sometimes called *absolutes,* relate

terms

to whole sentences rather than to particular words or phrases: *Obviously, she would like a job. Without a doubt, I will be there. She is fasting, although I don't know why.*

Shift

A shift is an unnecessary change from one kind of construction to another. Shifts can occur in tense, voice, number, person, and structure. (Chapter 17)

Simile

A simile is a figure of speech in which two dissimilar things are said to be alike. The words *like* or *as* distinguish a simile from a metaphor: *problems sprouting like weeds, the moon round like a Concord grape, a plot as complicated as an acrostic puzzle.* (Section 33d)

Simple Sentence

A simple sentence has one independent clause (main clause) and no dependent clause (subordinate clause): *The smell of the food reminded me of my childhood.* (Section 7e.1)

Slang

Slang is a kind of informal language that develops when people invent new expressions or change the meaning of existing expressions to create an individual and unique way of speaking: *pinkie* for *little finger, whirlybird* for *helicopter, cop out* for *refusal to commit oneself, yak* for *chat.* (Section 32a)

Split Infinitive

A split infinitive has a modifier between the *to* and the base form of the verb: *to slowly stroll, to desperately yell, to at the last second fall.* In most split infinitives, the modifier should be moved: *to stroll slowly, to yell desperately, to fall at the last second.* (Section 18d)

Squinting Modifier

A squinting modifier appears between two words, both of which it might modify: *The woman he called reluctantly made an appointment.* [*Reluctantly* could modify *called* or *made.*] Squinting modifiers must be repositioned: *The woman he called made an appointment reluctantly.* (Section 16b.4)

Subject

The subject joins with the predicate to form a clause. A subject consists of a noun (or a noun substitute) plus any modifiers. A simple subject is the

terms

subject minus its modifiers. *The interior of the car lit up.* [The subject is *the interior of the car;* the simple subject is *interior.*]

Subject Complement

A subject complement follows *be* or another linking verb and renames or modifies the subject of the clause: *He was a scrawny kid.* [*Kid* renames *he* and can be called a predicate noun or nominative.] *The conversation became serious.* [*Serious* modifies *conversation* and can be called a predicate adjective.] (See also **Linking Verb.**)

Subjective Case (See Case.)

Subjunctive Mood

The subjunctive mood primarily indicates that something is not a fact or that something should happen: *If I were qualified, I would apply for the job. The doctor insisted that Jack get a second opinion.* Unlike the indicative mood (*I was qualified* and *he gets*), the subjunctive mood has only one form for each tense and person. (Section 4f.3)

Subordinate Clause (See Dependent Clause.)

Subordinating Conjunction

A subordinating conjunction introduces a dependent clause and expresses relationships such as cause, contrast, condition, manner, place, and time. Common subordinating conjunctions are *because, although, if, as if,* and *when.* (Section 6b.3) For a more complete list, see 7c.1. (See also **Adverb Clause.**)

Subordination

Through subordination, writers show that one idea is dependent on another. Subordination can be achieved through dependent clauses, verbals, and appositives. For techniques that use subordination, see 33a.3–33a.6. (See also **Adverb Clause, Adjective Clause, Noun Clause, Infinitive, Participle, Gerund,** and **Appositive.**)

Suffix

A suffix is a syllable or sound that attaches to the end of a word to alter the word's meaning, to change the word from one class to another, or to change the word's form. The suffix *-itis* ("inflamed") added to the root *appendix* creates the word *appendicitis.* The suffix *-ly* changes the adjective *sad* to the adverb *sadly.* The suffix *-ed* changes the present tense verb *call* to the past tense *called.*

Superlative Degree

The form of an adjective and adverb used to make a comparison among three or more items is called the *superlative degree.* An *-est* ending and the words *most* and *least* indicate the superlative degree: *This is the largest hotel in the city. The video you selected is the one most frequently purchased. This brand of yogurt is the least fattening of all.* (See also **Comparative Degree.**) (Section 3c)

Syntax

Syntax refers to the arrangement of words to form structures—phrases, clauses, and sentences.

Tag Question

A tag question appears at the end of a statement and asks for verification. It is composed of an auxiliary verb and a pronoun: *The car has been repaired, hasn't it? You read the book, didn't you?* (Section 21g and ESLp)

Tense

Tense is the feature of verbs that indicates a meaning related to time. English is said to have three simple tenses (present, past, and future) and three perfect tenses (present perfect, past perfect, and future perfect). (Sections 4c and ESLh)

Transitional Expression

A transitional expression indicates the relationship between ideas: for example, *however* indicates contrast; *as a result* indicates cause/effect; *furthermore* indicates addition. Sometimes called *conjunctive adverbs* or conjuncts, transitional words and phrases serve to link independent clause to independent clause, sentence to sentence, and paragraph to paragraph. The following list includes the most common transitional expressions.

terms

Relationship	Appropriate Expressions
Contrast	however, on the other hand, on the contrary, in contrast, still, nevertheless, regardless, instead
Cause/effect	therefore, thus, consequently, for this reason, as a result, otherwise, thus, then, accordingly
Time sequence	first, second, third, next, last, finally, afterward, now, then, again, soon, formerly, eventually, subsequently
Restatement	in other words, in short, in summary, that is, again
Emphasis	in fact, indeed, of course, certainly, after all, surely, actually

Relationship	Appropriate Expressions
Addition	furthermore, moreover, likewise, also, in addition, besides
Summary	in conclusion, on the whole, all in all, in summary
Example	for example, for instance, specifically

Transitive Verb

A transitive verb expresses action and requires an object: *She <u>wrote</u> the letter. Mr. Williams <u>speaks</u> Japanese fluently.*

Verb

A verb is a word that indicates action (*swim*), occurrence (*happen*), or existence (*be*). (Chapter 4)

Verbal

A verbal is one of three verb forms functioning in a sentence as a noun or a modifier: infinitive (*to write*), present participle (*writing*), past participle (*written*). A verbal alone never functions in a clause as a finite verb. A verbal with a subject, object, complement, or modifier is called a verbal phrase. (See also **Infinitive, Participle,** and **Gerund.**) (Chapter 5)

Verb Phrase

A verb phrase is a verb made up of more than one word: *is calling, will consider, have been reading.*

Voice

The voice of a verb indicates whether the subject acts (active voice) or receives the action (passive voice). (See also **Active Voice** and **Passive Voice.**) (Section 4e)

terms

Index

Boldface indicates sections.